The Military Origins of Industrialisation and International Trade Rivalry

To my uncle, Samar Sen,
founder and editor of *Frontier* (Calcutta),
for courage

The Military Origins of Industrialisation and International Trade Rivalry

Gautam Sen

St. Martin's Press, New York

Library of Congress Cataloging in Publication Data
Sen, Gautam
    The military origins of industrialisation and international trade rivalry
    Bibliography: p.
    1. Commercial policy.   2. Economic development.
    3. Military policy.   I. Title.
    HF1411.S3326   1983   382'.3   83–9717
    ISBN 0–312–53236–9

Contents

Preface

This book was originally submitted as a doctoral dissertation to the London School of Economics and Political Science, University of London. Some revision (with the benefit of hindsight and advice) and shortening owing to reasons of space have shaped its present form. A number of case studies on State intervention and industrialisation in the thesis have been dropped, and interested readers may wish to consult the original for more extensive empirical evaluation.*

This book is primarily a work of interpretation, hence the number of creditors for my gratitude is understandably large and perhaps appropriately acknowledged by the list of names in the Bibliography. As a consequence, I feel partly absolved from claiming all errors of fact and judgement exclusively for myself, although I am sure that the truly novel transgressions are entirely mine.

In the first year of my research I was fortunate to have Michael Banks of the Department of International Relations at the London School of Economics as my supervisor. He first impressed upon me the real meaning of intellectual rigour. Thus, it was with great regret that I found my research interests diverging from his. However, since the Michaelmas Term of 1978 I was lucky enough to be jointly supervised by Professor Susan Strange of the Department of International Relations and Professor Meghnad Desai of the Department of Economics. I would like to record my gratitude to them both for their patience, encouragement and, most of all, judicious intellectual correctives to excesses of enthusiasm.

I owe a profound debt to a brilliant contemporary, Francesca Bettio, an economist at New Hall, Cambridge, for providing sustained and lucid intellectual support and giving over-generously of her time. I particularly wish to thank her for painstakingly helping me to 'decipher' the formal analytical methods which underpinned the findings of a number of crucial articles on 'similarities in production structures' surveyed in Chapter 1.

---

* 'The role of national defence in industrialisation and in international trade conflicts in manufacturing: 1800–1980' (submitted 1982).

INTRODUCTION

1 The issue

Disputes over international trade in manufactures have become widespread since the late 1960s, following the relative quiescence of the early post-war period. Neo-Mercantilist pressures are evident in most developed market economies in varying degree; restrictions like 'voluntary' quotas, reference prices, public and private cartels and industrial subsidies are commonplace. During the past decade there has been an intensification of industrial subsidy policy which appears to have replaced more direct forms of protectionism as the principal instrument for defending domestic industry against the threat of cheaper imports. The ideological counterpart of this neo-mercantilist impulse is the exhortation to 'buy British', 'buy French', etc. International trade in certain manufactures like textiles and clothing has been subject to control for over two decades but a growing number of industries (e.g. steel, transportation equipment, machinery) are following in the same direction.

In Britain some 600 imported products are already subject to restrictions; by the mid sixties almost a quarter of all Japanese products entering the US market were also subject to some form of discrimination, and over a hundred bills are before the US Congress demanding relief from import competition.[1] And governments are apparently willing to enact measures to defend domestic industry against the threat of cheaper imports. Yet, recent studies demonstrate that government responses to such threats to domestic industry have not been as protectionist as many observers had anticipated. The latter phenomenon is somewhat overstated, however, since the significance of indirect restrictions such as subsidies have not been taken into account fully, as distinct from more familiar measures like quotas, etc.

Thus, two central issues seem to be involved in the present disjuncture in international trade relations: firstly, the causes of these disputes over international trade which have become widespread since the late 1960s and continue to intensify, and secondly, government responses to them, both the various forms of evident protectionism and concurrently the apparent reluctance to pursue protectionism to its logical conclusion and break with the relatively liberal trading arrangements of the post-war period.

2   Existing explanations

Liberal trade theory is unable to provide a coherent interpretation of the disputes or the policies provoking them. The confusion in liberal thinking is, ironically, poignantly highlighted by the late H.G. Johnson, once the leading apologist of 'free trade' (see p. 194).

At the outset, it may be noted that there are two important assumptions underlying the theory of comparative advantage and the desirability of adjustment to trade which make it redundant, on its own terms, in the present situation. Firstly, it assumes full employment. The asumption of full employment is unrealistic since full employment has rarely been the norm in economic history. When there is unemployment any activity in which the country engages is beneficial, irrespective of its comparative advantage in that activity, since the gains from domestic production are greater than the losses suffered by excluding cheaper imports.[2]

Secondly, neo-classical trade theory is static, unable to explain changes in comparative advantage. It implies that if it is more profitable for a country to produce a particular product it should go on doing so, and not attempt to produce other products more profitably produced elsewhere. If that advice were to be followed, the existing division of labour at any given point in time would be 'frozen' indefinitely. Countries producing raw materials cheaply should not try to produce other goods, and vice versa. Indeed, some leading neo-classical theorists have advocated that most Third World countries would be better off trying to maximise their gains in producing primary commodities. The issue of industrialisation, which seems to be an undeniable prerequisite for higher living standards, does not seem to agitate them excessively! The two exceptions frequently cited, New Zealand and Denmark, are inappropriate. Both have a highly mechanised agriculture, permitting high levels of productivity. This would be impossible in a country where labour is the most abundant factor of production — an apt description for the overwhelming majority of Third World countries. In any case, if all Third World countries, in contrast to two small countries like New Zealand and Denmark, produced huge quantities of primary products there would not be a commensurate demand for them.

Trade conflicts have no place in the perfect world of nations specialising according to their comparative advantage but their occurrence in pluralist democracies finds a rationale outside the pure laws of economics in the theory of group behaviour.[3] According to Kindleberger, trade policy has rarely been based on economic calculations alone. Governments have to take into account the impact of trade adjustment on domestic social cohesion. Thus protectionism occurs because governments are compelled to respond to domestic pressures. In terms of this hypothesis, protectionist demands succeed in pluralist democracies because producer interests are better organised than consumer interests in these societies since the individual losses of dispersed consumers are comparatively much smaller. Furthermore, since dispersed consumers are less able to voice and sustain collective opposition to protectionism than clustered producer interests, the latter have greater influence over government trade policies.[4]

Thus, in accordance with liberal trade theory, the orthodoxy regards contemporary disputes over international trade in manufactures as one of 'friction', when comparative advantages shift and require adjustment. As a consequence they advocate adjustment assistance to help industry to accommodate changes in comparative advantage, and greater firmness of resolve in refusing to accept sectional demands for protection from employers and employees.

However liberal trade theory is unable to explain why the problem of international trade disputes and the need for adjustment between countries affects the same industries: in particular, why this problem has been a recurrent feature of international trade relations since the onset of industrialisation in the latecomer countries of the nineteenth century; and why the process of resolution has been conflictual rather than orderly and rational.

Liberal trade theory is addressed to the question of international trade disputes and adjustment, *per se*, but it does not take into account the recurrent and systematic pattern of such disputes. The theory of comparative advantage, on which the liberal interpretation of international trade disputes is predicated, may be internally consistent but it is at a loss to explain the historical reality whereby steel, transportation equipment, textiles and clothing etc. are the subject of conflict between several countries simultaneously. Why does global surplus capacity affecting several countries arise inex-orably, for instance? Why do countries fail to adjust and reap the benefits of economic rationality? The theory of group behaviour does not help in this context either since it is not addressed to the question of the identity of the industries involved. In any case, in the present period many of the industries provoking international trade disputes are in the public sector and therefore do not involve employer pressure. As for employment considerations, the case of textiles and clothing, discussed below (in chapter 5), will demon-strate convincingly that employment has not been a major factor in determining government trade policies in the long run. Further-more, the half-hearted approach toward adjustment assistance policy and its absence in many countries undermines the assump-tion that governments have regarded the threat of dissent from employees and their trade unions as a significant challenge. The apparent lack of concern, as opposed to rhetoric, about mass unem-ployment in many developed countries at present, the principal actors in international trade disputes, also subverts the avidly pro-moted supposition that all political parties have consistently regar-ded unemployment as a serious threat to their electoral prospects.

The Marxist interpretation of disjunctures in international trade relations needs only to be sketched briefly to highlight how the alternative theory proposed below offers a more satisfactory explanation, since both the Marxist and liberal approaches suffer from somewhat similar weaknesses. Whether Marxists interpret the issue of international trade disputes in terms of the problems of underconsumption, or accord priority to the falling rate of profit and regard the former as a secondary manifestation of the latter, the inexorable tendency of capitalism towards overaccumulation is considered to be the primary reason for recurrent crises of capitalism, and its corollary, conflicts over international trade.

According to the underconsumptionist version, the crisis in international trade relations is ultimately caused by the unequal distribution of income within capitalist societies which 'creates a tendency to overproduction'. The obstacle to the continuing expan-sion of capital is the 'low income of the masses in capitalist society'. Thus, crisis is provoked by the 'inability to realise surplus value in the sphere of circulation, the inability to sell what is produced'.[5]

By contrast, other Marxists have regarded the tendency of the rate of profit to fall as the primary cause of crisis. They identify a number of factors which operate in a period of expansion to activate the latent tendency of the rate of profit to fall.

> The technical composition of capital is rising with the increases
> in productivity, and with it, eventually, the organic composition
> of capital in terms of exchange value, which actualizes the latent
> tendency of the rate of profit to fall.[6]

During this period of expansion the uneven development of
capitalism is accentuated because the technical composition of capital and the growth of labour productivity proceed unevenly among
capitals. The reduction of the reserve army of labour and general
increase in wages during the expansion precipitate the crisis
although other factors could also provoke it (e.g. a sudden rise in
raw material prices). And, according to Weeks, 'the actual impulse
which turns the crisis into the form of a realization crisis is of
incidental importance.'[7] It is the latent tendency of the rate of profit
to fall, actualised by the reduction in the reserve army of labour and
intensified and, probably, precipitated by the general rise in wages
that is the ultimate cause of the crisis.

While the Marxist interpretation of such conflicts over international trade in manufactures is plausible on a macroeconomic
level, unlike the *ad hoc*, pragmatic explanation provided by liberal
analysts, the Marxists do not, like the liberals, consider why conflicts between countries occur over particular markets or industries.
Implicit in the Marxist interpretation is the idea that when a crisis of
realisation occurs in the national and international market, producers are in conflict over the total existing purchasing power in the
market(s) as a whole. The crisis which occurs in the international
market is merely an extension of the crisis which occurs in the
national market. Even if the crisis originates in the international
market, as Weeks argues the present one does, no allowances are
made for one important dissimilarity which exists between the two
markets and determines the form of the crisis. The international
market is constituted by a large number of similar economic
structures while the national market is comprised of one such
structure. Thus, it is possible for a steel industry to encounter no
competitor of significance within the national market. In the
alternative theory proposed it will be argued that because similar
structures of production exist in different national economies and
because such similarities are crucial to the existence and the role of
national states, conflicts arise between countries over the same
markets and products.

A further problem unaccounted for by Marxist interpretations is the occurrence of international trade disputes in a period not otherwise characterised by economic crisis. For example, international trade in textiles and clothing was the subject of dispute and negotiations, resulting in a formal arrangement during the late 1950s and early 1960s, when the developed market economies were not experiencing serious economic difficulties.

The primary shortcoming of both the liberal and Marxist approaches is the failure to address the issue of international trade disputes over the same products between several countries simultaneously. This problem can only be confonted by analysing the similarities in the structure of production between countries, detailed below (in Chapter 1), the reasons for its existence and its relationship to patterns of international trade and consequent disputes.

This book will deal only with the manufacturing sector because of its obvious significance in present trade disputes and also for reasons of space. The agricultural sector is not considered in GATT negotiations on trade liberalisation and is therefore unaffected by the on-going transition from relatively liberal trading arrangements to the more restrictive practices under purview. The growing importance of the service sector, which is a more recent phenomenon, would require a separate study.

3. An alternative theory: similar economic structures, the State and military impulses

The alternative theory proposed for analysing contemporary conflicts in international manufacturing trade relates to the spread of economic development internationally, ignored by existing analyses of trade conflict, and the role of the State.

At every stage of capitalist economic development, measured by, say, per capita income, there appears to exist a striking similarity in industrial structure. In other words, the relative importance of sectors in this industrial structure and inter-industry output flows is by and large the same. Even if the comparable stage of economic development is achieved at different historical periods the above similarity prevails. For example, the industrial structure of India today would be much the same as that of the USA at the same level of per capita income in an earlier period. The above conclusions, which have not been disputed in substance, are based on the work of Kuznets, later refined and elaborated at the World Bank.

This similarity in the structure of production is particularly evident for the investment-goods industries and the infrastructural ones (including transport and energy).

It has been suggested that most of these industries constitute an indivisible set crucial in both the initial stage (take-off) of industrialisation and in successive periods, either because of technological linkages (fixed coefficients of production) and/or inter-industry supply–demand interdependence. As a result of their strong interdependence and crucial role in industrialisation, this set of industries has been called 'industrialising industries'. In order to guarantee self-sustained industrialisation it is necessary to acquire this set of 'industrialising industries' since, (a) the products of each enter as an input for almost all the others and, (b) they are also inputs for final products in the consumer goods sector. This characteristic makes this group of industries strategic for achieving the goal of economic independence.

Although it is difficult to identify these industries once-and-for-all, owing to the influence of technological progress over time and the peculiarities displayed by different countries, the following list has been derived from input-output tables: iron and steel, chemicals, textiles, machinery, paper and paper products and transport equipment.[8]

Most of these industries are also of strategic significance for the production of military goods. The dual strategic significance for military self-sufficiency and national economic independence can be held to provide the rationale for the desire to acquire this group of industries.

An additional feature of this theory is the importance it attributes to the State. According to this alternative theoretical perspective, the State plays a crucial role in fostering and maintaining this pattern of a self-sufficient industrial structure. The reason for this is to be found in the competitive relations between states in the international political system.[9] Once the process of industrialisation has reached a significant stage in one country, others are compelled to respond by industrialising themselves, in order to preserve the balance of power — the balance of power, of course, being dependent on the relative levels of industrial strength.

It is this apprehension of industrial backwardness in a world of industrially and, therefore, militarily advanced nations that prompts the State to intervene to implant and speed up the process of industrial transformation. Thus, at bottom the motivation for rapid industrial change is almost invariably of a military nature. Other factors like the desire for economic autonomy are important, especially for small countries who cannot affect the politico-military equation, but even economic insecurity ultimately stems from the underlying militarization of international political relations.

In the 'latecomer' country the State assumes a pre-eminent role for a variety of reasons. The nascent local entrepreneurial class may be unwilling to risk the capital because of the market-size required to gain cost advantages from economies of scale. Moreover, the presence of industrialised competitors raises further barriers to entry, since most of the basic investment and infrastructure inputs can be imported because of imperfect transmission of technology, lack of local skills and the benefits of economies of scale already achieved by the 'firstcomers'.

Further, owing to the complex economic and technological links of the group of strategic industries, the successful import-substitution for some of them does not guarantee self-sustained growth, and therefore economic and military independence. State intervention to provide the complete set of strategic industries thus becomes inevitable. The State is compelled to guarantee the economic viability of this group of industries, either by providing state-owned facilities, or subsidising private industry.

3.1 Implications for international trade in manufactured goods

In the first instance, the production capacity which exists in firstcomer countries reflects the demand for imports from countries yet to industrialise. Since the benefits of economies of scale, both static and dynamic, can be reaped by longer production runs the latecomer countries will also need to establish a level of capacity, when they industrialise, that allows them to reach the competitive threshold already prevalent in the firstcomer countries, with the attendant need for adequate export markets as well. Thus, they in turn may establish a level of productive capacity in excess of local consumption levels and hope to carve out a share in the international market. A further element which accentuates the problems of excess capacity is the need to ensure the ability to produce adequate quantities during war-time. Thus, the planned capacity may well exceed strictly national peace-time needs.

The output of this excess capacity is unloaded on highly competitive international markets during peace-time. And similarly, with the postwar recovery the problem of overcapacity has become acute.The contemporary conflicts over international manufacturing trade faithfully reflect this dilemma. The recovery of the Federal Republic of Germany and Japan marked the beginning of tensions as they began to oust established countries like the USA (which survived with its industry intact after the war). The newly industrialising countries (NICs) followed and intensified an existing problem. As more and more countries industrialise, the greater the tensions over international manufacturing trade.

3.2 *The empirical evidence*

The evidence for similarities in the structure of production in different countries will be reproduced in detail in chapter 1. It is from the evidence discussed in this chapter that the group of strategic industries has been selected, according to the criteria already mentioned.

The importance of the State in economic development cannot be seriously challenged, as Gerschenkron has demonstrated.[10] In major instances of European industrialisation the involvement of the State and its acute awareness of military needs has been carefully documented.[11] The same is true for Japan; indeed, in the case of Japan, industrialisation was engendered by the State's efforts to create a domestic defence industry during the third quarter of the nineteenth century.[12]

In the period after the Second World War, the State has played a significant role in the recovery of European industry; the same is again true for Japan. In the NICs, State involvement in fostering the basic industries has been preponderant.

The importance of this group of industries in international manufacturing trade is apparent from the prevailing disputes over textiles,[13] iron and steel, shipbuilding, etc.[14] These have already been mentioned in the introduction. Among the group of industries identified as strategic, paper and paper products share all the characteristics which make for importance in international trade, but it does not feature prominently in trade disputes because of its high weight to value ratio; its trade is mainly in the form of wood and pulp, like other raw materials.

3.3 *Conclusion*

Disputes over international manufacturing trade are thus caused by the very process of industrialisation, which is a central goal of

national governments. To the extent that more countries industrialise successfully, the greater the tensions over international
trade markets. In the present period the political obstacles in many
Third World countries might, however, prevent successful industrialisation, thereby pre-empting a further intensification of trade
problems. According to Oskar Lange, this is an outcome which it
would be in the interest of the 'firstcomers' to promote.[15] The intensification of competition over markets in international manufacturing trade will also act as a brake, since the larger the number of
countries which have already industrialised, the more difficult it is
for those who follow.

The one novel and important element in the contemporary equation is the activities of manufacturing multinationals. The manufacturing multinationals have resisted the pressures towards the
abandonment of free trade. For them, tariff barriers and the like are
akin to additional transport costs which would inhibit their
freedom of movement. In particular, it would disrupt the existing
pattern of investment. Their conflicts of interest with national
governments (and labour) and their considerable influence make
the future of the international economy and the fate of neo-
mercantilist impulses uncertain.[16]

On the other hand, the political durability of the territorial-state
cannot be easily dismissed, although a possible mutation of the
international political system may be in the offing, as many have
been predicting. In the short run, however, the probable solution to
the problem of excess capacity in the world economy is cartelisation; indeed, this is what happened during the first thirty years of
the twentieth century. In the event cartelisation did not succeed,
and the onset of war imposed a solution through mass destruction.

3.4 Organisation of the book

The first chapter of this book is devoted to a detailed evaluation of
the issue of similarities in economic structures across countries. A
further issue analysed is the significance of exports at different
stages of economic growth, to underline the problem of surplus
capacity and conflicts over markets created by similar structures of
production. Finally, a number of industries strategic for economic
growth and the economic 'self-sufficiency' and military security of
the State are identified. These are the manufacturing industries
concerning which conflicts over markets will be analysed.

The compulsions inherent for territorial-states in the modern international political system are argued and reaffirmed in the second chapter. The central theme, which is not an issue of significant controversy, is the insecurity of territorial-states that motivates them towards the achievement of industrialisation and relative economic self-sufficiency once other industrial nations appear in the international system. The methods of likely State intervention, once industrialisation has been attained, to defend its fundamental economic structures are enumerated in broad terms.

In the third chapter a number of associated issues of indirect but substantive importance are discussed. Firstly, the military factors which determined the timing of the initial industrial changes in Europe before the actual industrial revolutions and the success of Britain in becoming the firstcomer country. In addition, it is argued that the timing and pace of industrialisation in the latecomer countries of nineteenth century Europe, Japan and the USA were dictated by the success of predecessor countries. The analysis in the fourth chapter is concerned to demonstrate the intervention of the State authority in territorial entities because of the insecurity of participation in an international system, in which firstcomer countries have achieved a vastly enhanced economic and therefore military potential through industrialisation.

The fourth chapter deals with the experience of State intervention in the process of industrialisation in a selection of latecomer countries. Three of them, Japan, Italy and the USA belong to the 'first round' of industrialisation; the other two, India and Brazil, belong to the 'second round' of the post-war period.

Evidence about a number of other countries (Germany, France and the more recent cases of the Republic of Korea and Mexico) which had been surveyed in the original thesis has been excluded from the present book for reasons of space. Japan has been included because it is the only non-European country which industrialised during the nineteenth century. Italy has been selected instead of France and Germany because the latter two examples are much better known. The case of the USA is included because it is a particularly illuminating example. The significance of State intervention in US industrialisation is usually underestimated since it is regarded as the *laissez faire* country *par excellence*.

The 'second round' countries discussed in the book, India and Brazil, have been chosen because they are two important developing countries professing contrasting economic ideologies. Their examples illustrate the significance of State intervention in the attempt to industrialise despite distinctive ideological perspectives.

The fifth chapter is devoted to a discussion of the conflicts over the world market for the group of strategic industries which the spread of industrialisation precipitates, the preliminary focus of the introduction. The shifts in market shares in the group of strategic industries since the late nineteenth century between countries and the outcomes which resulted will be surveyed in the discussion. The detailed data on shifts relate to the period 1899–1971 but an impressionistic analysis of trade relations since the nineteenth century and a brief discussion of more aggregate data for the post-1971 period will also be undertaken.

This chapter is concluded with an evaluation of the response of the State to relative economic decline and concomitant loss in market shares, primarily in the context of international trade relationships, i.e. departures from liberal trading arrangements as a consequence of uncompetitiveness. The responses of the two major declining countries, the US and the UK during the post-war period are considered in some detail. This analysis is preceded by a brief discussion of the propensities of the State, in general, to intervene in response to potential or real threats to its strategic industries.

The last chapter is concerned with the incipient structural changes in the world economy and pattern of exports in manufactured goods brought about by the activities of transnational corporations (TNCs). The impact of this development on the production structure of countries is analysed. Finally, the role of TNCs in exports and international trade policy in different countries, and therefore trade relations, is evaluated.

The last section is the conclusion, in which the preceding arguments are synthesised and summarised with some final remarks.

Notes

1. National Consumer Council (September 1978) p. 55; Allen (1967) p. 96; Also see Saxonhouse in Taylor, A. (ed.) (1973) pp. 137–64.
2. The possibility of retaliation by other countries in response to import barriers exists, but its practical effectiveness in the framework of a multilateral trading system is by no means predictable. The country imposing the trade barriers may not be a significant exporter to the country most affected by it. Furthermore, the expansion which the import barriers are intended to stimulate may permit a higher absolute volume of imports at a later stage.

3. Downes (1957).
4. Kindleberger (1959) pp. 30–47.
5. Weeks (1977) p. 282.
6. Ibid. p. 288.
7. Weeks (op. cit.) p. 289.
8. The three tests adopted as criteria for selecting the set of strategic industries are: backward and forward linkages, economies of scale and growth performance.
9. The exclusion of this political dimension from the neo-classical model explains its inability to apprehend the dynamics of change.
10. Gerschenkron (1966).
11. See, for instance, Clough (1939, 1964); and Rostow (ed.) (1965).
12. Kobayashi, (1922).
13. The dispute over textiles and an apparent solution somewhat pre-dates disputes in other products. The reason for this is the role of textiles in the initial stage (defined in the literature as 'early') of industrialisation, whereas the others follow at a later stage, and can be schematised in terms of 'middle' and 'late' industries. As the industrial structure of a country matures it becomes involved in the production of goods of the 'middle' and 'late' stages, and correspondingly markets them internationally.
14. See *Business Week, The Far Eastern Economic Review, Journal of World Trade Law, The World Economy,* etc.
15 In Dobb (1963).
16. See for example Frieden (1977).

1 Similarities in the pattern of economic growth

1.1 Introduction

The model developed in the following pages is based on the well-known work of Chenery and his colleagues, and other economists who have developed and extended it further. The work of these authors concerns the idea of similarity in modern economic growth referred to in the Introduction.

The theme of similarity is not new, but the more specific model of these authors has been a novel and important development. According to them, modern economic growth is characterised by patterns which are broadly similar for countries irrespective of the actual historical period when they occur, i.e. both firstcomers and latecomers display similar patterns. These patterns are observable in terms of (a) the relationship between the growth of GNP and the growth of different sectors like agriculture and manufacturing, and (b) the relationship between GNP and different manufacturing industries; both of these demonstrate repetitive patterns in different countries in different historical periods.

In the subsequent sections the implications of these patterns of growth for international trade in manufactures are analysed. The analysis is focused on the issue of import-substitution and the patterns of exports of industrial products. The determinants of industrialisation are also analysed to assess the true importance of import-substitution for the process of industrialisation.

Following the evaluation of similarities in the patterns of economic growth between countries in different historical periods, the firstcomers and latecomers, a comparison is made to determine specific similarities in the production structure of different countries. This comparison of similarities in the production structure is carried out in terms of three tests: (a) a measure of the linkages, both forward and backward, which connect a single industry with other industries, (b) the degree of triangularisation of the input–output tables, and (c) the comparability of the input coefficients of the countries sampled. The full methodology of these tests is elaborated in the text. On the basis of these tests the authors surveyed have concluded that a 'common fundamental structure of production in modern economic systems' is evident.

The relative importance of the various industries for economic growth and industrialisation is analysed in a final section. It is argued that a set of strategic industries exists which is strategic for growth on several counts and must be acquired for successful industrialisation. In fact, it is the regularity with which these industries are found across countries that accounts for much of the similarity in production structures in the latter.

1.2 Similarities in the pattern of economic growth and production structure across countries

1.2.1 *The theoretical debate*

The idea that modern economic development is characterised by similar patterns has been present in the literature on economic development for a long time and is widely accepted by scholars, both economists and non-economists, at least in its general formulation.

The theme of similarity, in a broad sense, is a basic tenet of Marxist thinking on economic development and progress. According to Marx, 'the country that is more developed industrially only shows, to the less developed, the image of its own future'.[1] The idea of similarity in this context stems from the Marxist view of the laws of motion of capital and its tendency towards extended reproduction, commonly described as imperialism. On an economic level imperialism has been regarded as the vehicle through which capitalism is replicated in non-industrial areas. However, the failure of imperialist expansion to initiate capitalist revolution in vast areas of the non-industrial world has led to the qualification of its presumed propensity as a force for change. The considerable literature which has emerged on this subject identifies contradictory political and economic factors which frustrate the process of change, perpetuating instead the pre-capitalist *modus vivendi* and intensifying the state of underdevelopment they were expected to destroy. Nevertheless, the idea of similarity asserted by Marx remains valid although the eventual reflection on the 'mirror' might take an unanticipated and devious path.

Rostow was one of the first liberal economists to validate

implicitly the idea of similarity. Rostow has asserted the existence of a 'certain rough sequence in the development process'. He has described the prerequisite of 'modern men' — changes in agriculture and 'the transfer of some part of the rent flow into the supply of capital for the creation of social overhead capital'. According to Rostow, development also requires efficient foreign trade institutions, the capacity to earn foreign exchange and, importantly, the ability of the 'modern men' to co-ordinate and respond to the potential spreading effects of the leading sectors.[2]

In another vein, the work of Kuznets is empirically illustrative of the phenomenon of similarity which has subsequently crystallised cogently in the work of the authors surveyed in this section. The quantitative work of Kuznets is thus a precursor to the more specific theme of similarities in the economic development of nations.[3]

1.3 The empirical investigation

1.3.1 *Methodology and concepts*

The debate on Rostow's work shows, however, that although the general ideas are appealing, they are in fact self-explanatory. The categories like 'take-off' which have been put forward to sustain the idea of similarities in economic development are too vague and ambiguous to provide an adequate standard for articulating the idea of similarity.[4]

The development and spread of new techniques for empirical research have given a more precise connotation to the idea of similarity, which does not necessarily collimate with the original concepts and categories of the previous debate. Although the research in this field is far from answering all the questions, satisfactory evidence is now available of the extent to which similar patterns of economic growth are observable in different countries, even at different time periods. Since the evidence is quantifiable it allows for the identification of similarities in terms of empirically defined categories which are less ambiguous.

At the outset, it is important to stress that the very nature of quantitative economic analysis limits the analysis to growth, as opposed to the phenomenon of development. The former has traditionally concerned the quantitative change over time of economic variables which can be measured; the latter encompasses instead socio-political changes that cannot be analysed by the econometric methods which have been employed.[5]

By similarities in the growth patterns of different countries is meant comparable relations between an economic variable chosen to represent the growth rate of the national economy and the growth rate of selected economic variables over a defined period of time. The former is traditionally identified by output or value added; the latter variables vary according to the area of interest. If the area coincides with production structure then the changing composition of growth over time of the different economic sectors will be preferred, together with changes in labour productivity, capital accumulation, etc. If the emphasis is on the demand side instead, it entails a study of the variables related to income distribution together with an analysis of the sector dynamics.

It is recognised in the literature that the dynamics of the different sectors of the economy, including the public sector and the export-import one, are fundamental for assessing the similarities in economic growth patterns. This assumption is based on the fact that every major change in the relevant economic variables must ultimately be reflected in the very economic structure. The assumption is supported by the definition of economic growth which, in the view of Kuznets, is the shifting over time of the relative importance of the different economic sectors owing to differential growth rates.

For the purposes of the present research the analysis of inter-sectoral dynamics is fundamental, since the idea of similarities in growth patterns is at the core of the model the research aims to substantiate. It is also sufficient for the purpose of demonstrating the relationship between economic growth and the potential for irreconcilable divergences of interests in trade between different countries as a consequence of economic growth. The emphasis of this book will be on the manufacturing sector, for reasons which have already been elaborated in the Introduction.

A search for similarities only within groups of countries starting off at the same time might, at first sight, appear the most appropriate approach in considering the effects of technological progress in production methods, the development of products and in the organisation of economic activity, as well as related socio-political modifications. In the language that has now become familiar, this is known as the distinction between the firstcomers and the latecomers.[6] Even abstracting from the operation of technological progress and socio-political modifications, the above conclusion could be reinforced by the significance of the constraints posed by already developed firstcomers to the developing latecomer (in principle this could also offer advantages to latecomers).

Anticipating the results it can, however, be stated that many similarities exist independently of the timing of the start of the process of growth. Indeed, the timing gives rise to differences as well, but the differences appear to be systematic. This vindicates in retrospect the method adopted by the authors surveyed. Chenery and his collaborators (and others) pursued the identification of similarities independently of the timing. The analysis of the differences has been undertaken only when they appeared to be systematic and significant.

The two-fold aim of identifying systematic differences while tracing fundamental similarities is fulfilled particularly well by the combination of two econometric techniques: the cross-section analysis and the time-series analysis. If one wants to see the relationship between per capita GNP and the share of industry in GNP, the time-series analysis of the share of industry over time will reveal a particular pattern for a given time period for each country (see Figure 1.1A). In order to see if the latecomers are likely to follow the same pattern a regression can be run between GNP per capita and the share of industry of each country for a group of countries at different levels of development; the figures of each country would refer in this case to a common year, say 1960 (see Figure 1.1B). If a superimposition of the cross-section pattern on the time-series pattern reveals a common trend, the hypothesis of similarity independent of timing is confirmed. If the cross-section series displays systematic deviations from the time series it establishes one or more systematic differences in the growth paths of the firstcomers as compared to the latecomers (see Figure 1.1C).

By and large, the findings in section 1.4 derive from the application of a combination of the two techniques. Either of them is used in isolation when the division between latecomers and firstcomers is deemed to be relatively unimportant, or when data are unavailable.[7]

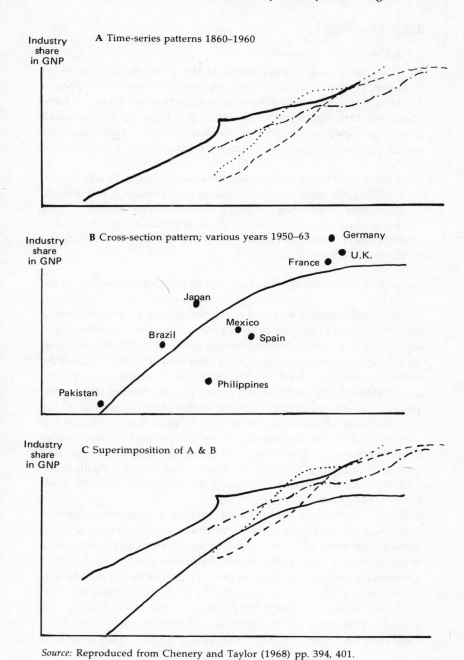

Source: Reproduced from Chenery and Taylor (1968) pp. 394, 401.

Figure 1.1 An illustration of the superimposition of cross section and time-series patterns

1.4   Findings

1.4.1 Cross-section analysis

With regard to the relative share of the three major sectors — industry, primary produce, and services in GNP — Chenery–Taylor (1968), adopting a cross-section regression analysis, have identified three patterns respectively for large countries, small countries exporting mainly manufactures and small countries specialising in the export of primary produce.[8]

> In the large countries industry rises rapidly from 16 per cent of GNP at an income of 100 dollars to 32 per cent at 400 dollars. Thereafter the increase is much slower and a peak share of 37 per cent is reached at 1,200 dollars. Primary production falls steadily and crosses the industry curve at a level of 280 dollars, where the share of each is 27 per cent.[9]

According to the authors there are few significant deviants from the pattern.

The small industry-oriented countries show a very much similar pattern. However, in the case of large countries, only per capita income levels (as a measure of the relative level of economic development), the population level (as a measure of the size of the country) and the fixed capital stock (as a measure of capital accumulation) appear to be important in determining the growth patterns of the industrial sector and the primary sector. In the second group of countries the export of manufctured goods has greater influence in determining the relative share of industry *vis-à-vis* primary production than capital accumulation has for the first group. This finding is easily understood when one considers the fact that small countries import a substantial part of their investment goods.

Finally, in the case of the small, primary production-orientated countries, the only difference to be found when compared to the pattern experienced by the previous two groups of countries is a much slower decline in the share of primary production in GNP. Conversely, this slow decline in primary production is matched by a slower rise in the share of industry, the former exceeding the latter up to an income level of $300 per capita. Not unexpectedly, this phenomenon is due to the export pattern of this group of countries. However, for a small country, the negative impact on the rise of the

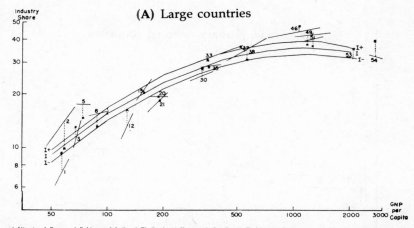

1 Nigeria 2 Burma 3 Pakistan 5 India 8 Thailand 12 Korea 15 Brazil 20 Turkey 21 Philippines 30 Mexico 33 Japan 35 Spain
37 Argentina 38 Italy 46 Germany 49 France 51 United Kingdom 53 Canada 54 United States

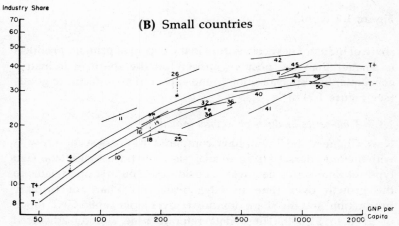

4 Haiti 10 Bolivia 11 Taiwan 16 Paraguay 18 Tunisia 19 Peru 25 Algeria 26 Portugal 32 Jamaica 34 Greece 36 Uruguay 40 Israel
41 Puerto Rico 42 Austria 43 Netherlands 45 Finland 48 Belgium 50 Norway

Figure 1.2 Cross-section regression for the share of industry in
GNP (see p. 22 for Figure 1.2(C))

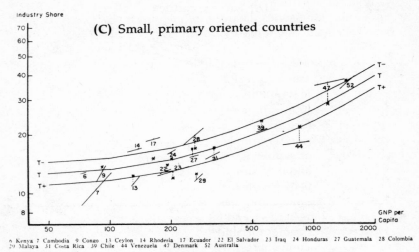

Source: Reproduced from Chenery and Taylor (1968) pp. 394, 397, 398.

Figure 1.2 (cont.)

share of industry of specialisation in the export of primary products is smaller than the positive impact (on the share of industry) consequent on specialisation in the export of manufactured goods (see Figure 1.2).

1.4.2 Time-series analysis of sectoral growth

Next, Chenery and Taylor have compared the cross-section results with the ones derived from an analysis of the time-series data. Two types of time-series data were considered. The first one relates to the growth over time of GNP itself, the share of primary production, and the share of industry over a per capita GNP range of $100 to $1,000. These data refer to nine already advanced countries — the firstcomers — and cover the same GNP range used for the cross-section analysis. The data were originally collected by Kuznets and stretch back to the nineteenth century. For the share of each of the two sectors considered, from a per capita income range of $100 to $1,000, the time series were plotted for each of the nine countries. The cross-section pattern of the share of each sector and of each of the three sub-group of countries (*L*, *SM*, *SP*), was then superimposed. The superimposition shows that the pattern of the share of each sector for the large country sub-group approximates well to the time-series data of the nine advanced countries. The only systematic difference evident is a slower decline of primary production in the post-war cross-section regression of the late-comers compared to the trend of the firstcomers who belong to the earlier period (see Figure 1.3).

Both the basic similarities and the systematic differences relating to the decline in the share of primary production in the post-war period are confirmed by a second superimposition of the cross-section and time-series trends. In this instance, the time-series data refer to the same sample used for the cross-section analysis. Time-series of GNP and the share of the two sectors were calculated for the period 1950–63 for the forty-eight countries sampled. Furthermore, a regression line has been run to derive an unique ('standard') time-series trend for all the forty-eight countries with respect to the same variables (GNP growth on industry and primary production shares). The 'standard' time-series regression line has been finally superimposed on the cross-section regression line.

In conclusion, it is worth mentioning that further tests have confirmed that a country will 'converge' to the standard pattern irrespective of the initial proportions between industrial and primary production.

1.4.3 Inter-industry growth patterns

The cross-section regression analysis has been repeated by the authors, substituting the share of the three main sectors in GNP (industry, agriculture and services) with the share of each of twelve manufacturing sectors. The data still refer to about fifty countries. The results lead to distinctions not only between large, small industry-orientated, and small primary-orientated countries, but also between three different patterns of industry growth-behaviour within each sub-group of countries. The three-fold classification of growth patterns for individual industries contemplates a distinction between early, middle and late industries, according to the climax of their respective impact on GNP.

The early industries — food, leather goods and textiles — appear to be the ones which 'supply essential demand of the poorest countries and can be carried on with simple technology'.[10] In the large countries 'they increase their share of GNP little above income levels of 200 dollars or so' and 'exhaust their potential for

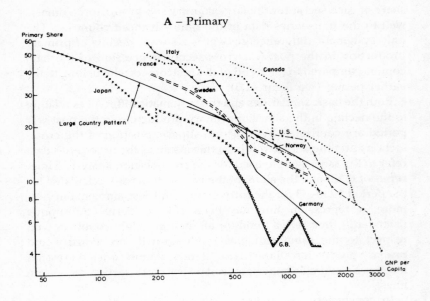

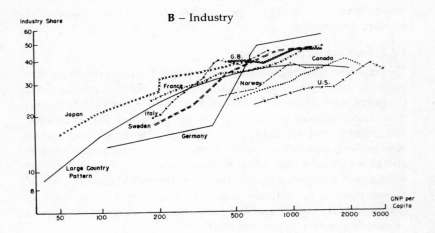

Figure 1.3 Historical patterns 1860–1960

Source: Reproduced from Chenery and Taylor (1968) p. 401.

import-substitution and export growth at fairly low income levels.[11] As a percentage of manufacturing output their share declines at fairly low levels of per capita income ($100 to $200).

The middle industries double their share of GNP at low income levels, but stop rising at income levels of $400 to $500. In a 'typical' large country these industries can be identified with non-metallic minerals, rubber products, wood products, chemicals and petroleum refining. The rise in the share of middle industries is substantially accounted for by import-substitution.

Late industries include clothing, printing, basic metals, metal products and paper, i.e., most consumer durables, as well as investment goods and intermediate goods necessary for their production. In large countries they always account for 80 per cent of the increase in the share of industry in GNP for values of per capita GNP above the level of $300.

Time-series data referring to western European manufacturing over the period 1901–59 collected and elaborated by Maizels (1963) confirm in detail the behaviour of the three industry groups, as predicted by the cross-section analysis for a typical country.[12]

In the case of the small-industry orientated country (SM) there is a slower rise of industry in all the three industry sub-groups as compared to the large country (L) pattern. According to Chenery, this slower rise is due to the effect of economies of scale. In the small primary-orientated countries (SP) the even slower rise of industry is attributed by the authors to the effect of resource endowment. The effect of economies of scale in delaying the industrial growth of SM countries, as compared to L countries is quantitatively equivalent to the impact of resource endowment in delaying the industrial growth of SP countries, as compared to SM countries. The impact of the two factors, economies of scale and resource endowment is particularly concentrated on the same group of industries, namely, basic metals, printing, rubber products, chemicals, textiles and non-metallic minerals, in both SM and SP countries. But the effect of economies of scale on the growth of industry is reversed in SM countries at high income levels because of the presence of exports. However, the even slower growth of industry in SP countries owing to the effect of resource endowment does not seem to be reversed when the per capita GNP reaches high levels.

1.4.4 *Export and import growth patterns*

The results stated above cannot but lead to the expectation of some regular pattern in the growth and composition of imports and exports once it is assumed (as effectively done by the study surveyed) that growth and composition of demand with the rise of income follow the same pattern for each country. The maintenance of the distinction between large, small industry-orientated and small primary-orientated is a natural consequence.

There exists a first important quantitative difference in the export and import profiles of large countries *vis-à-vis* both types of small country. The first relates to the quantitative importance of import-export activity as a share of GDP. For reasons connected to the size of the market, the opportunity cost of diversification of domestic production *vis-à-vis* trade, both imports and exports are less important for large countries than small ones. While the exports of large countries vary from 10 to 15 per cent of GDP, the corresponding figure for small countries is 20 to 30 per cent or more of GDP.[13]

As for the composition of both imports and exports, dealt with in the next sections, in coherence with the previous picture, the focus is on industrial products and the distinction between early, middle and late industries is also maintained.

1.4.5 *Dynamics over time of imported industrial products*

The changing pattern of industrial imports over time is of interest to the present research only in connection with domestic industrialisation. In other words, the interest is in the circumstances, timing and effects of import-substitution more than in the pattern of industrial imports itself. As will become apparent in the subsequent section, import-substitution was in fact, 'responsible' for more than half the growth of domestic supply.

Large countries initiate the import-substitution of a wide-range of industrial products at fairly low levels of per capita income. In a 'mirror' image to the pattern of growth described in the manufacturing and construction industries, the first products to be substituted belong to the early industry sub-group. Imports of intermediate products and investment goods, plus consumer durables predominate at an income range of $50 to $100. The import-substitution of most intermediate products (middle industry sub-group) commences at an income level of $100. Finally, the import-substitution of investment goods and consumer durables already exists at an income level of $100 to $400.

The existence of economies of scale is regarded by Chenery and Taylor as the most important factor in accounting for the delay by SM countries in acquiring a number of middle and late industries as compared to large countries. Naturally, the greater quantitative importance and slower decline of imports of products belonging to the same group of industries by the SM countries must be imputed to the same factor. This is more particularly evident in the heavy industries — chemicals, paper products, basic metals and metal products — than in other industrial categories. Import-substitution in these industries shows a delay of $300 as compared with large countries.[14]

For reasons which will become more apparent in subsequent sections there seems to be a trend towards an acceleration of import-substitution in heavy products enjoying economies of scale, as a main systematic difference from past experience. This consideration is applicable to both large and small manufacturing-orientated countries. It seems to be especially true for metal industries; in this particular case, the reason is the possibility of substituting intermediate metal products for intermediate rubber or wooden products because of technological progress. The classic example is provided by shipbuilding technology.

Finally, the small primary-orientated sub-group of countries is considered. As shown in the inter-industry growth pattern, the lag in import-substitution is concentrated in more or less the same sectors affected by scale economy disadvantages in the small industry-orientated countries. While import-substitution will eventually occur in the early and middle industry sub-groups (typically betweeen income levels of $400 to $1,000), it is not clear if the same will be true for the late industry sub-group as a whole. This uncertainty is attributable to the smallness of the sample available for small primary-orientated countries, namely only Denmark and New Zealand.

1.4.6 Dynamics of exports of industrial products

Since a later chapter will deal in detail with the question of industrial exports, this section will be confined to an elucidation of the fundamental features in order to complete the picture deriving from the development patterns discussed earlier.

The contemporary export pattern appears to be uniform for all types of countries in the per capita income interval of $50 to $100; in this range primary products are exported. From a per capita income level of $100 divergences begin to appear between countries. 'For the average country of population 10 million, industrial exports reach $10 per capita at an income level of about $250 dollars'.[15]

But while 'for the typical small country having high primary exports — the threshold level of $10 per capita is not reached until income reaches a level of $350 per capita' (e.g. Malaysia, Jamaica and the Ivory Coast), for the typical SM country industrial exports are above $10 per capita at an income level of $200 per capita.[16] As for large countries, although their overall pattern of growth of manufacturing is similar to the one shown by SM countries, their export levels are lower.

It is in the composition of exports that SM countries and L countries display the most pronounced differences. The latter start exporting industrial products enjoying economies of scale — basic metals, chemicals, machinery, etc. — at a lower income level. The former specialises at first in light, labour-intensive industrial products such as wood, textiles, processed food, clothing and footwear. The recent spread of multinationals has augmented this list of products exported in the early phases of economic growth. Often the export of the parts and components of products that has resulted from transnational production belongs to the late-industry sub-group. This recent development is particularly well illustrated by South Korea, Taiwan, Israel, Puerto Rico and Hong Kong. It should, however, be stressed that this development is of recent origin.[17]

The large country sub-group also exports the types of labour-intensive products listed above, in the early stages of development, apart from products which enjoy economies of scale.

To summarise, in the later stages of development as well as in the early one, the changing composition of exports for large countries more or less reflects the growth of domestic manufacturing capacity. The evidence on the export pattern of the already developed countries — the firstcomers — during their process of industrialisation has not been analysed systematically to provide satisfactory evidence of comparability with the behaviour of the large countries in the post-war period. The data are, of course, neither comprehensive nor wholly reliable. But the evidence available does not contradict the hypothesis that, by and large, the export growth patterns of large countries today are broadly comparable with the experience of large countries in the past; i.e. the experience of firstcomers and latecomers is largely similar. Nevertheless systematic differences can be recognised to exist since a large country developing now encounters a changed environment: the most self-evident one being the existence of an international market different in structure and size, with its attendant opportunities and constraints.

To return to the SM countries. If industrialisation, relying at first on the export of labour-intensive industrial products, is to continue successfully it seems to require a shift toward the export of heavy industrial products characterised by economies of scale. This emergent trend is perceptible in countries like Israel, Hong Kong and Singapore, which have begun the export of products like chemicals, transport equipment, etc.[18] Subsequent sections will provide theoretical reasons to show that this trend is the most plausible one for the future. Unfortunately, past experience relating to already developed SM countries, which include Switzerland and Belgium, does not provide significant evidence. In the case of Switzerland and Belgium, the integration with and proximity to large markets have had an important influence in determining growth and export patterns.[19]

Finally, for the SP sub-group of countries, a substantial shift from primary products to manufacturing is likely to occur at income levels between $500 to $1,000 per capita. At this level the wage rate is likely to be too high to give a comparative advantage in labour-intensive products. However, it is difficult to anticipate accurately the most likely export patterns at present since very few countries belonging to the SP orientated sub-group have already reached this per capita income level.

1.4.7 Determinants of industrialisation

Taking a sample of thirty-eight countries and census data spread over the interval 1950–6, according to the year of the census in each country, Chenery has analysed the pattern and causes of the relative growth of industries.[20] The manufacturing sectors have been broken down into sixteen industries, re-grouped as the following: group A (investment products) machinery, transport equipment, metals, non-metallic minerals; group B (intermediate products) paper, petroleum products, rubber, chemicals, textiles; group C (consumer goods) wood products, printing, clothing, leather, processed food, beverages and tobacco.

Avoiding distinctions concerning the characteristics of individual countries, a cross-section type regression has been run for each of the sixteen industries, relating the growth in each industry's per capita value added, taken as a dependent variable, to per capita growth of national income and of domestic population. The results show that for a 'typical' country 'at income level $600, the share of group A has increased to 35 per cent of all manufacturing, while group C has fallen to 43 per cent. Group B maintains a fairly constant share of the total'.[21]

Once the important factors in growth, the rise in income and the size of the country have been taken into account, three causes of each industry's specific growth pattern remain to be investigated: import-substitution, the changing composition of final demand and the changing composition of intermediate demand deriving from them. The methodology employed starts from the assumption that if none of the three 'causes' were operating, economic growth could be viewed as a perfectly equiproportional increase of both the demand for and output of each of the sixteen industries: the increase being equal to the rate of growth of national income. Moreover, since the cross-section regression analysis has revealed that the growth of per capita income and the size of population explain a substantial part of the growth of each sector, one could assume that these two variables account fully for an equiproportional growth of each of the manufacturing sectors. What the remaining three variables — import-substitution, growth of final demand and of intermediate demand — explain is the deviation of each sector from an equiproportional growth pattern.

Accordingly, the measurement of the impact of each of the three factors on the growth of specific industries relies on the analysis of the deviation of each industry's growth from the equiproportional rate. As an illustration suppose that the impact of import-substitution on the typical growth of the textile industry, relative to the growth of national income is to be calculated. An income interval of $100–$600 can be taken as an illustration of the effects of industrialisation. The typical propensity to import at an income level of $100 is derived from data on imports of textiles of a sub-sample of countries, reckoning incomes per capita close to the level of $100.[22] Next, a typical value of production and imports is derived for an income level of $600 from a different sub-sample of countries having per capita incomes close to that level. The typical import coefficient for this level of income is obtained by dividing their typical imports by their typical production values. On the assumption of an equiproportional growth rate, imports would increase sixfold and so would production, leaving unchanged the initial propensity to import, i.e. the typical one for countries at an income level of $100 per capita.

The value for the typical propensity to import at $600 is subtracted from the value of the initial (and constant in the hypothesis of equiproportionality) propensity to import, giving the deviation in the import coefficient due to non-proportional growth. This deviation is taken to represent the contribution of import-substitution to the non-proportional growth rate of the textile industry.

The same method is applied to the analysis of the deviation of final and intermediate demand from the equiproportional, sixfold increase in values. The procedure is repeated for each of the sixteen sectors.

The results show that in groups A and B (investment and intermediate groups) where imports provide 64 per cent of the total supply of commodities at an income level of $100, 'the substitution of domestic production for imports is the cause of the high growth rate, accounting for 70 per cent of the total deviation'.[23]

It is interesting to note that the same group of industries, A and B (except for non-metallic minerals) show higher values for the scale elasticities coefficient in a cross-section regression of each industry's value added growth rate on national income growth rate and size of the country. The data for the above regression refer to a sub-sample of thirty-eight countries at an income level of $300 per capita. The scale elasticity coefficient measures the association (taken as a casual link) between a percentage increase in the industry's rate of growth in value added and a percentage increase in the size of the market measured by the population variable. The high value of scale elasticities is taken to be indicative of the importance of economies of scale, which in turn explains both the high percentage of imports in the first phases of industrialisation and the high rate of growth induced by import-substitution. From the results obtained, Chenery concludes that 'these results contradict the usual assumption that changes in the composition of demand are the main cause of industrial growth'. If a country has an increase in income with no change in comparative advantage, the analysis suggests that only about a third of the normal amount of industrialisation will take place. Changes in supply conditions resulting from a change in relative factor costs as income rises, causes a substitution of domestic production for imports and, to a lesser extent, of factory goods for handicraft goods and services. These supply changes are more important in explaining the growth of industry than changes in demand.[24]

1.5 Similarities in the economic structure

1.5.1 Hypothesis and concepts

The existence of regular and comparable patterns of economic growth for the major sectors of the economy, and in particular for the manufacturing sector, points strongly to the existence of similarities in the structure of production itself. One can dispense here with providing a precise definition of the term 'structure'. All that is really needed is to specify the elements chosen as representative of the structure. The hypothesis of the studies surveyed, which have investigated the similarities of the structures of production in different countries, is that intersectoral demand can be selected as indicative of the production structure of an economy. Intermediate demand is defined as the produced — as distinct from primary — inputs which are consumed in the production of so-called final commodities. The primary, or non-produced inputs include labour, land and capital input flows, i.e. depreciation. The produced, or non-primary inputs, include all other inputs, e.g. tomatoes for the processed food industry or iron ingots for the transport equipment industry.

To restate the basic hypothesis, similarities in the intersectoral flows are assumed to be representative of similarities in the structure of production. The explanation for similar growth patterns ultimately rests on the assumption that either because of imitation, or a phenomenon of dominance (economic, political and cultural) every country experiencing modern economic growth will share with its predecessors a similar pattern of demand (summarised in its most general form by Engel's law), a similar set of technological alternatives and a broadly similar development of organisational alternatives.[25]

The data reveal, to anticipate the results detailed below, not only the existence of broadly similar structures for countries at the same level of development, but also a substantial comparability of the production structures for countries at different levels of development, i.e. varying per capita income levels. To put it another way, while economic growth is reflected in a systematic change of not only volume but also relative sectoral shares in GNP, the structure of production, as defined above, displays a much greater stability. One explanation could be the statistical method adopted to measure the 'similarities'. The indices are constructed in such a way that only the relative contribution of a sector or industry to the inter-industries flows is taken into account. This reduces the influence of the size of the country and its absolute income level on the inter-industries flow patterns. Nevertheless, it cannot obviate the fact that the relative importance of each sector and industry varies with the level of output. A second reason is the level of aggregation. The same ratio of value of inputs to value of output from sector to sector could conceal differences in the composition of products. Finally, a third reason, to be stressed later, might be the characteristics of the sample of countries selected, all of which are in the category of 'large'. It is likely that large countries have a fairly diversified economy, even at low income levels. However, it is assumed that the main reason for the existence of similarities at divergent income levels is the availability of a basic set of technologies, common to all countries, which can be adapted to the production of different bundles of goods relying on a limited number of industries for the production of basic inputs. This hypothesis will be developed further.

1.5.2 *The empirical evidence*

The analytical tools designed to reckon the inter-industry flows are the so-called flow tables and input-output matrices. Flow tables, in contrast to matrices, measure the absolute values of the inputs and outputs between sectors and industries, while input-output tables are normally expressed in coefficients that measure inputs as a ratio of the sector/industry output level, which is taken as a unity. It is obviously always possible to derive an input-output (coefficients) table from a flow table by dividing each input figure by the sector/industry output level. For the purposes of the following exposition it is unnecessary to specify which type of tables has been used, since the results do not depend on the original specification of the table itself. Some of the tests of similarity, however, can be carried out only on coefficient tables: consequently all references below will be to input-output tables, in order to simplify the terminology. The time period for which the amount of flows is calculated is one year.

The studies surveyed have carried out comparisons of the input-output matrices, the elements of which are measured in value terms, of sub-groups of the following countries: USA (1947), Japan (1950 and 1955), Italy (1950), Norway (1950), Spain (1957) and India (1964–5). The date in brackets indicates the year to which the matrix refers. In the case of Japan most of the studies consider the 1950 matrix, one of them considers the 1955 matrix.

Following the pioneering study of Chenery and Watanabe, all matrices have been made comparable and reaggregated in a number of industries which range from 22 to 37, of which two-thirds exhaust the manufacturing sector, while the total obviously encompasses all productive activities (including the tertiary sector).[26]

The comparability of the input-output tables has been tested against three main criteria: (a) a measure of the linkages, both forward and backward, which connect a single industry with every other industry, (b) the degree of triangularisation of the matrices and (c) the similarity between corresponding input coefficients in different matrices.

(a) Forward and backward linkages. According to this criterion, two matrices are considered similar if the degree of forward and backward linkages displayed by the same sector/industry is of comparable magnitude for the two countries under consideration.

Two methods have been adopted to assess the magnitude of linkages. The first one, originally developed by Chenery and Watanabe in 1958 for Italy (1950), Norway (1950), USA (1947), and Japan (1950), has been adopted by Santhanam and Patil who have extended the analysis to India (1964–5) as well.[27] Laumas has tested the results obtained by the two previous studies using a more sophisticated method and applying it to the matrices of the same countries, including India.[28]

Entries along the column of an input–output matrix indicate purchases of a particular industry from all other industries, i.e. the inputs used by a particular industry and supplied by the rest of the economy. It can therefore be assumed that a column represents some sort of aggregate production process for the industry concerned. A summation of all the entries in a column gives an absolute measure of the backward linkage. Further, the division of this sum total by the output of the sector provides an index of the proportion by which the industry concerned depends on the supply of other industries for every unit of its output. The index, read from the point of view of demand, quantifies the demand for other industries generated by a unit output of the industry under consideration. This index is termed U_j, where j denotes the industry selected.

Entries along the row of an input–output matrix indicate the sales of industry j to every other industry. Summing up the entries of every row and dividing it by the total demand for the products of industry j, an index is obtained (say W_j) which measures the dependence of other industries on industry j. Alternatively, it can be seen as an index of indirect use of products of industry j, as opposed to direct (final) use. This index is a measure of the forward linkages of industry j.

On the basis of the values of U_j and W_j industries have been classified as part of final manufacture (strong backward linkages and weak forward linkages), and intermediate primary production (strong forward linkages and weak backward linkages). Finally, two matrices satisfy the criterion of similarity if broadly the same industries fall under the same classification in each of the countries.

Results from Norway, Italy, the USA and Japan reveal that, with a few exceptions, the same classification of sectors is obtained for each country. The typical classification arranges industries as shown by Table 1.1.

India displays the major number of exceptions, partly because of its level of development and partly on account of aggregation problems. The level of development, for example, explains why the printing and publishing industry, the lumber and wood product industry, and the agricultural and forestry sectors fall under the category of final primary production instead of intermediate production, as for the USA, Japan, etc. In other words, the products of these industries tend to mainly satisfy final demand in India, while in the more developed countries like the USA and Japan they contribute substantially to intermediate demand. Another notable exception in India is the case of the chemical industry, which shows weaker backward linkages (although the difference is not as great because chemicals are a borderline case between intermediate primary and intermediate manufacturing in India). However, except for the cases mentioned, the typical classification of Table 1.1 holds for India as well, which points to the hypothesis that differences in the economic structure are not proportional to

Table 1.1 Types of productive sectors*

		Final				Intermediate		
	III	Final Manufacture	w	u	II	Intermediate Manufacture	w	u
	3	Apparel	.12	.69	13	Iron and steel	.78	.66
	4	Shipbuilding	.14	.58	22	Paper and products	.78	.57
	8	Leather and products	.37	.66	28	Petroleum products	.68	.65
Manufacturing	1	Processed foods	.15	.61	19	Non-ferrous metals	.81	.61
	2	Grain mill products	.42	.89	16	Chemicals	.69	.60
	5	Transport equipment	.20	.60	23	Coal products	.67	.63
	7	Machinery	.28	.51	11	Rubber products	.48	.51
	15	Lumber and wood products	.38	.61	12	Textiles	.57	.69
	14	Non-metallic mineral products	.30	.47	9	Printing and publishing	.46	.49
	10	Industry n.e.c.	.20	.43				
	IV	Final Primary Production			I	Intermediate Primary Production		
	A	*Commodities*			17	Agriculture and forestry	.72	.31
	6	Fishing	.36	.24	27	Coal mining	.87	.23
Primary production	B	*Services*			20	Metal mining	.93	.21
	25	Transport	.26	.31	29	Petroleum and natural gas	.97	.15
	21	Trade	.17	.16	18	Non-metallic minerals	.52	.17
	26	Services	.34	.19	24	Electric power	.59	.27

* The values of w and u are averages for Italy, Japan and the USA.
Source: Reproduced from Chenery and Watanabe (1958) p. 493.

differences in the levels of economic development. Nevertheless, it may be thought that the results would be substantially different in the case of some developing countries which, unlike India, are unable to diversify production because of the limited size of the domestic market. The results might not have been so favourable even when comparing developed and mature developed countries — say, Israel and the USA — if huge differences in size, accompanied by a more substantial specialisation of production are coupled with the differences in their levels of development.

The method described above for the measurement of forward and backward linkages specifies only the immediate inter-dependence among industries; i.e. the dependence of, say, iron and steel on machinery is based only on the direct purchases and sales between the two industries. But the iron and steel industry also depends on the machinery industry indirectly via, say, the chemical industry. The chemical industry supplies to the iron and steel industry products which are dependent on, *inter alia*, inputs supplied by the machinery industry. The same reasoning can be applied to the demand side. A method known as the inversion of matrices allows calculation from the original coefficients another set of coefficients which take into account not only the immediate but also the indirect interdependence among industries.

Laumas has applied the method of matrix inversion to the input-output tables of India, Norway, Italy, Japan and the USA with the dual purpose of testing and improving the results of the studies referred to above.[29] After obtaining the new set of coefficients which take into account the indirect as well as the direct input-output flows he has used them for calculating W_j and U_j indices. His studies do not entirely support the four-group classification of the Chenery–Watanabe and Santhanam–Patil studies.[30] The only industries which respect the original classification for all countries are apparel, leather products, textiles, iron and steel and chemicals. However, the hypothesis of a fundamental similarity in the structure of production, as detected by the linkage criterion, is supported by the following findings: (i) irrespective of the state of economic development all countries have a very high percentage of their intermediate production well linked, (ii) a set of thirteen industries exhausts the list of industries falling into the category which have strong linkages, both backward and forward, for the USA, Japan, Italy and Norway; the industries of the set account for the vast majority of the products used in intermediate production (73.5 per cent for Norway to 84.5 for Italy). In the case of India, eight out of the thirteen industries fall under the same category but they account for no less than 81.8 per cent of the intermediate demand in the country. This last set of industries, which the author labels 'key industries', include iron and steel, textiles, machinery, processed food, agriculture and forestry, chemical, trade and services and transport.[31]

(b) Triangularisation of the matrix. Consider an economy in which land and labour are the only primary inputs (i.e fixed capital, except land, is assumed not to exist) and the only products are raw cotton, textiles and clothing. The input-output table of such a country can be represented by the production sequence of raw cotton, textiles and clothing. The three industries depicted are arranged in the

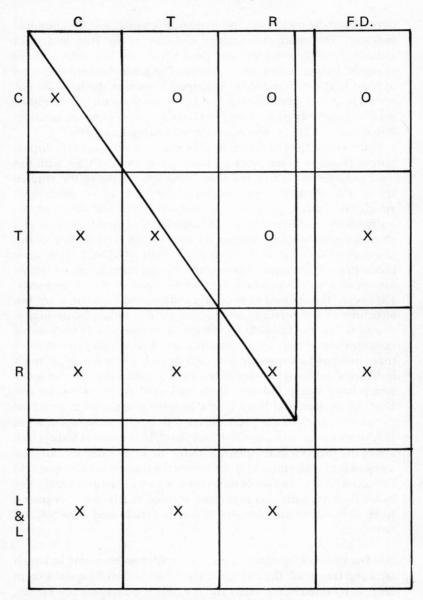

Figure 1.4 Triangularisation of the I–O matrix

Where C = clothing, T = textiles, R = raw cotton, L & L = labour and inputs, F.D. = final demand. The cross indicates a positive coefficient.

Note: The intermediate demand matrix, the relevant one for the purposes of the test, is made up by the entries within the square marked by the double line.

following order: C (cotton), T (textiles), R (raw cotton).

Reading the matrix in Figure 1.4, along the column it can be seen that the production process of clothing, most of which goes to satisfy final demand, requires inputs from textiles (cloth) and raw cotton (e.g. thread); apart from other intermediate products within it (e.g. clothing components). Textiles require raw cotton and intermediate textile products in its production process (in the case of intermediate textile products, say, patchwork cloth may be used, with a single firm sewing the individual pieces). In contrast to clothing, a substantial part of textile products go to satisfy intermediate demand. Finally, in the production of raw cotton, apart from land and labour only raw cotton is needed (e.g. in the form of cotton seed). The output of the raw cotton industry satisfies intermediate demand almost entirely.

Reading the matrix along the rows the mirror image can be seen: raw cotton supplying all the three sectors (for the sake of simplicity final demand is omitted), textiles supplying only textiles, the clothing sector and final demand; clothing supplying only clothing and final demand. This type of matrix depicts a 'natural hierarchy' of sectors, where the dependence only goes one way: from raw cotton (primary products, in the general case) to clothing (final products, in the general case). This is called a triangular matrix. Technically it is defined as a matrix in which the entries above the principal diagonal are empty (i.e. zero).

The possibility of conceiving an approximately triangular matrix for the process of production as a whole might, however, appear speculative. Ultimately, the production process is a circular one. Many intermediate products are linked by circular, as opposed to linear (one-way) dependence in which case the elements above the principal diagonal are positive.

Despite the existence of circular relationships it is always possible to re-arrange a casual ordering of industries in the 'natural hierarchy' order, leaving as many empty entries as possible above the principal diagonal. In the example of Figure 1.4 if the casual ordering was R, T, C, empty entries would be randomly distributed. The 'natural hierarchy' is obtained where the ordering is set as in Figure 1.4.

In this way it is possible to obtain two standards by which the structures of production across countries may be compared. The first is represented by the degree to which the input–output tables of every country approach a triangular pattern. A measure of triangularity can be the number of empty entries (i.e. zero) above the principal diagonal. This comparative exercise will also permit the identification of particular sectors which least conform to the triangular pattern in particular countries, i.e. 'which sectors in which countries least conform . . .'.[32] The second standard is provided by the ordering of the industries which in each country best approximate a triangular table. A rank-order coefficient is the statistical tool which quantifies the similarities of two different orderings.

Using the triangularisation technique Chenery and Watanabe have found their results supportive, on the whole, of the idea of a 'natural hierarchy' of industries, with the 'final manufacture' group on the top and the 'primary production for intermediate use' group at the bottom.[33] The 'intermediate manufacture' group which contributes most to the circularity of production is found to have its industries along the 'natural hierarchy' ordering. Most importantly, the ordering of the sample of countries surveyed by Chenery and Watanabe is surprisingly similar. The most comparable pair of countries are Japan and the USA: the least are Japan and Norway, but the quantitative differences in the rank-order coefficient is minimal. Santhanam and Patil have calculated rank-order correlations between the orderings of Japan, Norway, Italy and the USA in turn with India, to extend the Chenery–Watanabe results.[34] The comparability of the ordering of industries for India with each of the other countries is lower than for any pair of them. Again then, the differences in the levels of development seem to reduce the similarity of structures of production but do not cancel it.

Simpson and Tsukui have carried out a somewhat more sophisticated analysis of triangularity on the input-output tables of the USA (1947), Japan (1955), Spain (1957), Norway (1950) and Italy (1950).[35] Their findings not only confirm but add cogency to and enlarge the results of Chenery–Watanabe and Santhanam–Patil. Not only have they shown that the matrices of the countries considered can be triangularised by following a similar ordering of the industries; they have also shown that, except for the services sector, the triangular patterns tend to be organised in independent blocs of industries whose products are physically homogeneous. Again, despite variations, this tendency is well evident in each country's matrix.

To illustrate their findings, instead of giving precise but lengthy definitions of the terms used, the input-output tables of the five countries are reproduced as 'rearranged' by the authors. As is clearly evident from Figure 1.5 the structure is fundamentally triangular except for a few entries above the principal diagonal. It should be noted that an empty entry does not necessarily mean that no transactions occur between a pair of sectors. It simply means that their flow is not statistically significant compared to other flows and is therefore approximated by 0. The second feature of Figure 1.5, which is emphasised by the partitioning done by the authors, is the identification of four blocs of industry. The first one (industries 1–10) comprises only metal industries. The second (11–29) comprises all non-metal industries. The third (30–4) encompasses the energy industries, the fourth is the services bloc.

Their findings confirm the existence of triangular relationships within each of these blocs, although it is possible to find sub-blocs (e.g. machinery, electrical equipment, fabricated metal products, iron and steel) within which circular relationships predominate. Each bloc tends to be independent of the others, although not completely. Industries within each bloc neither buy from, nor sell to industries of other blocs. The true exception is provided by the fourth, and partly by the third bloc. Finally, the most important inputs within each bloc are homogeneous in nature: metals for the first, non-metals for the second, energy for the third and mostly labour for the fourth.

The authors have concluded that their findings not only strongly suggest the existence 'of a common fundamental structure of production in modern economic systems', but also illuminate the role played by technological factors in bringing about this similarity. In particular, the independence of metals and non-metals in production processes suggests limited substitutability, despite the enormous technological achievements since the beginning of the industrial revolution.

(c) Comparability of input coefficients.   Since it would be difficult to derive general conclusions from a comparison of individual input-output coefficients, the unity assumed for this similarity is either the column, in which case production similarity is tested, or the row to detect similarities in use.[36]

The method adopted by Chenery–Watanabe and Santhanam–Patil for the measurement of similarities in production entails the summing of the absolute differences between corresponding input coefficients of the two columns representing the same industry in a

Figure 1.5 I–O Matrices arranged in the triangular pattern

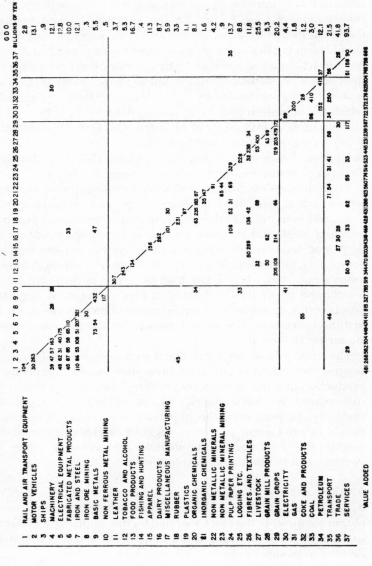

A – USA (1947)

Source: Reproduced from Simpson and Tsukui (1965) pp. 435, 438, 439.

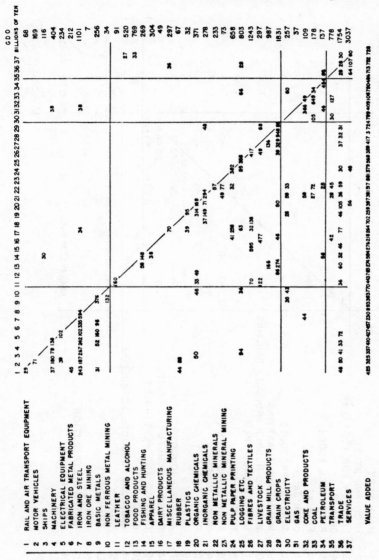

B – Japan (1955)

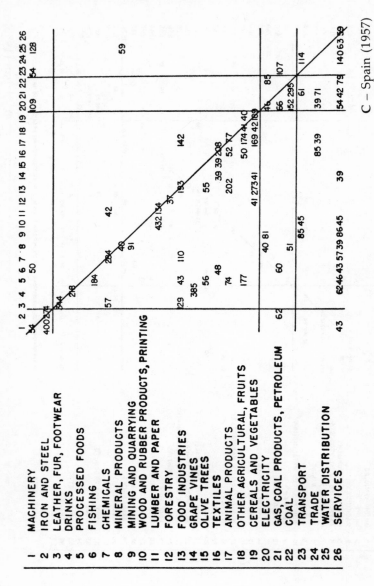

C – Spain (1957)

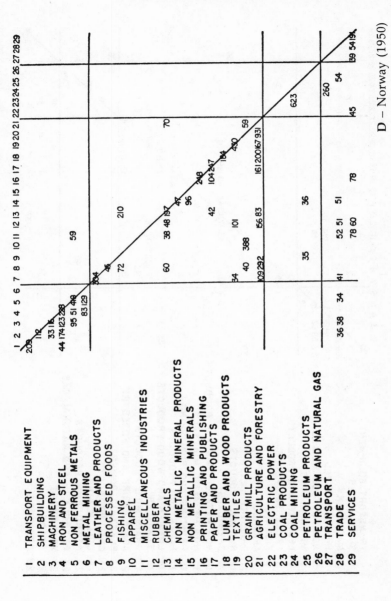

D – Norway (1950)

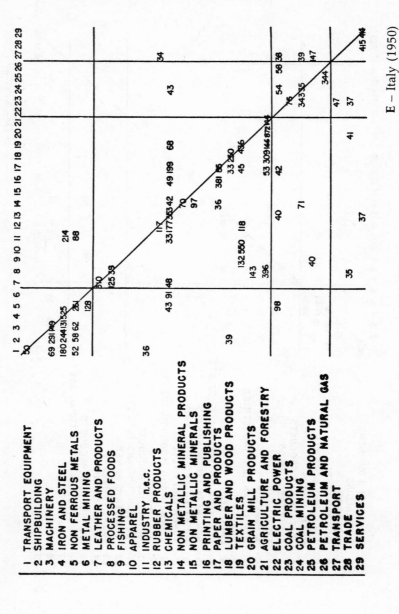

E – Italy (1950)

pair of input-output tables.[37] Next, the ratio of this sum total to the average (for the two tables) total inter-industry purchases of the industry considered is calculated. The index so obtained varies between 0, when the two sets of coefficients are identical, and 2, when the difference is maximal; the value of 1 has been chosen as the borderline for assessing the comparability in the production structure of each industry. On this basis, Japan and the USA appear the most comparable pair of countries, confirming the results obtained by the previous methods. Furthermore, and importantly from the point of view of this research, the comparability of the coefficients in the manufacturing sectors is significantly superior to that of other sectors. In quantitative terms, 'in the manufacturing sector nearly 80 per cent of all the two-country column differences are less than 0.30', i.e. significantly comparable.[38] Again, India's input-output matrix, analysed by Santhanam–Patil shows less comparability when coupled with any of the other countries. The same index is less than 0.80 in eight out of twenty-two industries when India is compared with the USA; seven for the pair India–Japan; ten for the pair India–Norway. This last result confirms the previous finding that Norway is the country most comparable to India.

Analysis of the differences by row (differences in the use of products) carried out by an analogous index reveals that for Norway, Japan, the USA and Italy the average differences are less than 20 per cent.

Finally, for India the index of similarity for the rows confirms the results obtained for the columns, i.e. Norway–India and Japan–USA are the most comparable pairs. The number of sectors which show significant similarities are about seven out of twenty-two in each case.

1.6 The identification of strategic industries

1.6.1 Methods

The idea that the process of economic development highlights the existence of a group of 'leading' or 'strategic' industries is not new in the economics literature. It is much evident in the work of Rostow as well as in Marxist literature.[39] The notion of strategic industries is also a recurring theme in the literature on economic development. It is also reiterated in the literature on industrial policy. The whole debate on the *'poles de croissance'* in France underlines its significance. However, the idea of similarity has been articulated, with some exceptions, vaguely and in an impressionistic fashion. In fact, it is difficult to restate the ideas of the authors systematically, leave alone specify the industries involved.[40]

The first ambiguity requiring clarification, before any attempt is made to distinguish strategic from non-strategic industries involves the very term 'strategic'. The concept strategic is most frequently associated in the literature with growth or development. However, the term 'growth', merely in its quantitative dimension (i.e. increase) is too narrow. It does not imply the wider structural transformations which accompany the process of growth. The experience of all developed countries demonstrates clearly that consistent overall growth over time is not merely a quantitative expansion of output. Even the changing composition of output over time, as illustrated in previous sections is the result of a series of structural transformations. The notion of development, on the other hand, is too broad and the concept of 'strategic' risks dilution in the context of such a complex phenomenon. In accordance with some authors who have considered the issue, and with the intention of using an empirically measurable concept, the term strategic will be used with reference to an economic transformation of the production structure which allows an economy to undergo self-sustained growth. Thus, the industries which will be described as strategic are those which not only contribute directly and successively to the growth of an economy over time, but also those whose growth guarantees and stimulates further growth for themselves and the remaining non-strategic industries.

There is another dimension to the concept of economic growth which Destanne de Bernis describes as the progressive 'filling' of a country's input-output table.[41] Similarly, De Cecco, drawing from past experience assigns to the process of economic growth the ultimate tendency of completing the domestic input-output flows.[42] In fact, the inter-industry growth patterns reported by Chenery and others, detailed in the preceding section, can easily be translated to fit De Cecco's proposition.

The tendency towards the completion of the domestic input-output table, assuring progressive self-sufficiency to a country in terms of modern production requirements, can also be seen as a political goal. As the previous section shows, the goal of growth itself — which can be regarded as universal — implies a broadly self-sufficient production structure in most important areas of the economy, even if self-sufficiency, *per se*, is not consciously pursued as a goal. However, self-sufficiency should not be understood to mean complete economic independence. Continuous changes in technological possibilities alone, both in production methods and product development, institute changing circumstances which alter the meaning of self-sufficiency. Of course, dependence on international trade is a parameter which affects all countries in varying degrees, limiting the extent to which economic independence can be achieved.

From the studies surveyed in the previous section it has been established that import-substitution is one of the main sources of growth for developing countries. In general, a growing domestic production capacity is the very source of self-sustained growth; i.e. a self-sustained growth which does not depend on external constraints or stimulus and generates the stimulus for growth internally.

To recapitulate, if both self-sustained economic growth and progressive, national, economic self-reliance are considered as goals, the implementation of one implies the achievement of the other. It follows that industries which are strategic for bringing about and nurturing self-sustained economic growth are, *ipso facto*, strategic for national economic self-reliance. Accordingly, the concept strategic will be used in this dual sense.

It should be noted that these observations, which have been formulated in the context of the theory of economic growth, have important consequences for a basic tenet of orthodox international trade theory. The hypothesis postulated implies that a country's pattern of trade is not toward specialisation as the H–O (Heckscher–Ohlin) theorem predicts, since the process of economic growth entails an increasing diversification of the structure of production and progressive self-reliance. Although the proposed findings and preliminary results of the present research can be regarded as supportive of the above conclusions, further discussion of the issue is deferred until a later chapter which will attempt to elaborate the implications of the model for international trade flows.

A further set of qualifications needs to be made before selecting the criteria to be adopted for the identification of the strategic industries. It has been evident (in the first section) that each individual industry experiences a different growth pattern in relation to the growth pattern of GNP; this suggests that it would be historically and theoretically incorrect to identify strategic industries independent of the particular stage of development. The picture is further complicated by the consideration that the progress of technological development might permanently alter the relative importance of an industry. In other words, an altogether different set of industries might be found to play a strategic role for the latecomers in comparison to the firstcomers. For example, the relative importance of coal mining has been reduced by the use of other forms of energy like oil and nuclear power. The first problem will be considered in detail later, for the moment only the conclusions to follow are anticipated. Although the classification of strategic industries for different levels of per capita income (different stages of economic growth) is a more satisfactory approach, it is possible to identify, with some exceptions, a more or less stable set of strategic industries independent of the stage of economic development. Undoubtedly, the results depend on the degree of aggregation adopted. Regarding the second problem of changing technology, it is possible to hypothesise that both technologies and patterns of demand are imported by developing countries from the more developed ones; and the latter exports the 'standard' technology in existence at any given point in time in the developed world. This is implicit in Vernon's product cycle theory of international trade.[43] Although there might be substantial differences in the technological content of a product sold by a developed country in a developing country, compared to its own or other developed-country markets, the results obtained by the authors investigating the comparability of production structures (section 1.4) indicate that they are not sufficient to expect substantial differences in inter-industry relations. It can therefore be assumed that developing countries tend to inherit the same hierarchy of sectors identifiable in the more developed countries. Hierarchy in this context does not mean the 'natural hierarchy' discussed earlier, but an ordering or quasi-ordering of industries according to their strategic importance. The previous conclusion about the possibility of identifying strategic industries independent of stages of economic development is consequently qualified in terms, not only of the presence of a stable set of industries in a single country (although, as will become apparent, some industries do not conform to this hypothesis), but, most of all in terms of their presence in countries at different levels of development at any moment.

The previous discussion shows that an acceptable conception of strategic industry is complex enough to require more than one criterion, quantitative or otherwise, which can guide a classification of industries.

Broadly, the two tests which an industry must satisfy in order to be classified as strategic are growth performance and structural importance. Two criteria are proposed for assessing the potential of an industry for inducing structural transformation — therefore the indirect contribution of each industry to the growth of other industries — the strength of backward and forward linkages and the presence of economies of scale. The third and final criterion proposed, growth performance, takes into account the direct contribution of a single industry to the growth of manufacture.

(a) Backward and forward linkages. The analysis below will be based on a more detailed evaluation of the results already surveyed in section 1.4 — i.e. the studies concerned with an appraisal of structural similarities in different countries. The backward linkage of an industry (say, j) gives an indication of the growth industry j induces in other industries (say, i) supplying its inputs. The strength of a linkage and its consequent growth-inducing effect is adjudged by the number of industries supplying its inputs and/or the magnitudes of the inputs supplied. If some of its inputs are imported, the existence of a demand for the imported inputs consumed by industry j provides a strong incentive for the establishment of domestic production facilities (say, i).

A strong forward linkage of industry j would reveal, conversely, the dependence of other industries on the output of industry j. In this case, structural transformation and the overall growth of the economy are stimulated and favoured by the growth of industry j, via the supply instead of the demand side.

The ease of communication which proximity to input facilities, deriving from forward linkages, and markets for output — backward linkage, with respect to industry j — provides an important element of the so-called external economies. The existence of these external economies illustrates the role of linkages in promoting economic growth, by instituting structural trans-formation and also making the growth self-sustaining.

It is possible to quantify the strength of linkages in more than one way, as shown in section 1.4; i.e. W_j and U_j are either calculated using the rows and columns of a conventional matrix or an inverted one. Preference for the second method has already been expressed since an inverted matrix takes into account both direct and indirect intermediate demand. Consequently, whenever the results obtained by Chenery and his collaborators — who have used the conventional method — disagree with the results obtained by Laumas — who has used the inverted matrix — the conclusions of Laumas will be given more weight. Finally, indirect evidence on the strength of linkages is provided by the existence of circular relationships and 'sub-blocs' within the matrix. In other words, industries which conform least to a hierarchical, triangular pattern contribute most to circularity. The strongest linkages are implied by 'sub-blocs', as illustrated by the tables of Simpson and Tsukui (Figure 1.5). Within every 'sub-bloc' each industry is connected to all the others by strong backward and forward linkages, making each a perfect complement to the others. Significant external economies can be assumed to operate within each 'sub-bloc'.

The measurement of direct backward and forward linkages has provided the most controversial results. Table 1.1 (also see section 1.4) summarises the findings of Chenery and Watanabe: nine industries — iron and steel, paper and products, petroleum products, non-ferrous metals, chemicals, coal products, rubber products, textiles, printing and publishing — are strongly linked, both backward and forward; a further set of nine industries — apparel, shipbuilding, leather and products, processed foods, grain mill products, transport equipment, machinery, lumber and wood products, non-metallic mineral products — have only strong backward linkages; six sectors — agriculture and forestry, coal mining, metal mining, petroleum and natural gas, non-metallic minerals, electric power — display only strong forward linkages. Laumas, who has calculated the strength of linkages by inverting the same matrix, only partially confirms the classification of the twenty-four sectors and industries by Chenery and Watanabe.

Laumas has found that the industries with strong linkages, both backward and forward, common to the developed countries (the USA, Japan, Italy and Norway) and the developing one included (India), are as previously shown: transport, trade and services, agriculture and forestry, processed foods, textiles, machinery, iron and steel and chemicals. Some other industries have strong backward and forward linkages for one or two countries, but not for all of them. They can be identified by a simple manipulation of the U_j and W_j indices calculated by Laumas; they are non-metallic minerals, grain mill products, paper and products, lumber and wood products and the coal industry.

As for the evidence of circular relationships, Chenery and Watanabe have found that the nine industries with the strongest backward and forward linkages, which belong to the intermediate manufacturing group, conform least to a triangular pattern; these findings are confirmed by Santhanam and Patil. However, the conclusions are not entirely satisfactory since the analysis is not exhaustive. Finally, Simpson and Tsukui's finding that matrices can be arranged in 'sub-blocs' along the principal diagonal has already been mentioned. A closer look at the matrices as rearranged by the authors makes apparent that the same group of industries inside each individual sub-bloc contributes most to inter-bloc circularity in all countries. Apart from trade and services and the energy blocs, three such groups of industries are conspicuous: the first within the metal bloc, the second and third within the non-metal bloc. Within the metal bloc rail and air-transport equipment, motor vehicles, ships, metal products and iron and steel show very strong circular links. Within the non-metal bloc plastics, organic and inorganic chemicals constitute another strongly interrelated group. In the non-metal bloc organic and inorganic chemicals contribute substantially to the circularity of the whole bloc. Finally, it is possible to distinguish a set of industries which depend on agricultural commodities and display considerable interdependence: pulp, paper, printing, logging, fibres and textiles, livestock, grain mill products and grain crops.[44] The three groups are evidenced in the matrix of Japan (see Figure 1.5B).

In conclusion, it should be stated that the circular relationships, therefore the strength of linkages, are greatly understated for industries which contribute most to fixed investment. This is because of the convention adopted in the construction of input-output tables whereby depreciation (of fixed investment) appears as a part of final demand and not as part of the intermediate demand of inter-industry flows on which the strength of linkages is based. Although it is difficult to make an *a priori* selection of industries which contribute to fixed investment, they can be identified, by and large, with the machinery (ISIC 36–37), transport (ISIC 38), metal products (ISIC 34–35), and the non-metallic mineral product (ISIC 33) industries.[45]

(b) Economies of scale.   It can be recalled from the discussion of section 1.4 that the experience of both SM and SP countries

highlights the role played by economies of scale in the process of industrialisation. As in the case of linkages, the existence of economies of scale is not only important for the industry affected by it, but also for other industries which depend on its inputs, final consumers aside. The effect of scale economies in a particular industry 'spreads out' across the production structure; i.e. some inputs become cheaper to produce. The availability of cheaper inputs enhances the growth of industries dependent on it. Moreover, the cheapening of some inputs *vis-à-vis* other inputs may prompt technological changes, thereby affecting the composition of inter-industry flows.

The acquisition of industries in which economies of scale are important benefits a developing country doubly. For reasons already stated in section 1.4 imports are likely to be conspicuous for products enjoying economies of scale. The import-substitution of these products through the creation of domestic production facilities is also likely to initiate the export of the same products. The full exploitation of economies of scale, from the economic and technical point of view, will probably entail surplus capacity in excess of domestic requirements. The resulting surplus output can be exported at low opportunity cost once the production facilities are already established. The developing country thus benefits doubly, through import-substitution and the simultaneous possibility of entering export markets and further easing balance of payments constraints to growth. The issue of economies of scale and their impact on international trade is of importance to the present research and will be reconsidered later.

Two distinctive kinds of evidence are available on the extent to which individual countries enjoy economies of scale. The cross-section regression run by Chenery on a sample of thirty-eight countries (see section 1.4) gives the correlation between size of the country — taken as a measure of market size — and the growth of each industry's per capita value added. Each regression gives a size-elasticity coefficient relative to a specific industry; the coefficient is taken as a quantitative indication of the presence of economies of scale due to the size of the market for the industry in question. The group of manufacturing industries which show higher than average values of size–elasticity coefficient for manufacturing as a whole is, in the order of magnitude of the coefficient:

(1)   petroleum products;

(2)   paper and products;
(3)   rubber;
(4)   metals (iron and steel, basic metals);
(5)   textiles;
(6)   machinery;
(7)   transport equipment and chemicals.[46]

Haldi and Whitcomb[47] have investigated the existence of economies of scale directly at plant levels on the basis of calculations from engineering and economic data. They have found that significant economies of scale exist in plants of the following industries:

(1)   cement (the most important of the non-metallic mineral products);
(2)   chemicals;
(3)   rubber;
(4)   petroleum;
(5)   aluminium (metal industry sub-group);
(6)   pulp and paper;
(7)   shipbuilding (sub-category of transport equipment).

Except for the case of cement, which does not reveal above average economies of scale in the findings of Chenery, and textiles, which have not been investigated by Haldi and Whitcomb, the same group of industries emerges from the two studies.

(c) Growth performance. According to the previously stated premise of the conception of strategic, what is required is an indicator of the direct growth performance which represents a 'typical value' for a sufficiently numerous sample of countries and which does not depend strictly on the country's level of development. The growth elasticities calculated by Chenery, using cross-section regressions for the same sample of countries used for computing the scale elasticities, satisfy both the requirements — i.e. of being both a 'typical value' and independent of the level of economic development. The growth elasticities measure the correlation between a percentage increase in per capita national income and a percentage increase in the value added per capita for each industry. Arranged below in descending order are the industries which display values of growth elasticity coefficients above the average value for manufacturing:

(1)   machinery (electrical and non-electrical);
(2)   paper and products;
(3)   transport equipment;
(4)   petroleum products;
(5)   metal products;
(6)   rubber;
(7)   chemicals;
(8)   non-metallic mineral products;
(9)   textiles.

It should be noted that textiles are a marginal case since the value of its growth coefficient is exactly equal to the average value for the whole of manufacture.[48]

Finally, one of the conclusions of section 1.4 stresses the dominant role played by import-substitution for overall industrial growth in each country. Examining the relevance of import-substitution for the growth of an industry further evidence is obtained on the importance of acquiring such an industry if overall national economic growth is to be enhanced. The technique used by Chenery to assess the role played by import-substitution for the pattern of growth of each industry has been described in section 1.4.7. Consequently, the industries for which import-substitution is a substantial source of growth, as compared to the manufacturing sector as a whole, will merely be listed without further comment in descending order:

(1)   petroleum products;
(2)   machinery;
(3)   transport equipment;
(4)   paper products;
(5)   rubber;
(6)   textiles;
(7)   metals;
(8)   chemicals.

In this instance, chemicals appear to be a borderline case since the percentage of the growth attributable to import-substitution is equal to the average for manufacturing.[49]

1.6.2 The strategic industries

It is evident that the results of all the criteria do not always converge in the selection of industries. A more dificult problem is posed for a final selection of industries by the divergence of results designed for the same criteria by different authors. This is particularly true for the linkage criterion. Consequently, each industry will be discussed separately and the selection of the set of industries will be based on (a) the number of criteria satisfied and (b) the maximum number of empirical tests devised for each criterion fulfilled.

A first group of three industries which, in varying degrees, appears by all indicators to satisfy all the criteria is steel, textiles and chemicals.[50]

A further group of three industries, machinery, paper and products, and transport equipment, appears to be a good candidate for selection as strategic. They seem to satisfy all the criteria according to the majority of indicators. The case of machinery is the most clear cut. Economies of scale are significant in the industry and it is also one of the fastest growing industries, contributing substantially to import-substitution. The results concerning the strength of linkages is somewhat more divergent. According to Laumas, the machinery industry shows strong linkages in both developed and developing countries. Evidence from the input–output tables rearranged by Simpson and Tsukui (Figure 1.5) suggests that it is a 'key sector' in the metal bloc. However, Chenery has discovered strong backward linkages, but weak forward linkages. Nevertheless, it is likely that indices based on a conventional input–output table underestimate the real strength of forward linkages since purchases of machinery are primarily in the form of fixed investment and hence classified as part of final demand and therefore absent from intermediate demand. Moreover, Laumas's results, which take into account both direct and indirect demand, are more appropriate than Chenery's insofar as the strength of linkages is concerned.

The divergences of the results for the paper and products sector again relate to the differences in the findings of Laumas and Chenery. The values of growth elasticity, and the size-elasticity coefficient and the importance of import-substitution points towards its inclusion in the set of strategic industries. In addition, according to Chenery, the paper and products industry displays both strong backward and forward linkages. But Laumas substantiates these results only for two countries, Norway and Japan. However, the convergence of all the other indicators (the highest values for economies of scale and contribution to direct growth) is decisive in determining its inclusion as a strategic industry.

In the case of the transport equipment industry, the last two criteria, economies of scale and growth performance, are satisfactorily met. According to the calculations of both Chenery and Laumas, the transport equipment industry does not have strong linkages. Nevertheless, a careful examination of Laumas's results reveals that the figures for both backward and forward linkages are, in most cases, only marginally below the average of manufactures for each country. Most important of all, the demand for transport equipment is primarily in the form of fixed investment; in its case the underestimation of the actual strength of the linkages is likely to be especially high because the bulk of transport equipment used in production or services is classified as fixed investment. This undoubtedly understates its importance for intermediate demand and hence, inter-industry flows. Thus, it may be reasonably assumed that the transport equipment industry is of strategic importance to the national economy.

For a further group of three industries — rubber products, petroleum and non-metallic minerals — the evidence is somewhat indecisive. Rubber products fully satisfy the criteria of growth performance and economies of scale. Chenery has found that rubber products also have strong backward and forward linkages. But the results provided by Laumas fail to confirm the findings of Chenery. In the case of rubber products allowances cannot be made to take into account fixed investment because its uses as a product are different.

The case of petroleum is similar to that of rubber products. In the case of non-metallic minerals (ISIC 33, primarily cement), the strength of linkages is underestimated because most cement products are used for construction purposes, as fixed investment. However, since the rate of depreciation (in physical terms) in construction — mainly buildings — is lower than for other types of fixed investment, the degree of underestimation of the strength of its linkages is lower. Thus, there is little to add to the findings of Laumas that non-metallic minerals have strong linkages in only two of the five countries of the sample. The size-elasticity coefficients for this sector are also below the average for manufacturing. The economies of scale for non-metallic minerals are also unimportant. It does not enter international trade in any significant quantities because of its weight/value ratio. However, non-metallic mineral products have a growth coefficient somewhat higher than the average for manufacturing. In conclusion, on the basis of the tests carried out in the studies surveyed, it is not possible to make a compelling case for its inclusion or exclusion from the group of strategic industries. For the moment the question remains open. Subsequent chapters will add further dimensions to the term 'strategic' and extend the clarification of its component industries.

Two other industries, processed foods and grain mill products (the latter is considered part of the former in some tests and is a sub-category of the former in the ISIC classification; 20/5), display strong linkages. According to Laumas, the values for the processed food industry of the linkages are much above the average. Grain mill products also have strong linkages in two out of the five countries. The results of Simpson and Tsukui (Figure 1.5) also show strong linkages for these two industries, in what is described as the agriculture-related sub-bloc. Thus, despite the contrary conclusions of Chenery, the linkage criterion can be considered to have been fully met. However, both these industries fail to satisfy the other two criteria, size-elasticity and growth performance. Chenery and Taylor have classified them as 'early' industries, which it will be recalled exhaust their growth potential at fairly low levels of income.[51] Thus, while both these industries can be regarded as vital for the functioning of the economy as a whole, they do not contribute sizeably to, or guarantee self-sustained growth, i.e. the process of industrialisation.

On the basis of the tests conducted, the evidence reached on the rest of the manufacturing industries, although contradictory at times, warrants their exclusion from the set of strategic industries. These industries comprise: apparel (sometimes labelled clothing), lumber and wood (category 25–26 of ISIC), non-ferrous metals, coal products, leather and leather products, printing and publishing and miscellaneous manufacture.

To resume, six industries form the strategic set: *iron and steel, chemicals, textiles, machinery, paper and paper products and transport equipment.* The remaining nine industries have been excluded.

It is worth noting that the majority of the industries comprising the strategic set and also the ones for which the evidence is inconclusive can be classified as capital goods, in the sense that they contribute primarily to intermediate demand (variable, produced capital) and/or fixed investment demand (fixed capital). They also include the so-called heavy industries. Conversely, the industries excluded are light industries, or form the bulk of consumer goods (non-durables).

Notes

1.   Marx (1954) p. 19; but rather surprisingly the implications of this insight of Marx are not carried to their logical conclusion in Marxist analyses of international trade disputes.
2.   Rostow (1965), p. 20–1.
3.   Kuznets (1957).
4.   Rostow (1965).
5.   For the purposes of the present research the concept of economic growth is more relevant than economic development. My interest is exclusively in the quantitative changes in international trade variables as a consequence of economic growth and the attendant trade frictions which such changes provoke. The concept of economic development would also preclude consideration of countries like the Federal German Republic and Japan, the growth of whose economies has been the major source of international trade conflicts in the contemporary world.
6.   Gerschenkron, A. (1966).
7.   Sections 1.4.1 to 1.4.3 are based on the study by Chenery and Taylor (1968); 1.4.4 to 1.4.5 are based on Chenery and Hughes (1972) and Chenery, Ohlin *et al.* (1977); 1.4.6 is based on these last studies and Helleiner (1973). Finally, paragraph 1.4.7 is based on Chenery (1960).
8.   Data refer to the period 1950–63 and comprise a sample of forty-eight countries at different levels of development. Chenery and Taylor (op. cit.) have chosen a population level of 15 million as the dividing line between large and small countries. Small manufacturing-orientated (SM) countries and small primary-orientated (SP) countries are distinguished by their respective export patterns. Large countries include the USA, Japan, Italy, France, Great Britain, the Federal Republic of Germany and Canada. The small manufacturing-orientated countries selected by Chenery and Taylor (op. cit.) are Haiti, Bolivia, Taiwan, Paraguay, Tunisia, Peru, Algeria, Portugal, Jamaica, Greece, Uruguay, Israel, Puerto Rico, Austria, the Netherlands, Finland, Belgium and Norway. Finally, the small primary-orientated countries are Kenya, Cambodia, the Congo, Ceylon, Rhodesia, Ecuador, El Salvador, Iraq, Honduras, Guatemala, Colombia, Malaya, Costa Rica, Chile, Venezuela, Denmark and Australia. (See Table 11 p. 414 of Chenery and Taylor for the full list).
9.   Chenery and Taylor (1968), p. 399.
10.   Chenery and Taylor (1968) p. 409.
11.   Ibid.
12.   See the reference to Maizels (1963) in Chenery and Taylor (op. cit.) on p. 409, footnotes 32 and 34.

13.   Chenery in Ohlin, *et al.* (1977) p. 460.
14.   Ibid. p. 413.
15.   Chenery and Hughes (1972) p. 79.
16.   Ibid. p. 80.
17.   These arguments have been developed by Helleiner (1973) and by Cohen (1975) with reference to Asia. The involvement of multinational corporations in the export of components and goods from locations in the newly-industrialising countries, mostly in the form of intra-firm trade across international borders adds a new dimension to world trade and the process of readjustment in the firstcomer countries. According to Helleiner over 63 per cent of US manufactured imports are intra-firm trade (see Chapter 6). Consequently, the management of surplus capacity world-wide might take the form of cartelisation; this 'solution' would be internal to the transnational system instead of inter-state intervention in the form of, say, protectionist nationalism. There is already a precedent, although ultimately unsuccessful (since it became submerged in and transformed by two world wars), in the cartels of the post-1900 era; see Vernon (1971) pp. 86–90.
18.   Chenery and Hughes (1972) p. 85; also see Kaldor (1967) p. 32.
19.   Maizels, A. (1968), p. 18.
20.   Chenery (1960) p. 632.
21.   Ibid. p. 638.
22.   The derivation of such 'typical' value is done by means of a regression.
23.   Chenery (1960) p. 643.
24.   Ibid. p. 644.
25.   Assuming a common organisation of economic activity (a market structure, broadly speaking) and, overlooking for the moment differences in resource endowment which influence both technology and prices, the differences in technology or in the composition of demand are reflected in the physical combination of inputs and the structure of relative prices, i.e. the two elements which concur in determining the value of the inter-industry flows. Since the existence of regularities found in the growth patterns confirm that common demand and technological patterns accompany the growth of national income, and since the comparability of organisational structures is an established fact, there are strong *a priori* reasons to expect similarities in the value of intersectoral flows, whether measured in physical or value terms for countries at comparable levels of development, i.e. similar income per capita level. It should be added that when similarities are found and flows are measured in value units it can be inferred that both the technological and price structure are similar or that differences in the first are offset by differences in the second. However, from a statistical point of view,

the probability of such a distribution of differences is low. And the presence of international competition alone, apart from the independent evidence of the similarities across countries for each of the elements taken separately, suggests that if compensation of differences does occur the magnitudes involved are not great.

26.   Chenery and Watanabe (1958).
27.   Santhanam and Patil (1972).
28.   Laumas (1976).
29.   Laumas (1976).
30.   Chenery–Watanabe (1958), Santhanam–Patil (1972).
31.   Laumas (1976) pp. 57–60.
32.   Chenery–Watanabe (1958).
33.   Ibid.
34.   Santhanam–Patil (1972), Chenery–Watanabe (op. cit.).
35.   Simpson and Tsukui (1965).
36.   An industry column represents some sort of aggregate production process, while the row lists all the industry's sales.
37.   Chenery–Watanabe (op. cit.); Santhanam–Patil (op. cit.).
38.   Chenery–Watanabe (op. cit.) p. 500.
39.   Bettelheim's critical comments on Emmanuel's Unequal Exchange (1969) and the work of Destanne de Bernis can be taken as examples; Destanne de Bernis (1966).
40.   Among the exceptions are Hirschman (1958) and Destanne de Bernis (ibid). Hirschman, prompted by the findings of Chenery and Watanabe, reviewed earlier, suggested that industries with the strongest backward linkages should be given priority in developing countries. The strength of the linkages is also one of the criteria proposed, by the present study, for identifying strategic industries; the reasons for which will be given in the following pages of the main text.

The article by Destanne de Bernis (ibid), which has been translated from French into English for the present author, partly inspires the ideas on strategic industries. Destanne de Bernis himself does not list clearly measurable and unambiguous criteria which can be used to distinguish strategic and non-strategic industries. But his ideas are extremely suggestive and go further than those of other authors. Also relevant are the work of Rosenstein–Rodan (1943) and Nurkse (1961), whose discussion on development and the need for 'balanced growth' are a possible theoretical counterpart of the empirical studies on which the present work is based. In particular, the issue of external economies is prominently discussed by Nurkse; also see Scitowski (1959) and Bardhan (1978).

41.   Destanne de Bernis (1966) p. 446.
42.   De Cecco (1971) p. 975.

43. Vernon (1966).
44. Electrical equipment and machinery are usually aggregated under machinery by Chenery. This convention has been maintained by the other authors. Similarly, organic and inorganic chemicals are aggregated under chemicals. Finally, rail, road and air transport equipment, motor vehicles and ships are classified as transport equipment.
45. See Chenery (1960) p. 637.
46. See Chenery (1960) p. 633 and p. 646.
47. Haldi and Whitcomb (1967).
48. Chenery (1960) p. 633 and p. 638.
49. Ibid p. 643, column 6 of table 7.
50. There remains a problem in classifying the metal products' sub-group (ISIC 35). For the second and third criterion tests have been carried out on ISIC categories 34 and 35, labelled metal products; they comprise iron and steel, non-ferrous metals and metal products. The linkage criterion has measured only iron and steel and non-ferrous metals. These measures establish the respective classifications for iron and steel and non-ferrous metals. However, since separate evidence is not available for metal products it is impossible to decide its appropriate classification.
51. Chenery and Taylor (1968).

2 National defence, the economy and the role of the State

2.1 Introduction

The present chapter is principally concerned with two related issues: firstly, the role of the State[1] in the national economy, both in terms of promoting industrialisation, and ensuring the viability of the economy subsequently; secondly, the relationship between national defence and the strategic industries and their influence on the economy as a whole. The organisation of the chapter is described below.

The first section briefly recapitulates the findings and conclusions of the preceding chapter. The next two sections analyse the context in which State involvement in the national economy is situated. This discussion concerns the imperatives of the international political system and the essential behavioural traits of the national actors, and the impact of industrialisation on the interaction between them.

The subsequent section elaborates the relationship between national defence and the economy, and their influence on technology and the national economy as a whole. This is followed by a discussion about the dynamics of the process by which it occurs.

This discussion is followed by an analysis of the role of the State in the economy. The analysis is conceptualised on two levels: the stage at which the State intervenes to establish the group of strategic industries (considered synonymous with industrialisation), and attempts to ensure their viability subsequently should they be threatened.

The modes of State intervention are then described. Finally, the policy impact of State intervention is disaggregated on a number of distinctive levels.

2.1.1 Recapitulation of the findings and conclusion of the preceding chapter

Two important conclusions emerged from the previous chapter.

Firstly, the existence of similar structures of production in different national economies at the same stage of economic growth, measured by, say, per capita income was demonstrated. This similarity is evident even if the countries concerned reach the same stage of economic growth at widely separated periods of time, i.e. a country reaching a particular stage of economic growth (measured by per capita income) will have the same structure of production as another country which experienced the same stage of economic growth at an earlier period of time, and had now reached a more advanced stage; for example, if India had the same per capita income in 1980 as the USA in 1880, her structure of production in 1980 would be similar to that of the US in 1880. Indeed, the path of the economic growth of the three categories of industry which advance in succession — early, middle, and late — is also likely to follow a similar pattern; the early, middle, and late industries follow a fairly orderly progression in all countries, growing in relative importance at successive levels of per capita income.

The evidence analysed also highlighted some systematic differences between countries. These systematic differences relate to the size of the country and resource endowment and affect the timing of the progression of economic growth. For example, a small manufacturing-orientated country tends to reach the same stage of economic growth at a higher level of per capita income than a large country; similarly, a small primary-orientated country increases its share of manufacturing output in GNP at an even higher level of per capita income than a small manufacturing-orientated one. The patterns of export are also dissimilar. Nevertheless, the structure of production tends to converge at higher levels of per capita income in the first two groups of countries.[2]

Secondly, there exists a group of industries which can be considered strategic for industrialisation and economic growth. These 'industrialising industries', as Destanne de Bernis calls them, are of great importance in the production of all other manufactured goods.

This group of industries, which produces manufactured intermediate inputs is virtually synonymous with the so-called 'heavy industries', essential for self-sustained economic growth. In a sense, industrialisation can be interpreted as the process by which these industries become established in an economy; industrialisation has also been viewed as the 'filling' of the industrial matrix, in which the importance of this group of industries has been demonstrated in the previous chapter. A number of other industries are also of importance, as the analysis of the previous chapter highlighted, but the strategic group of the six indentified are pre-eminent in the industrial hierarchy[3]

Thus, the significance of this group of industries for economic growth, *per se*, is evident. Any country desiring to achieve self-sustained economic growth and industrialisation acquires this set of industries. And because of the importance of this group of industries in the industrial matrix, successful industrialisation automatically makes a country largely self-sufficient in basic industrial inputs, i.e. intermediate manufactured products. Successful industrialisation consequently institutes a significant degree of national economic independence. This national economic independence obviously does not abolish international trade and imply complete autarky, but it does have implications for the theory of comparative advantage. However, it introduces a relative economic self-sufficiency, and hence, greater political independence.

At this point it would be appropriate to draw attention to a shortcoming of the analysis of the previous chapter concerning the group of strategic industries. The apparently invariant identity of the group of strategic industries assigns an unjustifiably static character to the process of industrial and technological change in the history of economic growth. The reasons for this shortcoming will be discussed later, and arguments will be advanced to affirm the dynamic nature of the process.

2.1.2 *International politics and the national actor: the primacy of national defence*

The dominant reality of the international political system is the competition between national actors. At its most general level, the competition is for power and influence and it takes many forms, the most significant of which is the competition for military power. Whatever the constitutive structure of the international political system, barring universal empire which would transcend the system of territorial states, the dominant reality is rivalry and competition between national actors, and the currency of transaction between them is power;[4] and the highest denomination of this currency of power is military capability.

The importance of military capability is reinforced by its dual role in international politics. The primary importance of military power relates to its operational use in actual conflict, or as a deterrent. However, its significance as a conditioning factor in other forms of rivalry and conflict cannot be underestimated. While the relevance of military power in a particular conflict may be open to debate, its general influence is undeniable. For example the bargaining strength of a country over questions of territorial limits at sea (usually of commercial significance) depends largely on its naval power. Its ability ultimately to enforce unilateral decisions of its own, or resist those of other countries, limits and defines the negotiating positions held. Similarly, the potential threat of military intervention influences the attitudes of many countries toward the economic interests of certain countries in their own country.

The existential condition of an international society or political system constituted by territorial states may then be characterised as competition and struggle. It is this existential condition of competition and rivalry which substantially pre-determines the basic impulses governing the mutual behaviour of the entities comprising the international political system.[5] In this competition and rivalry military capability occupies a poignant role, whether as an actuality in operation, or as an underlying phenomenon conditioning other modes of behaviour by the mere fact of its availability. This is the view of most students of international relations, whatever the particular emphasis or qualifications; the primacy of politics which this view asserts is reaffirmed below on methodological grounds.

2.1.3 *The primacy of politics*

The primacy of political considerations in governing the behaviour of the State is apparent in its determination to institute industrialisation because of international political rivalry. The stimulus of capitalist economic interests in prompting militarism and imperialistic behaviour only occurs with the advance of capitalist industrialisation to a higher stage. Lenin's thesis on imperialism is aptly titled, 'Imperialism, the Highest Stage of Capitalism'.[6] In terms of traditional international relations theory, the issue of national security is prior to all others. Imperial economic ambitions are undoubtedly important, but they express the particularistic group interests which also comprise foreign policy goals of countries, whereas national security considerations constitute the most overarching interest for the country. However, imperial economic ambitions assume a disproportionate significance in advanced capitalist countries since it is the single most powerful expression of domestic group interests.

The primacy of the group or political entity which this view asserts has also been argued by the French Marxist Regis Debray. Comparing the nation with the invariable family triangle, whatever the social organisation of the triangle, he argues that:

> . . . the nation is in one sense a historically determined mode of existence, and to this extent a variable; yet what the nation expresses, that of which the nation is made, is an invariable. So while it is quite true that the nation is an historically transient category as something arising out of the ruins of feudalism, etc., historically determinate and hence variable, yet it is so as one phase of a primary determinant that remains invariable: the cultural organization of the human collectivity in question.[7]

According to Debray, the 'enclosure' — the collectivity — 'arises in the first instance against the idea of a fundamental chaos, chaos in the entymological sense of lawlessness, scattering, absence of organization'.[8] Thus, the security interests of the territorial state are pre-eminent.

2.1.4 Socialist countries and national defence

This book is concerned only with the problems of manufacturing export in the market economies of the non-socialist world, but the discussion on State intervention in the economy (particularly in the group of strategic industries) is equally applicable, if not more so, to the socialist countries. Indeed, the behaviour of the centrally planned economies is especially relevant in demonstrating the importance of the group of strategic industries for defence and their significance in setting the parameters of civilian economic development; since the State and the economy are synonymous in these economies, the involvement of the State with industry as such need not be demonstrated.

Briefly, the preoccupation of the centrally planned economies with the issue of national security is well known. Both the Soviet Union and the People's Republic of China are intensely preoccupied by the question of national defence capability. It is also known that successive regimes in centrally planned economies have attempted to build a strong defence capability to the detriment of consumer goods. And the thrust towards the acquisition of a defence capability has stimulated the growth of the group of strategic industries with which we are concerned.[9]

2.2 The impact of industrialisation on international political relations

In the modern era, the competition and rivalry between national state actors has been transformed by the advent of industrialisation. Most fundamentally, the process of industrialisation has radically changed the currency in which territorial units transact the business of power struggles and rivalries.[10]

It can be stated without fear of controversy that in the modern world, the military capability of national actors is measured with reference to their industrial potential.[11] Other factors like skill, leadership, valour, even luck may be relevant, but the only reliable index for assessing the military capability of a national actor is its level of industrial development.

The absence of a sound national economic base seriously qualifies the possibility of meaningful participation in the international political system. It is a matter of empirical fact that the industrialised world plays the preponderant role in the international political system; the less industrialised countries of the world are effectively almost excluded from participation in the decisions which affect the functioning and direction of the international political system. Much more important, in the absence of a sound national economic base the independence of national actors cannot be considered to be guaranteed.[12] The vulnerability of industrially inferior civilisations and territorial entities to the predatory proclivities of the industrially advanced is a matter of historical record. In particular, the past two centuries have demonstrated the decisive importance of industrial and technological muscle for the defence of national independence. In contrast to the possible inequalities of the pre-industrial age, the degree of superiority enjoyed by the industrially and technologically advanced, in terms of political and military power, has become disproportionately large in the industrial world.[13]

The balance of power in the international political system and the relative power of national actors is therefore primarily predicated on the relative levels of industrial and technological advancement (other things being equal). The achievement of industrialisation may not be a sufficient condition for national security and meaningful partici-pation in the international political system, but it is a necessary one, i.e. it is a prerequisite.

Thus, the history of the industrial revolutions of the past two centuries can also be seen as the history of international political rivalries. And the government as the agency which mediates the relations between the country and the outside world consequently finds it incumbent to ensure the ability of the country to uphold national security and participate effectively in the international political system by assuring the industrial progress of the country.

The determination of the State to achieve and maintain relative economic self-sufficiency in the interests of national security is unambiguously demonstrated by two examples in industry and agriculture.

Virtually every major developed and a growing number of developing countries are attempting to develop civilian nuclear energy as a means of reducing dependence on imported supplies and exhaustible domestic natural resources, i.e. petroleum and coal. The efforts have continued unabated despite the high development costs and apparently unresolved safety problems and concomitant domestic opposition. For a number of countries these costs are not as great because the basic technology is a spin-off from nuclear weapons programmes. But the problem of safety and the enormity of the dangers associated with it, were dramatically illustrated by the Three Mile Island episode.[14] Domestic opposition, which also concerned the issue of weapons, has had a profound political impact, e.g. in the political life of the Federal Republic of Germany. But the State appears heedless. Nuclear energy alone is considered the main response in the medium-term to dependence on vulnerable imported supples, and also promises unlimited energy for the future.

The insistence of EEC countries and Japan on maintaining national food production capacity, particularly in staple products like grain, rice, meat, etc., is also primarily due to the desire to ensure a substantial measure of self-sufficiency. Of course, certain political parties benefit from the existence of conservative rural constituencies but parties without such affiliations have also allowed them to persist. It was this insistence which led to virtual exclusion of agricultural products from successive GATT negotiations. This determination of the State acquires a particular cogency as food becomes an increasingly useful weapon in international diplomacy.[15]

There is no reason to suppose that such national policies toward energy and food supplies cannot exist in manufacturing industry, especially in the group of strategic industries which are of direct relevance for the production of defence goods as well.

It is therefore argued that industrialisation in most major countries has been rooted, historically, in the attempt to acquire a military capability. However, an industrial potential does not always translate into military capability, in the sense of armed forces, etc. In certain periods countries have not been able to translate their industrial potential into military capability (e.g. Japan after the Second World War. But such a situation has usually arisen because of a previous military defeat.

2.3 National defence, the strategic industries and their influence on technology and the economy

The crucial argument of this chapter is that the characteristics of the structure of production which exist in industrial economies and the similarities observed to exist between them arise substantially from the efforts of governments to industrialise in response to the pressures of international political competition. More specifically, it is contended that the characteristics of the structure of production (and the similarities between economies) are essentially determined by industries acquired for national defence purposes by government.[16] The fundamental attributes of industrialisation and the basic contours of the civilian manufacturing economy are importantly predetermined by previous government efforts to establish industries for defence and economic autonomy.

In other words, the self-sufficiency in intermediate manufactured products (primarily belonging to the group of strategic industries), which the process of industrialisation evidently implies, may seem somewhat curious at first sight, but becomes quite logical when viewed from the perspective of the State's desire to acquire an autonomous national defence capability. This relationship was most readily observable before the advent of the industrial revolutions proper in Western Europe when more immediate defence requirements prompted State involvement in industrial production. The civilian economy, in all its immense diversity and sophistication may seem far removed from the distinctive purposes of defence, but it is ultimately underpinned by a group of industries which originated under the catalytic stimulus of defence needs.

The above argument implicitly asserts an important premise regarding the role of consumption and production in industrialisation, i.e. civilian consumption is supply-determined. The provision of cheapened and standardised intermediate manufactured inputs because of the non-market stimuli of military requirements creates and propels the civilian market. In particular, the cheapening of goods has been the key factor in the creation of the large-scale markets which characterise the industrial age. As Hobsbawm has observed:

> it is the factory system which (in turn) produces in such vast quantities and at such rapidly diminishing cost, as to be no longer dependent on existing demand, but to create its own market.[17]

This premise would find favour with Marxists and some unorthodox neo-classical economists like Galbraith, but is at variance with the orthodox neo-classical insistence on consumer sovereignty. According to orthodox neo-classical economists production techniques are virtually infinite, the particular technique of production chosen deriving from demand conditions. In a recent study, Joel Mokyr reached the conclusion that

> ... the traditional notion that supply and demand were somehow symmetric in industrialization is unfounded. The determination of 'when', and 'how fast' are to be sought first and foremost in supply, not demand related processes.[18]

In fact, Mokyr was charitable in imputing the more reasonable view of a symmetric influence of supply and demand to the traditionalists. Their theoretical position implies preponderant stress on demand.

The premise adopted here is more specific than either of the presuppositions above. It is argued that it is the basic inputs (mainly of the set of strategic industries) which are supply-determined, with the State assuming an important role in creating the supply for military purposes. But the actual mix of products in the civilian manufacturing economy need not be supply-determined; consumer sovereignty, or preference can perfectly determine the actual mix of products manufactured. The 'sovereign consumer' has a fairly closely circumscribed choice regarding the intermediate inputs which are incorporated in the product purchased, but he can choose as between products, i.e. he can choose between a motor cycle and a car, or even between two types of machines for the cycle and a car, or even between two types of machines for the manufacture of the same product, but his choice of the materials embodied in it is fairly limited.

The impact of military needs on the fundamental characteristics of the structure of production in the first industrial economies is detectable in the relationship between, what Lewis Mumford terms, war and the machine. He has described 'the stimulation of invention and innovation by military needs.' Napoleon III offered a reward for a 'cheap process of making steel capable of withstanding the explosive force of the new shells. The Bessemer process was the direct answer to this demand'. But the most profound invention was the gun; 'the gun was the starting point of a new type of power machine: it was, mechanically speaking, a one-cylinder internal combustion engine'. Because of it, a number of events followed: first, it increased the consumption of iron and stimulated mining; second, 'war established a new type of industrial director who was not a mason or a smith or a mastercraftsman — the military engineer. . . . It was to the Italian military engineers from the fifteenth century on that the machine owed a debt quite as high as it did to the ingenious British inventors of James Watt's period'; third, heavy fortifications were developed, and road-building, canal-building, and bridge-building became necessary adjuncts of warfare; fourth, it increased the demands on industry for standardized arms and equipment, thus accelerating factory organization . . . and so Mumford sums up by asking 'How far shall we go back in demonstrating the fact that war has been the chief propagator of the machine?'[19] It is therefore held that the needs of war and weapons substantially dictated the choice of materials and techniques which subsequently become commonplace in European industrial production.

In the contemporary world, the development of atomic fission and the revolution in all forms of communications and information technology because of computers, electronics, and most recently, the silicon chip, all initially inspired by advances in military 'science', promise to transform society.

At this juncture it would be useful to reiterate that it is at the initial stage of industrialisation that defence-related purposes greatly influence the character of the incipient manufacturing economy. The creation of industries for military purposes lays the basis on which the civilian manufacturing economy subsequently

grows. This does not, of course, mean that no civilian manufacturing economy exists prior to the defence-related effort of the
State to build an industrial base. It only means that the process by
which the civilian manufacturing economy acquires its direction
and its technological momentum, and its mass basis receives its
catalytic stimulus from the original defence-related efforts of the
State to create the group of strategic industries.

The progressive development of the civilian manufacturing
economy subsequently acquires a dynamic of its own, outstripping
the military sector which stimulated its creation in both size and
value. Few countries spend more than ten per cent of GNP on
defence, a circumstance illustrative of the size and importance of
the civilian manufacturing sector of the national economy. But a set
of overall parameters has already been imposed, within which the
civilian sector grows. At the same time, it should be recognised that
once the civilian manufacturing sector becomes established it
cannot but react upon the economy as a whole, by virtue of its sheer
size, altering its direction and modifying its fundamental features in
some respects.[20] Yet, the group of strategic industries is strategic for
defence purposes and only becomes strategic for the civilian
manufacturing economy because the latter derives ultimately from
the former.

2.4 Dynamics of the process of acquiring the group of strategic industries

Industrialisation is held to spread internationally through a process
of imitation. The industrialisation of a firstcomer invests it with
industrial and technological advantages which reinforce its military
capability and thereby raise its status in the hierarchy of the
international political system. Other countries then respond by
imitating the firstcomer, acquiring industries for military purposes
and consequently initiating the process of industrialisation. The
phenomenon of imitation, however, is not a one-way process; over
time, the firstcomer(s) may find themselves imitating particular
advances made by latecomers.

It is also necessary to clarify that the process of industrialisation
does not entail the simultaneous establishment of all the group of
strategic industries. While individual plants may exist to cater for
specific military needs the overall growth of the group of strategic

industries in their civilian dimensions occurs more progressively, as outlined in the previous chapter. However, a tendency to telescope economic growth is evident, not only in the contemporary period, but also in the experience of countries which industrialised after Britain in the nineteenth century. This is mainly due to the enhanced role of the State in the latecomer countries, leading to an element of 'planning' in anticipation of future market potential. The State, unlike private entrepreneurs, is willing to bear the burden of temporary losses by building excess capacity in the interests of economies of scale, which would be justified by future growth of the market. Nevertheless, the sequential expansion of industry along the path of early, middle, and late industries does occur. This self-sustained growth is precipitated by the expansion of civilian demand, with its impact on the interdependent linkages between sectors.

The apparently invariant identity of the group of strategic industries gives a misleading impression because it seems that these industries are determined a priori, i.e. the same for countries in the nineteenth century as today, regardless of historical specificity. The reason for this problem is the analytical procedure adopted in the studies discussed. Owing to the paucity of nineteenth-century industrial data the researchers surveyed adopted a cross-section analysis, observing the industrial structure as it existed then (i.e. 1950s). Thus, the particular industrial structure in contemporary developing countries was projected backwards in order to infer the situation in the nineteenth century. However, it is a reasonable assumption that the industrial structure in developing countries today is different in important respects from the one which existed in the nineteenth century. For example, the contemporary prominence of the chemical industry in the structure of production is likely to be more recent than the retrojection of the cross-section analysis suggests.

Finally, another shortcoming of the studies surveyed is the high level of aggregation used in categorising each industrial sector. The level of aggregation obscures the dynamic nature of the group of strategic industries, i.e. changes in the character and relative importance of sectors within the broad industrial categories. This process has been evident, historically, in the replacement of iron by steel, the supercession of rail transport by other modes, including road, etc.

Nevertheless, while the product utilised may change, its purpose does not: for example, a tough and resilient material like steel will probably always be necessary, as will the need for mobility whatever the mode of transport. However, the revolutionary transformations in technology introduced by nucler power and the silicon chip, most recently, may alter some of the purposes themselves. But it is significant that both these developments can be traced to military needs.

2.5 The role of the State in the economy

The involvement of the State in the economy can be conceptualised on two levels: at the onset of industrialisation, where the State is attempting to create an industrial capability, and subsequently, in assuring the viability of the economy. The former primarily relates to the State in latecomer countries, the latter to all countries where industries have become vulnerable, including the firstcomer(s).

It is held that the intervention of the State in the economy to establish the group of strategic industries and ensure their viability when threatened (by international trade competition or internal contradictions) is primarily motivated by the concern for national defence. It is also motivated by the desire to achieve national economic autonomy. However, the desire to achieve national economic autonomy can be interpreted as stemming from the political insecurity which characterises territorial units in the international political system, an insecurity most poignantly crystallised in the compulsion to create and maintain an auto-nomous defence capability. Thus a general desire for the maximum attainable economic autonomy is really a function of the more specific compulsion towards acquiring and maintaining a national defence capability.[21]

This impulse towards the institution and maintenance of maximum attainable national economic self-sufficiency is illus-trated by policies towards two of the group of strategic industries, textiles and paper products. Unlike the other four industries of the strategic group (iron and steel, transport equipment, machinery and chemicals) these two sectors are not of direct relevance to defence needs. But, as the evidence presented in the previous chapter affirms, they are of strategic economic significance to the economy. Their presence consequently defines an important component of relative national economic self-sufficiency, despite the limited direct relationship between them and defence. However, as it has been argued earlier, the desire for such economic autonomy is ultimately a function of perceived national security imperatives. There would be no need for either defence capability or economic autonomy in manufacturing if international rivalries did not exist.

Evidence presented in the fifth chapter also highlights the determination of State authorities to go considerably beyond the protection of textiles, by also defending the clothing sector. This may of course be due to the interdependence between textiles and clothing manufacture. Although the latter may not be strategic in the sense described, it is of indirect importance to the existence of the former. Textile goods are sold primarily to the domestic clothing sector and cannot be exported in large quantities since other countries also possess a textile industry which caters for their own clothing sector. A similar logic also holds for the paper and products industry which has no direct significance for defence capability.

Finally, the importance of relative national economic self-sufficiency touches upon an issue which will be elaborated later in this chapter. This is a goal which all countries seek to achieve even if the possibility of acquiring a national defence capability is qualified by other circumstances, e.g. status as a small power, relevant to the appraisal of most developing countries in the twentieth century.

The goals of State intervention in the economy — and society — are, of course, broader in intent and wider in scope. Whether society is viewed in class terms, in which the State primarily represents the interests of the dominant classes, or in liberal pluralist terms, in which the State is neutral, articulating the interests of different groups and social coalitions, the motives of State intervention in the economy are undoubtedly more variegated than national defence alone. From the process of nation-building, the provision of law and order, a national currency and system of taxation to the modern welfare-state, the role of the State in the economy and society expresses many interests.

However, the primacy of national defence considerations is indisputable. Since the viability of the national territory is a prerequisite for the achievement of all other goals, the State accords an absolute priority to national defence needs. The willingness of governments to subordinate all other goals to the exigencies of national defence is clearly evident in periods of actual war. And State actors have historically viewed the dominant condition of the international political system as one of permanent threat of war, if not actual war. Indeed, some observers of the international political system argue that peace is the exception and war the norm.[22] In this context, governments regard national defence as an absolute priority, whatever the degree of preparedness considered necessary in particular circumstances.

The analysis of State intervention in the economy is concerned with the impact of defence needs on the process of industrialisation. Thus, it is limited to the relationship between military needs and the creation of the group of strategic industries. It is not concerned with the role of defence expenditures in industrialised economies, i.e. State defence expenditure to overcome, what some perceive, as an inherent tendency toward underconsumption in capitalist economies. In fact, the issue of ensuring the viability of the group of strategic industries, which relates to an already industrialised country, is also distinct from the role of defence expenditures in the economy as indicated above. The latter is concerned with the dynamic interplay of defence expenditures and the economy, whereas the former only concerns the conditions necessary for the maintenance of a defence capability, i.e. in the form of the group of strategic industries.

2.5.1 The State in latecomer countries

The catalytic stimulus of military exertions reached a climactic stage in the late eighteenth century in Europe. The cumulative interaction between war, plunder and trade, accompanied by agrarian change, brought Europe to a stage where dramatic industrial and technological advances were now possible — the most dramatic changes since the discovery of settled agriculture. For a variety of reasons (to be discussed in the next chapter) Britain became the first country to cross the threshold of industrialisation, thereby threatening and prompting her European neighbours to join the race to industrialise.[23]

In the two preceding sections (before the section on the State) it was argued that the fundamental characteristics of the structure of production (i.e. primacy of the group of strategic industries) are essentially determined by the impact of military requirements. And the importance of the group of strategic industries for military purposes accounted for their predominance in the industrial structure. The spread of similar structures of production has been attributed to the process of imitation, as the State in latecomer countries strives to acquire locally industries which are important for defence and relative national economic self-sufficiency.

2.5.2 Specific reasons for State intervention

The necessity for State intervention in the economy because of the perception of national defence needs and the goal of economic autonomy, instead of allowing private enterprise to proceed independently, is highlighted by the timing of State intervention to ensure industrialisation. The industrialisation of Britain progressed relatively slowly compared to the pace of industrialisation elsewhere later. Since Britain was the first industrial nation it did not perceive any serious military threat from the existence of other more advanced countries and the State in Britain intervened relatively little, allowing industrialisation to proceed at a 'natural' pace.

If the State in France, Germany, Italy, Russia, and Japan had allowed industrialisation to proceed at the same pace, intervening on the same limited scale as Britain, industrialisation would not have occurred in the relatively short span of time that it did in these countries. In the case of Britain, intervention in the economy reflected much more accurately the cross-pressure of internal class conflict. The preponderance of domestic pressures (i.e. class conflicts, etc.) would have led to a more leisurely pace of industrialisation elsewhere too. Only the perception of external threat from the prior presence of already industrialised countries prompted considerably enhanced State involvement with industrialisation, and explains the rapidity of progress. Thus, while the process of industrialisation and economic growth is influenced by endogenous factors specific to the internal dynamics of society, the timing and its character are primarily determined by the impact of international political rivalry and perception of national defence needs. The political rationale and legitimacy of State intervention, its consensual inter-class basis is defence of the national territory.

The necessity of State intervention in the process of industrialisation in the latecomer countries is also predicated on several economic factors.

The presence of industrialised competitors raises barriers to entry in markets for the latecomers since most of the basic investment and infrastructural inputs can be imported because of the imperfect transmission of technology, lack of local skills and the benefits of economies of scale already achieved by the firstcomers.

In fact, the optimum level of production is likely to be established by the firstcomers — producing for local and export markets — raising the cost of entry. The initial cost of production for some of the group of strategic industries, as with other infrastructural activities, is also likely to be high because of inherent economies of scale, making the capital investment necessary too large for private entrepreneurs; the time horizon for returns may also be regarded as too long by private capital. In addition, owing to the complex economic and technological linkages of the group of strategic industries, the successful import-substitution for some of them does not guarantee self-sustained growth, and therefore economic and political independence. The intervention of the State to ensure the creation of the complete set of strategic industries thus becomes inevitable.

Finally, the State aims to ensure the existence of an installed capacity in the group of strategic industries which contains sufficient surplus to satisfy potential wartime levels of demand. As a consequence, the State is obliged to provide incentives to ensure the existence of this surplus.

2.6 Other explanations of State intervention in the economy of the latecomer countries

2.6.1 The Marxist view

The Marxist view that the desire to achieve and maintain internal control and unity to promote the interests of the nascent capitalist class motivates State sponsorship of industrialisation and the creation of industries for military purposes is to be acknowledged. National unification has usually required military power to overcome the resistance of existing local centres of authority.[24] However, the impact of this particular stimulus on State policy towards the creation of industries relevant for military purposes is likely to diminish once the process of national unification is complete. As compared to the initial problem of subjugating previously autonomous local entities, the subsequent situation essentially involves policing.[25] In any case, the issue of internal security is less urgent in terms of the motivation to establish defence industries, since the level of technology involved on both sides is likely to be similar. The asymmetry of military capability almost always relates to the superiority of other territorial units.

Indeed, the emergence of an external threat, real or imagined, can provoke internal conflict initially because of the very attempt to impose national unification in response to the prior external threat.[26]

Thus, the process of nation-building and the unification of the national market, which Marxists have traditionally viewed almost exclusively in terms of the interests of the emerging capitalist class, can also be seen as a means of consolidation which allows the State to cope with the dynamics of the international political system, i.e. preliminary to industrialisation.[27] In fact, Henry Barbera suggests that the

> . . . process of building nations found its inspiration and momentum in mercantilism and nationalism. Mercantilism is a policy aimed at fusing state and society by replacing the medieval combination of religious universalism and political localism for the territorially bounded nation in order to promote thereby its power over all other political units both domestic and foreign in a context of rather intense rivalry.[28]

This was a view also shared by Eli Heckscher in his authoritative study of mercantilism.[29] The class struggles which the process of nation-building also articulates does not detract from the primary causative role of international political competition.

2.6.2 *The liberal view*

While liberal analysts recognise, with misgiving, the need for State intervention to ensure a national defence capability, the primacy of defence, *per se*, in prompting State intervention to institute industrialisation would not be acceptable to them. The necessity of State intervention in the range of industries comprising the strategic set, or perhaps even its historical reality would be contrary to liberal assumptions. A liberal analysis of the involvement of the State in promoting industrialisation would stress factors like imperfect competition, the infant industry argument, externalities, etc., although the degree of intervention required is viewed more restrictively. But this argument is incomplete, since it does not consider the political imperatives which make industrialisation urgent. The intervention of the State to promote industrialisation in latecomer countries is essential for economic reasons, as the liberals argue and as affirmed earlier in the chapter. However, the desire to industrialise is itself based on political imperatives, namely, the pressures of international competition.

The desire to acquire the material benefits of industrialisation and economic growth has also been considered significant by some observers in motivating the State, especially because of demonstration effects. However, the goal of material prosperity does not contain the urgency of the fundamental objective of national defence. The concern for national prosperity becomes a matter of importance once the country has actually experienced the fruits of industrialisation, not in advance of it. While it is undoubtedly true that industrialisation did bring higher living standards and prosperity there is some dispute regarding its initial impact. According to some historians, living standards in the conditions of overcrowding and squalor in the urban centres were worse in the early phases of industrial capitalism than in the countryside from which the newly emergent proletariat came.

2.7 The State and the viability of the economy

A recent Marxist debate has made a distinctive attempt to explain the intervention of the State in contemporary industrial societies in terms of the inability of capitalism to provide the conditions of its own existence privately. The areas of State intervention to compensate for the deficiencies of private capital which have been specified in the debate are somewhat more inclusive than the group of strategic industries, but they do coincide partly with them, and consequently these arguments require examination.

According to the 'state derivation' debate the functions of the State in the advanced capitalist countries can be derived from the 'needs of reproduction of capital as a whole — total social capital'.[30] Their analysis of 'nationalisation and the public sector in its discussion of the State provision of the general conditions of production' is relevant to this study.[31]

The evolution of economic conditions in the advanced capitalist countries is considered to have imposed new functional tasks on the State in its relationship with private capital. The capitalist process of reproduction, it is argued, generates the need for the State, removed from the process of competition, to provide the general material conditions of production which cannot be singly provided by individual capitals.[32] It is held that historically the tendency of capital is to posit fixed capital as the form adequate to itself, 'to release production ever more clearly from its natural basis and to transfer the conditions of production (particular and general) into the general condition of social reproduction mediated through exchange value'.[33] The separation of private capital from its natural bases as a result of its growing sophistication compels the State to compensate by expanding its functional tasks. The State has to take measures to protect the environment, ensure the creation of alternative sources of energy and raw materials — with the depletion of or unadaptability of traditional sources. Above all, a functional compulsion arises to provide infrastructural activities: health, education, research, transport, building of towns, etc.

As a general point it is self-evident that the sphere of State activity has expanded vastly, and could be interpreted as supportive of the State derivation debate thesis.[34] But two problems are apparent: firstly, the involvement of the State in these activities is not entirely novel, although it has now become more systematic and comprehensive. For example, the State was involved in the provision of education, health, building of towns, etc. in the nineteenth century because of the high costs, externalities, and short-run unprofitability. Similarly, the Factory Acts of the nineteenth century, like transfer payments today, were a means of preventing capital from self-destructive depredations against labour. Secondly, the exclusive preoccupation with direct forms of ownership — i.e. nationalisation — is inappropriate, especially where the group of strategic industries is concerned. The intervention of the State to ensure the viability of some of the group of strategic industries has taken the form of nationalisation, but in other instances, subsidies have been granted instead. The preoccupation with direct forms of ownership accounts for the exclusion of a number of industries from the analysis of the State derivation debate. It should be recalled that the State in latecomer countries was also involved in the creation of the group of strategic industries whenever necessary; for example, in the nineteenth century, as shown earlier. The State derivation debate overlooks this earlier involvement because of its preoccupation with direct forms of ownership.

The issue of inter-capitalist international rivalry and its impact on the policies of the State towards the achievement of self-sufficiency, both in raw materials and basic manufactured inputs, is acknowledged by the State derivation debate but insufficiently stressed.

The idea of ensuring the viability of industry is anathema, in principle, to liberal economists. While liberals accept the need for certain types of State intervention, they do not accept the idea of generalised intervention implicit in ensuring the viability of the group of strategic industries. For example, liberal analysts acknowledge the need for State intervention in some limited areas directly concerned with the production of armaments, but it certainly does not include the range of industries which comprise the group of strategic industries. The intervention of the State in response to the impact of international trade is perceived as legitimate only in terms of minimising the social and political costs of adjustment. Hence, the intervention of the State in response to the disruptive social impact of trade is regarded as temporary.[35]

However, the persistence of the similar structures of production in diverse countries undermines the notion that State intervention is temporary and prompted only by concern for the social and political costs of adjustment in response to changing patterns of comparative advantage. There has been some reallocation of economic activity and the modification of the mix of products because of cheaper imports, but these industries have not been allowed to adjust themselves out of existence.[36] Undoubtedly, the social and political costs of trade adjustment, in terms of unemployment and regional deprivation, may be significant for governments indebted to the immediate pressures of electoral politics, but it cannot be an adequate explanation for the survival of these industries in the long run. It is here that the explanation of perceived military security and national economic autonomy become highly suggestive.

In the contemporary phase of capitalism, the expansion and permanence of State intervention in the group of strategic industries — both ownership by the State and subsidy — stems from the competitive pressures of proliferating State-sponsored or subsidised industry in other countries. In the past the State in latecomer countries sponsored these industries, but did not need to support them indefinitely. But the attempt by a growing number of latecomer countries to capture a share of the market through State sponsorship, in order to overcome the advantages enjoyed by the established firstcomer countries, has provoked a widespread response in the form of more permanent State involvement in the latter; and the proliferation understandably tends towards universality since all countries are obliged to join once the phenomenon begins to spread.

In conclusion, it should be admitted that the Marxist and liberal views analysed above are not entirely mutually exclusive. Given the heterogeneity of perspectives in the two 'schools', the delineation imposed above for analytical purposes is somewhat artificial.[37]

Thus, it can be persuasively argued that it is the perception of national defence needs and the goal of relative economic self-sufficiency which prompt State intervention to create and ensure the survival of the group of strategic industries. As it has already been shown, the acquisition of the group of strategic industries is also the process of industrialisation itself. And industrialisation automatically entails a substantial measure of economic self-sufficiency; that it also coincides with desire of the capitalist class for greater national autonomy merely reinforces the resolve of the State. However, it is argued that industrialisation initially occurs because of the catalytic impact of national military needs, for which industrialisation and economic self-sufficiency are both a by-product and a necessity.[38]

The analysis concerning the motivation of the State to industrialise and defend the group of strategic industries has been couched at a high level of generality. It needs to take into account the differential impact of the international political system on different countries and delineate the historical experience of countries implied by it. Obviously, the opportunities and constraints encountered by large, medium and small countries must necessarily differ. All countries, like oligopolies and small firms in the market, share certain broad features. Just as oligopolies cannot abolish the international market, the most powerful country cannot transcend the international political system. But the constituent units of the international political system can be differentiated according to the functional equivalent of 'price-makers' and 'price-takers' in the market. Thus, the goal of national defence and its corollary, relative economic autonomy, have distinctive meanings for countries of differing size.

If the general hypothesis advanced on State intervention and the economy is re-interpreted to take into account the actual options available to countries of varying size a number of qualifications are required. Before proceeding any further, however, the notion of size itself should be clarified. The classification of countries according to population size, the criterion adopted in the first chapter, is not wholly satisfactory in the context of international political and military relations and should be employed with some caution. The geographical and population size of a country are relevant in assessing its location in the politico-military hierarchy of nations, but the smallness of territory and/or population can be compensated by other factors, e.g. industrialisation itself, leadership, skill, etc. apart. Nevertheless, size in this sense, remains an absolute constraint despite the latitude of possibilities still potentially available. Thus, Israel may indefinitely retain its superiority in relation to larger neighbouring countries, but it cannot conceive of challenging the USSR, or perhaps, even Turkey; even its local dominance is dependent on outside support. A hierarchy based on size, however compensated by other factors, does therefore exist and it is this reality which must be reconciled in detail to the general hypothesis advanced earlier.

In the context of size constraints, the pursuit of national defence, *per se*, and the goal of relative national economic self-sufficiency might be distinguished. Furthermore, it would be useful to view the former on two policy levels for analytical purposes. The goal of national defence is, at minimum, the protection of territorial sovereignty and it can be pursued by sponsoring industrialisation (with a concomitant defence capability) and/or international alliances.

In many circumstances medium and, more particularly, small powers may find that their security is threatened by a larger country. In such a situation their dependence on international alliances is inevitable and the significance of national defence capability diminishes correspondingly. In relying on alliances, small powers usually also depend on allies for the supply of weapons and armaments. In any case, it would not be meaningful or possible, in terms of costs, to compete with the industrial and military capability of the larger power which might threaten it.

But the historical experience of State intervention in industrialisation, leading to the emergence of similar and relatively self-sufficient production structures and the protection of the national economy established, is common to all countries. This may be more problematic for small powers but the impulse towards it, as the evidence presented in chapter one demonstrates, is undeniable; small powers attempt to compensate for their limited local market, by exports, for example. Why then do virtually all countries pursue relative economic self-sufficiency, even when a national defence capability is not an altogether feasible goal?

Even if national defence capability is infeasible for many countries, economic autonomy is regarded as desirable because industrialisation offers security (prosperity apart) in an uncertain world. It provides a degree of protection against the ever-present danger of international economic disruption and external shock. Such disruption and shock are much more persistent than the greater danger of war. Thus all States seek the maximum measure of economic autonomy, to insulate themselves, as far as possible, from the vagaries of the outside world.

In the twentieth century, the enhanced volatility of the international economic environment has made this an extremely desirable option. The chaos of west Asia affects uninvolved third parties, for example. This is therefore the primary motivation for relative national economic self-sufficiency of the majority of otherwise militarily weak countries of the twentieth century.[39]

2.8 Modes of State intervention in the group of strategic industries

The methods by which the State has intervened either to create or ensure the viability of the group of strategic industries have varied in different countries in different periods. As far as the creation of the group of strategic industries is concerned the involvement of the State need not always be a self-conscious one, although nearly always it is the case. At the most general level, procurement for defence purposes, which it will be argued was the initial stimulus towards industrialisation in the case of Britain, has an important impact.

Direct subsidy and tariffs. The latecomers in the nineteenth century, with respect to Britain, used two major policy tools. In France, Germany, Russia, and Japan both direct subsidy and tariffs to provide protection have been important methods of fostering the growth of the group of strategic industries. The particular mix of policies employed has varied. For example, in the early period of industrial development the State in France displayed a penchant for tariffs as a means of promoting industrialisation, although it later engaged in widespread subsidisation.

Public ownership. The public ownership of industry, particularly those belonging to the strategic group like iron and steel, transport, etc., has been widespread in the developing countries of the Third World, but it was less important in the first round of industrialisation in most of Europe. Nevertheless, the practice of direct State ownership was important in the first stages of Japanese industrialisation; some European countries also had State-sponsored (i.e. nationally owned) enterprises in the period before full-scale industrialisation actually occurred: foundries, forges, arms factories, etc.

The public ownership of sectors like transport, especially railroad, was not uncommon in nineteenth-century Europe, but it has become more general in its reach. The impact of State subsidy and ownership in latecomer countries and the consequent intensification of competition in international trade has compelled the State in some firstcomer countries to intervene more directly in order to cope with shrinking markets, falling profits and the general decline in industrial primacy.

Preferential procurement. The policy of buying from local, and preferably, nationally owned firms, is practised by all governments. If the State is compelled to make purchases from abroad it only does so when the technological gap is so vast that the cost of immediate local production would be exorbitant. At the same time, governments constantly strive to initiate local production whenever projected future national needs are likely to be substantial.

Discriminatory taxation. The use of discriminatory taxation in favour of industry has become widespread in western countries, as an alternative to allegedly undesirable direct State intervention, although the latter option becomes unavoidable when persistent problems arise. However, the State is increasingly prone to manipulate the level of taxation in favour of industry. For example, generous depreciation allowances, not unknown in the past, have been employed to shift the burden of taxation to the consumer.

Export subsidies. The promotion of industries through export subsidies and tied aid may be motivated by balance of payment considerations, but it is also important in itself for industry. The latter is particularly important to the group of strategic industries which tend to experience problems of overcapacity. The tying of aid also creates a long-term relationship between the importing country and the exporter, the former becoming constrained in its

future choices by previous decisions made owing to the inducement of aid; i.e. even if the aid were to cease, the importing country
could not easily shift to another source of supply without incurring
the loss of abandoning purchases previously acquired.

Education and research. The more diffuse impact of education
sponsored by the State is also noteworthy. The successes of
Germany and Japan in the nineteenth century in the field of
technical education have been the subject of comment. In the
contemporary world, in contrast to the leadership of a few countries
in the nineteenth century, education in all its forms is both publicly
funded and fairly massive in scope. The training of manpower and
research are thus encompassed in State policy in support of
economic growth and a viable national economy. The direction of
research on scientific and technical matters undertaken at universities and institutes is greatly influenced by State policy in
promoting particular areas of study.

The more direct subsidy to research and development in the
underwriting of costs embodied in products procured by the State
is also of great importance, both as an element of subsidy to
industry and in its spin-off consequences for the economy. This
aspect of public economic support is of unquestionable significance
for the sectors of the group of strategic industries which produce
armaments for the national defence establishment.

State intervention in the economy also takes the form of
involvement in managerial decisions. In a number of developed
countries programmes for rationalisation and centralisation have
been pressed on industry through a mixture of persuasion,
coercion and financial inducement.

Notes

1. State here refers to Government, not the country as in territorial-
    state.
2. The sample of small primary-orientated countries is limited and their
    long-run tendency cannot be deduced affirmatively yet.
3. Textiles, iron and steel, machinery, chemicals, transport equipment,
    and paper and paper products.
4. There has been much debate about the concept of power, but for the
    purpose of this discussion it is sufficient to view power as a basic pre-
    condition or capability, i.e. industrialisation. Questions concerning
    the use of a particular form of power and the associated problems are

not of concern here, and go beyond this discussion. See von Clausewitz (1968); Aron (1967); McLelland (1966); Sprout (1962); Kahn (1960); Morgenthau (1960); Knorr (1956).

5.   See Hopkins and Mansbach (1975).

6.   Lenin (1973).

7.   Debray (1977) p. 26.

8.   Ibid. p. 28.

9.   See Nove (1972) and Gurley (1976); Carr and Davies (1974) pp 454–9; also see Skocpol (1979).

10.   The relationship between the emergence of the modern state system itself and industrialisation has many facets. For example, the drive for political unification in Europe and Japan was partly motivated by the desire for industrialisation as a means of participation in the international political system; equally, there were other factors.

11.   See Knorr (op. cit.) above.

12.   It is true that the industrially superior do not invariably succeed in undermining the independence of weaker states since the outcome of conflicts also depends on the configuration of power in the international political system and the prevalent alliances: the US in Vietnam, for example. Nevertheless, weak countries have an understandable compulsion towards self-reliance. Thus, it is the perception of vulnerability because of industrial backwardness which motivates the desire to industrialise.

13.   See in particular Fuller (1946) pp. 91-2; Wright (1942) **1** p. 313.

14.   'Three Mile Island Damage Confirmed', *Financial Times* (23 July 1982) p. 4.

15.   See Wallerstein (1980).

16.   The significance of iron and steel, transport equipment, machinery and chemicals for defence purposes is readily understandable and uncontroversial. However, the case of textiles and paper products, which also comprise the group of strategic industries, requires explanation. This issue will be discussed below; for the moment the distinction between defence purposes, *per se*, and national economic autonomy should be borne in mind.

17.   Hobsbawm 1977 p. 47.

18.   Mokyr (1977) p. 1005.

19.   Mumford in Barbera (1973) p. 5.

20.   Nevertheless, the preponderance of military influences on the economy, as a source of change is evident in the amount of resources devoted to defence research. See Kennedy (1975); also UN 'The Economic and Social Consequences of Disarmament', (1962) p. 3.

21.   It may be objected that if industrialisation is promoted by the State for military purposes, once sufficient industrial potential has been acquired for military needs there is no further incentive to continue. The question of a 'partial' industrialisation to cater for military needs

only does not arise because of the inherent economies of a scale which entail a high minimum capacity; there may be no market for this capacity, but its installation is unavoidable. In addition, the experience of wars in the late-nineteenth and twentieth centuries has shown that the demands of armament production in actual wars absorb considerable portions of the civilian economy. The size of the civilian economy is therefore a positive factor in the prosecution of war. It is also an acknowledged fact that the margin of 'surplus' which can be appropriated by the State during periods of war is a function of the relative prosperity of the economy, measured by per capita manufacturing output. See Kecskemeti (1958) pp. 225-45 and Hawtrey (1930).

22. See Claude Jr. (1962); also Bull (1978).

23. The question arises why other civilisations with a history of technological accomplishment did not succeed in achieving industrial change, e.g. China. In the case of China it seems that although many inventions were available they were not in general use. One reason for this situation was undoubtedly the official policy of suppressing what were considered potentially destabilising influences. See Elvin (1973).

24. There were rebellions in post-Meiju Japan for example; see Lockwood (1954).

25. It would not therefore require the heavy equipment of inter-state military conflict.

26. See Norman (1975).

27. The political unification of most countries has preceded the effort to industrialise.

28. Barbera (1973) p. 127.

29. See Heckscher (1934) also Moore Jr. (1966).

30. Holloway and Picciotto (1978) p. 19.

31. Ibid. p. 21.

32. Ibid. p. 64.

33. Quoted in Ibid. p. 92.

34. See Kidron (1968); Shonfield (1957); also Maddison (1967), Chapter IV.

35. See Kindleberger (1959); Saxonhouse in Taylor (ed.) (1973); Mitchell (1976); Macbean (1978).

36. The textile and clothing industry might have been expected to be relocated to parts of the developing world, but agreements like the LTA and MFA ensured the survival of these industries in the developed world. The developed countries of the world have only acceded to a reduction in their share of the international market, but have not surrendered their domestic markets.

37. For an excellent critical synthesis of Marxist analysis of the capitalist state see Jessop (1982).

38.   There exist countries which enjoy high standards of life without acquiring the group of strategic industries. The failure to ensure economic independence means that these countries become effectively integrated into larger systems of economic and political power, e.g. some of the oil-producing countries.

39.   I am grateful to Bob Rowthorn for pointing out the importance of this distinction in comparing the nineteenth and twentieth centuries, but I do not know if he would agree with the formulation above.

3 The catalytic influence of military impulses on economic growth

3.1 Introduction

The present chapter is devoted to an appraisal of the evidence concerning the catalytic influence of military needs on the process of economic growth. At this point a number of important analytical and historical distinctions implicit in the more synthetic discussion of the previous chapter require to be amplified.

In the previous chapter it was asserted that the catalytic impact of military needs was significant in precipitating industrialisation and determining the structure of manufacturing production. It was also argued that the spread of the similar structures of production which are known to exist (demonstrated in chapter 1) was essentially attributable to imitation, whereby the latecomer countries followed the path trodden by the firstcomer(s). The first imperative elaboration of the arguments relates to the overall socio-economic context in which the catalytic impact occurred in Europe before the onset of industrialisation. The second relates to the concrete historical process of the spread (i.e. the phenomenon of imitation) of industrialisation in Western Europe. Finally, it is considered necessary to perceive the role of the State on a somewhat higher level of generality in order to achieve closer correspondence between the conceptual definition of the role of the State and the diversity of actual historical manifestations of its role.

These three issues will be dealt with in descending order before proceeding to an appraisal of the relevant evidence concerning the catalytic influence of military needs.

The catalytic impact of military requirements, as the principal determinant of the structure of production, should not be misunderstood to be the *cause* of industrialisation itself. The impact of military needs was catalytic in that it influenced the *form* and *pace* of industrialisation but it did not constitute the cause.[1] The primary underlying cause of the rise of industrial capitalism in Western Europe was the decline of feudalism. The precise nature of the inner dialectic (i.e. the class contradictions, the growth of trade, and the increasing commercialisation of agriculture) which led to the disintegration of feudalism, the subject of a celebrated debate, is not of concern here except that it did occur.[2] The decline of feudalism is therefore to be considered the ultimate cause of the rise of industrial capitalism, whereas the influence of military needs was the occasion for the change. As Mandel has described Marx's conception:

> The production of weapons for the dynastic wars from the fifteenth to the eighteenth century was a major source of accumulation and *one of the most important midwives of early capitalism* (emphasis added). As a stimulus to accelerate industrialization or to extend the capitalist market, arms expenditure and war has played a considerable role in the acceleration of industrialization or extension of the capitalist market throughout modern history.[3]

The particular analysis of the present study is, however, more specific in its interpretation, but it is worth noting that the importance of arms and war for industrialisation has not gone unnoticed, although it may not have been articulated systematically, or even widely accepted.

The intensified military endeavours themselves were probably caused, in large part, by the very decline of feudalism and the growth of mercantilism as its secondary manifestation.[4] While the catalytic impact of military needs may, arguably, have been a necessary condition historically for industrialisation it certainly was not a sufficient one. In principle, the particular stimuli to industrialisation could have derived from other sources, although it is difficult retrospectively to imagine how else it might have happened. Negatively, by itself, militarisation is not enough to ensure industrialisation and this can be easily established by a cursory survey of relatively militarised societies which have nevertheless failed to industrialise because of a backward agriculture, and the attendant low levels of commercialisation and productivity. In the modern world even a country like India, despite its sizeable indigenous armaments industry, cannot achieve full industrialisation for these reasons: its low agricultural productivity and commercialisation. It is also interesting to note that the first non-European country to industrialise successfully, Japan, was also the only one where feudalism was declining, with almost fifty per cent of output produced for the market and high levels of productivity.[5]

On an abstract level, the conceptualisation of the catalytic impulse of military needs, in precipitating industrialisation and substantially determining its form, as first occurring in one country and subsequently spreading elsewhere through a process of imitation, is unavoidable as a means of viewing the overall progression of change, but it is not wholly satisfactory when analysed at a more concrete historical level. The transition from declining feudalism (or pre-capitalist commodity exchange, as Sweezy describes it) to industrial capitalism in Western Europe was a more generalised and complex phenomenon and the apparent implication that it first occurred only in England and then spread to other Western European countries is untenable. In this respect the very idea of a firstcomer in the European context merits qualification.

In fact, other parts of Western Europe like France and the Netherlands had reached a stage of sufficient economic and social maturity to achieve generalised industrialisation. France, the Netherlands and England had all acquired the prerequisites of an increasingly commercialised and productive agriculture deriving from the successful resistance of the peasantry to the perpetuation of older forms of exploitation.[6] As far as the specific preoccupation of this book is concerned, the stimulus of military needs was also present in these countries as well. The question then arises why Britain first? Although the answer to this question does not affect my arguments since British ascendency could be taken as given — i.e. the starting point of the analysis — a number of comments can be put forward in response to it, in order to illuminate the actual historical process.

Britain enjoyed a number of socio-economic and fortuitous advantages. Within the advanced social formations of Western Europe Britain had reached the highest point of maturity. During this era of pre-capitalist commodity exchange the growth rate of French trade and manufacture was similar to that of Britain. However, by 1750 it was clear that if industrialisation was to occur it would first take place in Britain, which by then exceeded France in per capita trade and manufactures. France had not recovered from the great economic depression of the seventeenth century and the 'Dutch had retired to that comfortable role of old-established business, the exploitation of their vast commercial and financial apparatus . . . and their colonies'.[7]

The origins of this initial advantage could be sought further in the past, but for the purposes of the present study it would be more relevant to dwell on the reasons for the continued supremacy of eighteenth- and nineteenth-century Britain. This continuing supremacy could be aptly expressed in the biblical aphorism: to him who hath shall be given. The initial advantages of Britain became further manifest in the successes of her imperial ventures, which accentuated the relegation of her continental rivals. The prosperity of French overseas trade, for example, was greatly hindered by British naval activities. One fortuitous reason for the unprecedented sway of British imperialism, which reinforced her economic advance, was a more efficient naval and military strategy.[8]

In addition, France, Britain's chief rival, continued to suffer serious domestic upheavals. The political revolutions which neutralised Absolutism had been fully consolidated in Britain by the end of the seventeenth century, whereas the struggles of the rising bourgeoisie of France were still to conclude.

The stimulus of military needs propels industrialisation, but it requires peace at subsequent stages to consolidate the gains made during years of war, in order to acquire the civilian momentum which underpins its generalised advance.[9] This period of recuperation was denied to France until the end of the Napoleonic wars. By then Britain's domestic economic strength was unrivalled and her imperialist position unassailable. Britain's imperialist policies were also uniquely characterised by the aggressive mercantilist promotion of national trading interests. It was the existence of this growing external market which fuelled British economic growth.[10]

In conclusion it is only necessary to stress that the significance of Britain's role as the firstcomer lies in the establishment of the first manufacturing civilian economy rather than the novelty of its experience in manufacturing production as such. Thus, the distinction between England as the firstcomer and the continental countries as latecomers is essentially one of degree; the latecomers who imitated England were not adopting a qualitatively new type of society completely unknown to them, except in the sense that the scale and penetration experienced by the advent of industrial capitalism, as opposed to mercantile capitalism, was new. In any case, it should be borne in mind that the historical distance which separated Britain from her immediate rival, France, was less than two generations.

The promotion of national trading interests referred to above leads to the final issue: the viewing of the role of the State on a higher level of generality in order to reach a more complete picture of the diversity of historical experience.

In the previous chapter the discussion concerning the involvement of the State in promoting industrialisation essentially related to the experience of latecomer countries. It will be recalled that the exertions of the State in latecomer countries to industrialise is considered to have been prompted by the prior existence of other industrialised countries. In the nineteenth century it was the corporeal presence of industrial England which motivated the State in other Western European countries to promote industrialisation (i.e. the group of strategic industries) for reasons of perceived national security. Of course, for each country the perception of a threat to national security issued from all predecessor industrial countries in general and, probably, from an individual country in particular; i.e. Japan *vis-à-vis* north Atlantic countries and Italy *vis-à-vis* France. The dictum of Gerschenkron that the greater the backwardness of a country the greater the likely involvement of the State in the process of industrialisation does not go far enough. Its political corollary is: the greater the proximity to areas of conflict and tension the greater the probable effort by the State of that country to achieve industrialisation. But the involvement of the State in the economy predates this distinctive phase in which industrialisation was a clear goal in the latecomer countries.

The wars from the seventeenth century onwards are regarded as having provided the catalytic stimulus for the installment of industrial capitalism, and wars are eminently an area of State activity. In this period of mercantile rivalry, and pre-capitalist commodity exchange, however, the state's involvement in the economy was indirect; it mainly took the form of purchase of war materials and supplies. The State did occasionally operate arms factories, foundries, forges, etc., but the scale and significance of this activity was limited;[11] there was no consciousness of introducing fundamental economic change of the kind represented by an industrial revolution.

The involvment of the State in the economy in England, the firstcomer country, was essentially of this variety and was an experience shared with other European countries during this period of history. This shared common experience is in notable contrast to the much greater State involvement in the actual process of industrialisation in latecomer countries during the nineteenth century. In Britain, during the first period the stimulus to economic activity came primarily from purchases and the licensing of monopolies for the acquisition of war materials and supplies. Later, as it has already been observed, the aggressive promotion of national trading interests through imperialism came to constitute the main bulwark of State assistance to industrialisation:

> The result of this century of intermittent warfare was the greatest triumph ever achieved by any state: the virtual monopoly among European powers of overseas colonies, and the virtual monopoly of world-wide naval power.

Hobsbawn further comments that 'behind our industrial revolution there lies this concentration on the colonial and "underdeveloped" markets overseas, the successful battle to deny them to anyone else'.[12] The process of change (schematised in the model below) induced by military activity in the first period was carried forward in England by the conquest of markets in the second period.

In the previous chapter the relative passivity of the State in England towards the progression of economic growth and industrialisation was noted: i.e. during the stage described immediately above as the second period of State involvement in Britain. For example, the high cost of railway construction in Britain could have been avoided by State intervention to make provision for the purchase of land at reasonable cost and measures to pre-empt the unnecessary duplication of lines. This relative passivity is attributable substantially to the absence of political urgency since she was the firstcomer.

There are also specific economic reasons for State intervention in the process of industrialisation.[13] Some of these factors apply only to latecomer countries, e.g. the presence of industrialised competitors. But one important economic factor is relevant for the firstcomer: the need of a growing economy for larger markets. As one can see, the British State ensured the existence of outlets in colonial markets. Of greater significance were the markets in Europe and north America which required British capital and technology to initiate the growth of industries. The existence of these markets, before industrialisation was actively pursued there, made State intervention less important for Britain, the firstcomer, than for others who followed.

3.2 Internecine wars and mass warfare

The origins of the military stimulus to economic growth and industrial capitalism can be traced to the internecine wars and mass warfare dating back to the sixteenth century. According to calculations made by R. Ehrenberg '. . . in the entire sixteenth century, there were only twenty-five years without large-scale military operations in Europe';[14] during the seventeenth century only seven years passed without major wars.[15] And the period beginning in 1689 and ending in 1815, spanning over one and a quarter centuries, has been described as the era of the Great Wars.[16] In this period Britain, the most important participant in international economic and political rivalries, was engaged in wars for some seventy-five years.

Beginning with the War of the Grand Alliance between 1689–97, the era ended with the close of the Napoleonic wars in 1815. The War of the Spanish Succession occurred between 1702–13, followed by the War of Jenkin's Ear and the War of the Austrian Succession (1739–48). This was immediately followed by Anglo-French rivalries in north America (1749–55) and the Seven Years' War (1756–63), and the War of American Independence, including the Maritime War (1775–83), ending with the opening of the Napoleonic wars in 1793 — which concluded in 1815.

The Absolutist States of the period, to quote Anderson, 'were machines built overwhelmingly for the battlefield'. According to Anderson the first regular national system of taxation to be imposed in France was levied to pay for the first regular military units in Europe. In Spain eighty per cent of State revenues were devoted to military expenditure. Even the modern type of administrative monarchy is considered to have originated because of military operations. Indeed

> by the mid seventeenth century, the annual outlays of continental principalities from Sweden to Piedmont were everywhere predominantly and monotonously devoted to the preparation or conduct of war, now universally more costly than in the Renaissance.

As late as 1789 two-thirds of French State expenditure was allocated to the military establishment. As Machiavelli put it: 'a prince should have no other thought or aim than war, nor acquire mastery in anything except war, its organisation and discipline, for war is the only art expected of the ruler'.[17]

It was also the Absolutist State that pioneered the professional army, which with the military revolution of the late sixteenth and seventeenth centuries (introduced by Maurice of Orange, Gustavus Adolphus and Wallenstein) grew prodigiously in size[18] (see Table 3.1). According to one scholar of that period,

> in the first half of the seventeenth century, even a wealthy nation found it burdensome to keep eighty thousand men under arms in time of war, and the famous captains of the mid-century believed that fifty thousand men constituted as large an army as could be handled. By the War of the Spanish Succession France had four hundred thousand men under arms, while her enemies deployed even more. Faraway Russia had one hundred thousand while Prussia has forty thousand, and it was not unusual for a single general to command a hundred thousand men.[19]

In Britain, for which the navy was always more important, Basil Williams has estimated the number of land troops at twenty thousand or below in 1745 to a peak of about sixty-eight thousand by the Seven Years' War; it also had Irish contingents numbering twelve thousand.[20] However, it should be borne in mind that the size of land forces under English control (and therefore constituting a source of stimulus for English industry) was considerably larger. The colonial armies in late-eighteenth century India, for example, were substantially composed of local recruits. Indeed it has been calculated that at no time during its imperial rule of India did British contingents exceed twelve thousand — the rest were drawn locally. The total figure throughout the British empire cannot have been inconsiderable (see Table 3.2).

The size of navies and naval vessels also grew apace with the intensification of mercantile rivalry. During the late seventeenth and early eighteenth centuries the number of ships in different navies began to increase. In 1661 Colbert's France possessed only thirty warships, at his death they numbered one hundred and seventy-six, with another sixty-eight planned or under construction. But it was the British navy which had begun its rapid expansion under James II that was the largest by 1715.[21] In 1685 the tonnage of the British navy stood at a hundred thousand tons, by

Table 3.1 Sizes of various European armies since before the industrial revolution

	UK	France	Germany	Russia	Austro-Hungary
1661	5,200				
1688	28,000				
1712				108,000	
1725/30	17,000			196,000	
1740					30,000
1756				163,000	
1764/65	40,000			313,000	
1783		127,000			
1792	57,300				
1800/05	306,700	743,000	160,000	433,000	220,000
1809/12	108,700	280,000	331,000	540,000	280,000
1827/36	138,000	445,000	346,000	870,000	286,000
1846/51				730,000	
1855				888,000	
1860	229,500				
1865/66			441,000		647,000
1869/71		426,000	937,000	834,000	
1874				794,000	
1880		498,000			
1888/89	212,000	525,000		770,000	323,000
1890			492,000		

Source: Mulhall, M.G. (1899) *The Dictionary of Statistics*, London, fourth edition, pp. 68-71.

Table 3.2 The total land forces of the British Empire in 1889

British regular army	212,000
Reserve and Militia	205,000
Volunteers	222,000
Yeomanry	14,000
Irish Constabulary	13,000
Anglo–Indian army	145,000
Indian police	190,000
Colonial forces	15,000
Total	1,016,000

Source: Mulhall, M.G. (1899) p. 68; quoted in Table 3.1.

the end of the 1750s it had reached three hundred and twenty-five thousand tons[22] (see Table 3.3). The number of seamen, more important than native land troops, fluctuated between forty thousand and seventy thousand, at which it stood in 1762.[23]

Table 3.3 The Royal Navy of Great Britain 1603–1890 (the growth of tonnage and manpower)

Year	Vessels	Tons	Men	Cost per annum
1603	42	17,000		180,000
1685	179	104,000	10,000	390,000
1760	325	321,000	51,000	5,611,000
1803	450	461,000	180,000	12,037,000
1850	585	570,000	48,000	6,438,000
1890	373	680,000	65,000	13,700,000

Source: Mulhall, M.G. (1899) p. 415; quoted in Table 3.1

Already by 1700 the mercantile marine numbered some six thousand ships, of around half a million tons; it employed one hundred thousand seamen and comprised a tenth of all capital investments, excluding real estate. In this context, the importance of ships as the single largest piece of capital equipment making a variety of demands on the economy should be stressed.

The growing importance of rivalry at sea beginning in the seventeenth century is a matter of historical record. Both the navy and the mercantile marine were participants in this conflict, the latter often being commandeered for actual battles at sea. In this connection the role of privateers in prosecuting sea warfare requires to be noted. The magnitude and intensity of rivalry at sea would be underestimated without accounting for their involvement.[24]

3.3 The catalytic impact of military needs on industry

First and foremost, a powerful stimulus is administered to the level of demand for certain types of industrial goods. The requirements of any organised military force are always large in magnitude. The magnitude of this demand is a strong stimulus to the expansion of existing facilities and the creation of new ones. It seems clear that the needs of the military have been particularly important for virtually all the group of strategic industries in the manufacturing sector.[25]

The interdependence of the structure of production is an acknowledged phenomenon, already discussed in the previous chapter. Thus, the stimulus of defence needs on one or a few sectors can be instrumental in initiating the development of other sectors. For example, the factory production of textile goods was stimulated because of military orders for a large and standardised output: uniforms, etc. The lowering of unit costs made possible by the production of a large and standardised output for military consumption allowed this factory-based textile industry to cater for the civilian market. The expansion of the textile industry then necessitated the enlargement of output in other sectors which had previously served primarily the military and a limited civilian market. The growth of civilian demand for iron and the development of an important chemicals industry owed much to textiles. The growth of the textile sector reacted upon the demand for substances to whiten cloth and iron machinery to produce the expanded output of cloth in factories.

Second, and related intimately to the first, is the influence on the organisation of production. The need to expand facilities or create new ones and standardise the production of goods for military purposes institutionalises the important idea of rationally organised systems. The mass production of standardised goods impels factory production since the task of equipping, clothing and feeding mass armies can no longer be accomplished by the decentralised and impromptu methods of earlier times.

The magnitude of military demand and the need for standardised output precipitated by the constant warfare and mass armies of the seventeenth, eighteenth, and early nineteenth centuries is held to have hastened factory production and the cheapening of goods at the outset of the industrial age.

Another feature of the organisation of mass armies is the

sense of discipline it instills in large segments of the population. The discipline of army life is an appropriate training for the discipline of factory production. Finally, the urgency of military requirements also spurs technological innovation and invention in the production of weapons and the development of materials necessary for their production. It is important to note that the source of the invention is not crucial: what is significant is the innovation and utilisation of inventions. Some inventions are a direct response to the needs of warfare, others can be in existence and are only developed and applied when the particular need arises. In general, however, inventions occur within a specific socio-economic context which elicits effort in a particular direction (i.e. an invention usually expresses a necessity for it), although the effort may not be a self-conscious one.[26]

3.3.1 Demand

The demands of military consumption were extremely important for iron, and later steel.[27] 'It is evident for example that the iron industry expanded considerably in the second half of the seventeenth century.'[28] Forges for the making of iron were widespread in Europe at this time, frequently employing several hundred in making guns, cannon etc.; the use of gunpowder and guns necessitated the large-scale use of iron for the production of guns, cannon and cannon-ball. In 1660 France had thirteen foundries, all producing cannon; the only other significant source of demand was for scythes.[29] In England

> war was pretty certainly the greatest consumer of iron, and firms like Wilkinson, the Walkers and the Carron Works owed the size of their undertakings partly to government contracts for cannon, while the South Wales iron industry depended on battle.[30]

In England and Scotland, King and Parliament promoted iron manufacture with charters and special grants.[31] The output of pig iron, substantially consumed by armaments and ship-building (although iron vessels were still a thing of the future) grew from 13-14,000 tons in 1700 to 250,000 tons by 1806.[32]

The industrial capacity behind the war machines grew rapidly with the demands.[33] Some areas like Suhl, Nürnberg, Milan, Tåburg, Rocheford, Sussex, Dauphiné, Tula, Solingen, Toledo, Brescia, Pistoia were among the many famous for quality products. In fact virtually every town in Europe boasted gunsmiths whose workshops produced quality products. In Germany alone there were seventy enterprises making weapons with distinctive trademarks.[34] In the seventeenth century, before any significant use of iron in civilian industry, Colbert had created arms factories in France, Gustavus Adolphus in Sweden, Peter the Great in Russia —one in Russia employed 683 workers.[35] These isolated examples of factory production anticipated that of the famous Jack of Newbury in England.[36] The arsenals were owned by the State or private entrepreneurs; for example the State-owned naval installations like Toulon and Rochefort. The state-owned arsenals were linked to privately owned workshops and forges. At Rochefort all the cannon was made in privately owned arsenals.[37]

Thus the stimulus of military needs deriving from the manufacture of armaments, guns, cannon, ships, etc. and machinery to produce them was of great significance. As for its magnitude, to quote Mumford:

> the most wanton and luxurious household cannot compete with a battlefield in rapid consumption. A thousand more uniforms, a thousand more guns, a thousand more bayonets: and a thousand shells fired from cannon cannot be retrieved and used over again. In addition to all the mischances of battle, there is a much speedier destruction of stable equipment and supplies.[38]

The textile industry, like the iron and metallurgical sectors was also affected by the demands of military consumption:

> by the end of the seventeenth century uniforms had become the rule for the soldiers of all nations. The English redcoats, the Prussian blue and the French green, yellow, white and blue regiments won fame on a dozen battlefields. As Sombart has pointed out, this suggests an expansion of the textile industry. Quantities of cloth of standard quality and color had to be woven and worked into uniforms. The manufacturers of rough woollen cloth were prosperous in France when most of the textile industry languished under the strain of taxes and low demand, and there was a lively trade in woollen cloth from Saxony, Silesia, and England to Hamburg, Frankfurt, and Holland, where elaborate equipment for dyeing and finishing adapted the material for military use. An estimate of the demand can be derived from the fact that an army of 100,000 men required 20,000 pieces of cloth every two years. Considering that all Brandenburg consumed in this period only 50,000 pieces a year for civilian use, and that 100,000 troops used about half of the textile production of West Riding, this figure assumes its proper importance.[39]

The 100,000 army of Louis XIV placed the first large-scale order in textile history for absolutely standardised goods. And when the sewing machine was tardily invented by Thimmonet in Lyons in 1829 it was the French War Department that first sought to use it.[40]

The stimulus of military demand for iron and textiles was a direct one and its role in initiating standardisation and mass production (thereby reducing unit costs) is consequently easily evident. The same direct stimulus was also experienced by shipping and road transport. In order to demonstrate the influence of military needs on the three other groups of strategic manufacturing industry the phenomenon of interdependence of demand needs to be established.

The interdependence of demand for intermediate manufactured products (i.e. the group of strategic industries evident in the industrial matrix) has been referred to earlier.[41] The degree to which this interdependence sustained mutual output in the group of strategic manufactured industries can be reviewed historically. First, a brief explanation concerning the nature of the inter-dependent relationships between the industries.

The impact of the military demand for iron was responsible for the establishment of the coal industry; the latter in turn initiated modern rail transport, which in turn stimulated both coal and iron production, hastening economic growth in general. Of course, both coal and rail transport were themselves of extreme military importance. The early chemical industry was essentially a creation of the rising demand for textiles. In the first period of the industrial revolution in England, before the age of iron, coal and the modern railways proper, beginning in the 1830s, the growing textile industry's need for machinery also stimulated production of iron. Both machinery, and paper and paper products (so defined in official classification) are, of course, the basis for the growth of other industries. In the case of iron for example,

> [it] stimulated not only iron-consuming industries but also coal (of which it consumed about one quarter in 1842), the steam engine, and — for the same reasons as coal — transport.[42]

The growth of all other strategic intermediate manufactured products (i.e. iron, steel, transport, chemicals, textiles etc.) creates the demand for machinery. Indeed, before the advent of the modern railways, shipping was an important source of demand for machinery as the largest and most complex piece of equipment in use at the time.

The demand for paper and paper products is also substantially an indirect one. The use of paper undoubtedly grows along with the growth of other industries, as a medium of communication, packaging, etc. In addition the increase in literacy and the expansion of education which attends economic growth and industrialisation also raises the quantity consumed. In this context, the function of education in promoting national integration, instilling patriotism (essential social conditions for participating successfully in the international political system) and creating a more skilled work force are highly relevant. In particular, education was a conscious instrument of state policy in Europe and elsewhere. In general though, from a purely military point of view, it is difficult to imagine a 'paperless' — without communications — economy in the nineteenth century prosecuting war. In the contemporary period the availability of other means of communication potentially qualifies the significance of paper and paper products in this respect, although its industrial uses are likely to endure for some time to come, i.e. for packaging, etc. if not information storage, which can be accomplished by other means.

In this context it is interesting to note that in negotiations with Scandinavian countries in 1966, EEC members stressed

> that it is absurd that big modern states should depend almost exclusively on foreign countries for their supplies of paper and paper board, products which play an unchallangeable part in the fields of instruction, defence, marketing, etc.[43]

This was the basis for the agreement between the parties. Recently, trade conflicts over this industry have been causing concern.

The stimulus of military needs for iron (and later steel) and textile industries has been reviewed historically: the interdependence of the iron and coal industries, and the influence of the former on the latter can now be traced. It will be argued that it was the demand for iron, primarily for military purposes, which was instrumental in promoting the modern coal industry.

Before the rise of the modern coal industry and its universal use the main form of fuel was charcoal. Charcoal was used for puddling iron and as domestic fuel. It was the shortage of charcoal precipitated by the growing production of iron that prompted the development of coal energy, and the development of techniques necessary for mining it: for example the use and subsequent development of the Newcomen pump for expelling water from the mines. Basil Williams records that in England ever since the time of Elizabeth I there was anxiety about the depletion of charcoal and the destruction of forests in Sussex. Indeed, according to him, iron production had begun to decline 'not due to any lack of native ore, but to the depletion of the forests considered essential for reducing iron into a metal fit for working'.[44] By 1720 there were only fifty-nine blast furnaces producing 18,000 tons of pig iron; this was only slightly above the 14,000 tons produced in 1700. The Sussex industry caused particular misgivings because the rapid consumption of wood reduced the supply for ship-building and the fuel supply of London.[45] The Coundouillet brothers of the Rochefort arsenal had to be given access to the royal forests to continue producing iron. In the end the destruction of forests led to experiments with coal in iron furnaces from the seventeenth century onwards and 'when a century later, the problem was finally solved by Abraham Darby in England, coal became a key to military as well as to the new industrial power'.[46]

In conclusion one can add that this interdependence between the iron and coal industries was crucial for two reasons: firstly, as it has been shown, the demand for coal, as an alternative source of energy, was created by the growing production of iron. Much more important, its subsequent expansion was directly correlated to the rising demand for iron. Indeed their interaction produced the second phase of the industrial revolution in England which generalised the use of both.

Secondly, the change from charcoal and wood to coal occurred over a period of several centuries and, without the decisive impingement of dramatically increased iron production, could have remained unaltered for some time to come, delaying the industrial transformation which occurred in Western Europe. To stress the point above it can be argued that in the absence of rising iron consumption the need for a new form of energy might not have arisen when it did.

The importance of the national defence stimulus for the transport industry (transport and transport equipment) is self-evident. In the era of mass warfare and heavy military equipment mobility is central to military strategy. Even the successes of the Roman imperium were crucially predicted on their mobility, made possible by their extensive network of roads. The importance of shipping in modern conflicts has already been discussed, and its economic impact on other sectors has also been noted. The importance of the railways for military strategy for Europe and elsewhere (e.g. Japan) will be detailed later when the military-industrial strategy of latecomer countries is analysed, but some indication of its significance can be provided by the behaviour of the German General Count von Moltke during the Franco–German War of 1871. He deployed some 100,000 Germans behind the Prussian front to protect the railways.[47] It is now recognised that the spectacular German successes were due considerably to their efficient mobilisation, whereas the defeat of the French is partly attributed to a converse failure. The subsequent policy of the French State towards the railways was transformed by this experience.

The case of Britain, the firstcomer and the progenitor of the railway, is somewhat distinctive in this respect. The railways were considered important for mobilisation and the transportation of troops, but sea transport was much more significant for British military strategy because of her island geography. Nevertheless, the army's initial interest in the railways was prompted by the desire to move troops between cities to suppress internal upheaval. And, 'from 1852 on, transport and concentration schemes were constantly worked out and kept up to date; every improvement in railroads was made use of to accelerate movement to sea outlets'.[48]

Finally, the modern chemical industry, like the iron industry, owed much to textiles.[49] Of the three branches of chemicals the demand for heavy chemicals like sulphuric acid and alkalis was almost entirely due to the expansion of textiles. The use of sulphuric acid to whiten cloth originally developed because 'there was not enough cheap meadowland or sour milk in all the British Isles to whiten the cloth of Lancashire once the water frame and mule replaced the spinning wheel.[50] The production of artificial fertilisers (e.g. phosphates) and coal tar and mineral dyes, pharmaceutical products, cosmetics and plastic matter, the second branch, developed with the growing maturity of the industrial revolution. The importance of artificial fertilisers, for example, was enhanced in the context of a modern, rationalised agriculture. The eminently derived demand character of chemicals is discernible from their diverse use.[51] One direct military use of chemicals which predates the industrial revolutions is, of course, explosives, belonging to the third branch.

3.3.2 Technology

The technological stimulus of military demands during the first
round of the industrial revolutions has been both direct and indirect.
The need for a particular improvement like steel capable of
withstanding the force of shells resulted in the Bessemer process;
alternatively, it can be imagined that existing inventions were applied
when the need arose. More generally, numerous and diverse changes
taking place at the outset of the industrial revolutions in Western
Europe can be attributed to the overall rise in demand consequent
upon military needs. The task of listing specific advances because of
military needs would be beyond the scope of this brief introduction,
but some indication can be given of the diversity and importance of
advances incumbent upon military imperatives.

The origins of modern metallurgy have been traced to the
famous swordsmiths of Damascus, Toledo and Milan renowned for
their 'refined metallurgy and their skill in manufacturing armaments, forerunners of Krupp and Creusot'.[52] The first great advance
is considered to have occurred with the introduction of gunpowder. In the early thirteen hundreds came the first cannon, and
then more slowly muskets, pistols, the organ gun and the machine
gun. And the gun, Mumford argues, was the starting point of a new
type of power machine.[53] The standardisation and mass production
of muskets came at the end of the eighteenth century: in 1785 Le
Blanc in France produced muskets with interchangeable parts. In
1800 Eli Whitney manufactured a similar standardised weapon on
contract for the US government. Another observer, Usher, has
commented that the technique of interchangeable parts, which was
established in general outline by this development, was a
fundamental condition for the great achievements which followed
in other fields, e.g. the invention of the sewing machine and the
harvesting machine.[54] Thus the constant and large-scale demand of
the military appears to have been crucial in sustaining achievements like these, by making them both necessary and profitable.

At the same time standardised production became established
for the building of ships for the British Navy. Under the guidance of
Sir Samuel Bentham and the elder Brunel 'various tackleblocks and
planks were cut to uniform measure: building became the
assemblage of accurately measured elements'.[55] According to
Hobsbawm, war and the British Navy made an inestimable
contribution to technological innovation and industrialisation. In

supplying the government or large quasi-government bodies (e.g. the East Indian Company)

> it was worth a businessman's while to introduce revolutionary methods. . . . Time and again we find some inventor or entrepreneur stimulated by so lucrative a prospect.[56]

Henry Cort, who revolutionised the manufacture of iron, began his career as an agent for the Navy and it was for his contribution to military security that he earned the gratitude of his fellow countrymen.[57] Similarly, the pioneer of machine tools, Henry Maudslay, worked for the Woolwich Arsenal, and both he and Mark Isambard Brunel, the great engineer, made their fortunes through naval contracts; Brunel had also been earlier employed by the French Navy.[58] The Government establishments also pioneered numerous developments themselves; canning and the conveyor belt, for example, during the Napoleonic Wars.

On a more general level there are gains from translating military advances to non-war uses: psychological testing, field surgery, sanitation, and more recently, radar; also upgrading of the workforce through on-the-job training, and the diffusion of job techniques.

3.3.3 Organisation

The advancement of organisational methods was also promoted by military experience. This occurred on two levels: firstly, the mass character of military demand stimulated the rationalisation of the production process itself, and secondly, the army itself, with its highly structured and disciplined organisation provided a model for industrial and social organisation. The mass demand for uniforms and cannon, for example, entailed co-operative manufacture on an increased scale: the old-fashioned handicraft methods were no longer equal to the task. The division of labour became particularly well established within the arms factories and the grinding and polishing of machinery was worked by water-power.[59] This pressure of military demand not only precipitated factory organisation, it persisted throughout its development.

> As warfare increased in scope and larger armies were brought into the field, their equipment became a much heavier task. And as their tactics became mechanized, the instruments needed to make their movements precise and well-timed were necessarily reduced to uniformity too.[60]

Thus with the progress of factory organisation came standardisation on a scale, in armament production, exceeding that of all other 'technics' except printing. This process also increased managerial skills, helped credit expansion and the concentration of capital.

Finally, it was warfare rather than industry and trade that anticipated in outline the machine age: 'the topographic survey, the use of maps, the plan of campaign — long before businessmen devised organization charts and sales charts — the coordination of transport, supply, production (mutilation and destruction), the broad divisions of labor between cavalry, infantry, and artillery, and the division of the process of production between each of these branches; finally, the distinction of function between staff and field activities — all these characteristics put warfare far in advance of competitive business and handicraft with their petty, empirical and short-sighted methods of preparation and operation. The army is in fact the ideal form toward which a purely mechanical system of industry must tend'.[61] Thus military organisational methods were crucial in institutionalising the important idea of rationally organised systems.

Notes

1. The significance of military needs for the form which industrialisation takes will be assessed later in this chapter. For the present it might be noted that the impact of defence-related activity on industrial societies is in many respects self-evident. The pace at which industrialisation occurs is also important since latecomer countries face political constraints not encountered by the industrialised firstcomers. Indeed the desire for rapid industrial transformation in industrially backward areas stems from a fear of the predatory proclivities of firstcomer countries.
2. Hilton (1976); Anderson (1974); Dobb (1946).
3. Mandel (1975) pp. 274-5.
4. Norman (1975).
5. Anderson (op. cit.) pp. 414-15.
6. Hilton (op. cit.) p. 27; Dobb (op. cit.).
7. Hobsbawm (1969) p. 51.
8. Wolf (1951) p. 173.
9. There are numerous writings on the impact of military activities on economic growth, but most of them relate to the direct economic consequences. In the present context it is only being argued that such military endeavours during the seventeenth and eighteenth centuries laid the foundations of subsequent economic transformations by

determining its form and timing. However, the state in the nineteenth and twentieth centuries has been profoundly influenced by defence needs, as it will be argued later, in striving to achieve industrialisation. Whether industrialisation benefited from the more direct expenditures on defence, as distinct from defence needs providing the political motivation to industrialise, is a more controversial matter. Although there are good grounds for believing that such defence expenditures were beneficial to industrialisation in a number of instances (e.g. nineteenth-century Japan). For a sample of the literature on the subject of defence and the economy see Reich NYRB (1982) p. 38; Weber (1980); Kaldor in Jolly (ed.) (1978) for a dissenting view; Deane in Winter (ed.) (1975); Kennedy (1975, 1983); Benoit (1973); Barber (1973); Nef (1950, 1947, 1944); Fuller (1946); Wright (1942); Mumford (1934); Kobayashi (1922).

10. Hobsbawm (op. cit.); Davis (1979).
11. Henderson (1961).
12. Hobsbawm (op. cit.) pp. 49-50; 54.
13. See chapter 1.
14. Ehrenberg quoted in Anderson (op. cit.) p. 33.
15. Clark quoted in Anderson (op. cit.) p. 33.
16. Williamson (1922) pp. 153-4.
17. For all quotations in this paragraph see Anderson (op. cit.) pp. 32-3.
18. Ibid. p. 29.
19. Wolf (op. cit.) pp. 171-2; also see Corvisier (1979) for a detailed account of the size of armies and the relationship between civil society and war.
20. Williams (1962) p. 124.
21. Wolf (op. cit.) p. 172.
22. Hobsbawm (op. cit.) p. 50.
23. Williams (op. cit.) p. 222.
24. Wolf (op. cit.) pp. 200-3.
25. Hobsbawm (1977) chapter 15.
26. Mathias (1979) p. 82; also Landes (1969); and Milward (1970) pp. 33-6 for a broad assessment of the impact of the two World Wars on the British economy.
27. The subsequent sections examine the specific dimensions of the catalytic impact of military endeavours on industrial changes during the period immediately preceding European industrialisation.
28. Wolf (op. cit.) p. 178.
29. Mumford (op. cit.) pp. 87-8.
30. Hobsbawm (op. cit.) p. 50; Williams (op. cit.) p. 117.
31. Wolf (op. cit.) p. 178.
32. Williams (op. cit.) p. 117.
33. Wolf (op. cit.) p. 177.

34. Ibid. p. 178.
35. Mumford (op. cit.) pp. 89-90.
36. Ibid.
37. Wolf (op. cit.) p. 178.
38. Mumford (op. cit.) pp. 91-2.
39. Wolf (op. cit.) p. 180.
40. Mumford (op. cit.) pp. 91-2.
41. See chapter 1.
42. Hobsbawm (op. cit.) p. 71.
43. Casadio (1973) p. 72.
44. Williams (op. cit.) p. 113.
45. It has even been argued by Wolf (op. cit. p. 173) that the reason for the increasing mildness of wars in the late seventeenth and early eighteenth centuries was partly due to the scarcity of indispensable raw materials like charcoal, among other things. Also see Nef (op. cit.) p. 179.
46. Mumford (op. cit.) p. 87.
47. Todd in Howard (1976) pp. 116-17.
48. Colin (1912) p. 318; also see Howard (1976) for the significance of transportation for military strategy.
49. Hobsbawm (op. cit.) p. 69.
50. Landes (1969) p. 108.
51. Ibid. p. 269; also see Mathias (op. cit.).
52. Mumford (op. cit.) p. 46.
53. Gun casting also greatly stimulated improved foundry technique.
54. In Mumford (op. cit.) p. 90. The semaphore telegraph was also first used in war, i.e. The American Civil War.
55. Mumford (op. cit.) p. 90.
56. Hobsbawm (op. cit.) p. 50.
57. Ibid.
58. Ibid.
59. Mumford (op. cit.) pp. 87-90.
60. Ibid. p. 90.
61. Ibid. p. 89.

4   State intervention in latecomer countries

4.1   Intervention in the group of strategic industries: the first round

The importance of international political competition and nationalist impulses in engendering the desire to achieve industrial transformation cannot be doubted, a reality recognised, though not systematically explored, by a number of economic historians. Rostow, for example, has described this phenomenon as 'reactive nationalism'.[1] A broad survey is presented below to illuminate the specific dimensions of this reactive nationalism in terms of State policies towards industrialisation and the establishment of the group of strategic manufacturing industries which it implies.[2]

At this juncture one issue requires clarification: State intervention need not necessarily take the form of specific aid to each of the group of strategic manufacturing industries. The phenomenon of interdependence between sectors presupposes that aid to certain sectors also stimulates others. For example, almost every State appears to take active interest in the condition of railways and shipping. The policies of the State towards this sector (transport and transport equipment) through the nineteenth century had a very favourable impact on iron and steel, machinery and energy (coal mainly). Indeed the role of a 'leading sector' is known to be crucial for economic growth. In the nineteenth century the leading sector was the railway, a fact amply documented by economic historians; Rostow, for example, bases his analysis of nineteenth-century economic growth in terms of the railways as the leading sector. Similarly, Hobsbawm regards the railways as the driving force behind economic growth in mid-nineteenth century Britain.[3]

Before proceeding to a detailed consideration of State intervention in Italy, Japan and the USA it would be appropriate to provide a brief illustrative discussion on France and Germany.[4]

The first phase of State activity in France during the period under review concerned the establishment of the political and judicial framework within which economic change could occur. In France this process of creating a unified political and economic order took place after the revolution of 1789. Before the revolution there were 360 regional codes in France, four customs of law, and also a multiplicity of divisions in tolls, tariffs, legal and administrative systems and in weights and measures. In the post-revolutionary period the guild monopoly of crafts was broken and individuals were free to engage in whatever activity they wished. Even before the revolution of 1789 the guilds had been reconstructed by Colbert, ever mindful of the need for economic strength to reinforce the power of the State, and had to work under a system of 'national control which was instituted at the same time. An elaborate system of rules to ensure quality was set up by Government and to these all work had to conform, and royal inspectors were instituted to see that the rules were observed';[5] rules so elaborate that they filled eight quarto volumes. The existence of certain large establishments was also the outcome of Colbert's policies. He arranged for the creation of a number of new manufactures and privileged establishments outside the control of guilds. Thus there was provision for large-scale enterprises directly under the control of the State, from which they derived the licence to exist.

The French State subsequently embarked on a host of policies to promote industrialisation: 'the process of introducing into France — of grafting onto a foreign organism — the machines that sprung spontaneously from the fertile soil across the channel was an artificial one'.[6] It had a positive attitude towards the importation of artisans by bestowing bounties, etc. Among the beneficiaries were the Englishman, John Holker, and the inventor, John Kay, who fled England; English workers were also imported from Manchester. The French also made attempts to persuade Watt and Bolton to emigrate to France. Inventors in France were aided and exhibitions of new mechanical contrivances were organised. France endeavoured to popularise the use of machines by holding industrial fairs and furnishing technical training, for example, in the Conservatory of Arts and Crafts (established in 1820) and the Central School of Arts and Manufacturers (established in 1829). The state provided subventions to industry, instituted tariffs and even owned and managed part of the transport system and industry.

Napoleon, for example, did everything in his power to encourage French industry. He was concerned partly to pre-empt domestic revolt, but he was especially concerned to restore France's position *vis-à-vis* England. Napoleon also framed his imperialist policies with this view in mind, i.e. the promotion of French manufactures.

[He] wished to restore France to its ancient pride of place. France must therefore adopt machinery, and Napoleon must find markets for the manufacturers. French goods were to go over Europe as freely as French soldiers and he expected his officials to follow up his victories and fill the shops of conquered countries with French products.[7]

Large orders were placed on his own behalf and for his Court, inventors were rewarded and loans provided to entrepreneurs. Between March 1807 and October 1809 1,175,925 francs were loaned of which only 250,221 were repaid. When the Jacquard Loom was invented he ensured its purchase by the town of Lyons and gave its inventor a three-thousand franc annual pension. With the aim of encouraging the diffusion of modern know-how and improved technology, Prefects (heads of departments) were sent to the model factory at Passy to learn to work the flying shuttle. A Scotsman named Douglas was set up in a government workshop to make machines and to teach French workmen their use. A large grant was given to him and the bigger manufacturers were organised into a commission to observe the progress. Circulars were also sent to provincial Prefects pointing out the advantages of machines, enclosing Douglas's circulars, and offering financial inducements to potential buyers. Napoleon also founded the Society for the Encouragement of National Industry.

A new financial and administrative system was also introduced, creating a strict system of national accounts. Napoleon acted through the Councils of Commerce which he had set up in all principal towns in 1801; alongside these were set up Chambers of Manufacturers to provide advice on trade and manufactures.

In retrospect it seems clear that France's national economics of the nineteenth and twentieth centuries were presaged by the State economics of the preceding three centuries. They shared with its progenitor the idea that 'the strong state must be a great producer, and the corollaries of that doctrine — protectionism, colonialism, and state aid to business';[8] harnessing the resources of the state for war.

The strongest French advocates of the doctrine of the national economy were Charles Ganilh, F.L.A. Ferrier and Louis Say. According to Ganilh

... national greatness depends on production ... and production, is the result of all the forces, and all the power of the nation for work. To judge the wealth of a nation, a measurement of the goods that are consumed should not be taken, but rather measurement of the ability of the nation to produce these goods. . . . A purely agricultural nation cannot rise to the heights of power among the states of the world; it must become industrial and commercial.[9]

He suggested tariffs and subsidies to promote national industry, and insisted that foreign commercial transactions should be allowed when the country is mature, taking the form of exchanges for what the nation has in surplus to its needs.

In Germany the impoverishment caused by the Thirty Years War left all initiative with the State; the State alone possessed the energy and the resources. The subsequent history of German economic development, rising to great heights during the Chancellorship of Bismarck 'was a conscious development. It began from above, was carried out by an autocrat in each state, and was systematic and designed to a definite end.'[10]

Following the Thirty Years War industries introduced by immigrants were fostered by a strictly protective system. There was a prohibition on the import of cloth, and prohibition on the export of wool. Frederick the Great superintended all industry, from the largest to the smallest. He founded iron and cloth factories. The home market was reserved for German merchants and all foreign goods were practically excluded. During the decade 1763-73 Frederick founded 264 establishments for the velvet, silk, satin, woollen, leather, iron and sugar industries;[11] the equivalent of £300,000 was spent establishing the velvet and silk industries. Frederick announced 'that if an economic enterprise is beyond the powers of my subjects, it is my affair to defray the costs and they have nothing further to do than to gather the profits'.[12] Thus a mercantilist policy was developed during this period — a policy dating back over a hundred and fifty years.

It was the challenge and experience of the Napoleonic Wars and the defeat at the Battle of Jena in 1807 — as a consequence of which Prussia was shorn of half its territory and devastated, reduced to a population of four and a half million and a 600 million franc indemnity extracted — that last spurred great changes. The subsequent history can be usefully divided into two periods: 1815–67 and the post-1871 period. In the first period the task of creating the framework of political, economic and legal unification was pursued with energy, heralding the modernisation of the Prussian State. The State

> reformed education, founding new universities where culture and civic duty should be taught. It united Prussian territories with a low tariff outside and free trade within. It freed the serfs. It abolished guild restrictions and permitted free choice of trades. It reformed municipal administration and it executed great legal reforms.[13]

In 1833 the Zollvereine was established, but Germany did not become a fully unified nation before 1871. It was not until the advent of the railways that full political and economic unification was complete.

Pride in nationhood and the desire to assert national rights had taken root in Germany:

> the Germans of the eighteenth and early nineteenth century were poets, philosophers and musicians. It was the age of Schiller and Goethe. The new Germany was basically different from the old Germany. The struggle was not for 'intellectual or political ideals, or ideals of any kind, but a struggle for sheer mastery in the realm of matter and for political ascendancy amongst the nations'. A cult of force had grown up, and the State was elevated to a position of importance which it had never held before. . . the all-powerful State, not indifferent to industrial progress as the government in *laissez-faire* England, but eager to aid the progress of industry by all means, by tariffs, by bounties, by preferential rates.[14]

The rise of the capitalist system of production occurred in the second period, accelerating from about 1860 onwards. This was made possible, in the first instance, by the extension of market areas, with the overcoming of local tariff barriers within the German states in the first period, and especially the subsequent State policy of introducing universal railroad transportation; one key specific measure was the institution of special rates for coal and iron. The importance of the State-sponsored boom in railroad construction cannot be underestimated. It lowered prices, raising demand and enhancing industrial activity.[15] In addition the protectionist tariffs, the promotion of technical education and research were significant in creating a solid foundation for industrial progress.

Without doubt the attitudes and the policies of the German State towards industrialisation were fundamentally influenced by international political rivalry, particularly with Britain. In this regard the ideas of List, who died twenty-five years before the Franco-German War of 1871, were transcendant. List's acute concern for industrial progress and its implications for international political competition, and his belief in pragmatic State intervention in the economy were later to be adopted by Bismarck. The idea of a world struggle with England and the US were ever-present in Bismarck's mind and evident in his policy statements and actions; the tariff of 1879, for example, was clearly motivated to build German industry in the face of English competition. The influential pronouncements of Treitschke in 1876 concerned this apprehension of Britain and hope of overcoming her supremacy.[16] The influential German Navy League was frequently vocal about the need for a powerful navy to protect German commerce against Britain. The tensions between the two powers in the early twentieth century were essentially provoked by the emergence of a strong German Navy. Thus Bismarck's policies were a definite break with the traditional doctrines of free trade and political harmony.

4.2 Italy

As in the case of France and Germany, Italian nationalism and international political rivalry were extremely important in precipitating State involvement in achieving industrialisation. In Italy, as in France and Germany, it was felt that economic success would restore national greatness. The ideas of writers like Domenico Romagnosi and Federico Confanlonieri espousing this theme became influential, eventually 'generally accepted by men of affairs, both in business and in statecraft'.[17] In the event the involvement of the State in industrialisation was substantial. It bore half the cost of the railways, largely created the metallurgical industry, and was responsible for the growth of shipbuilding and the establishment of the merchant marine.[18]

4.2.1 Banking

The Italian State created a well-organised banking system to cater for the needs of industry, e.g. the two banks, the Societi Generale di

Credito Mobiliare and the Banca Generale. The latter was involved in financing iron and steel industries, city construction and the railways; both were involved in other enterprises, e.g. steel production at Terni. The Italian National Bank also gave its blessings to the investment bank, the Banca di Credito Meridionale. The banking system however collapsed in 1893 but the long-term consequences of the collapse were not adverse for Italian economic development because during the intervening thirty years

> . . . the nation got its public buildings, some of its railroads, and some industry partly through the losses of the depositors and the shareholders of the bankrupt institutions. Unwittingly and unwillingly they had helped to provide capital for the economic development of the land.[19]

The banking system was then rehabilitated and two of the resulting banks, the Banca Commerciale Italiana (Milan) and the Credito Italiano (Genoa) became the two most important banking institutions in Italy. They engaged in making short-term commercial loans, and also long-term financing of metallurgy, electricity and shipping. These institutions remained close to the Italian political establishment and reflected the economic priorities of the State.[20]

4.2.2 Tariffs

After the unification, Cavour adopted low tariffs in keeping with the tradition of the Kingdom of Sardinia, but it was recognised that tariffs were necessary for industrialisation. And in the aftermath of the Great Depression in 1874 Italy embarked on a policy of tariffs, following the path of France and Germany. The Commissions which were set up to study the problem of tariffs in 1878 and between 1884-6 both concluded that tariffs were indispensable. In 1878 specific duties were imposed per product rather than *ad valorem*; this included a measure of protection for cotton textiles. But Italian interests were dissatisfied and high tariffs were adopted in 1888; already in 1887 high rates had been imposed on cotton and imports had fallen. The rates on some products were increased by 200 or 300 per cent: iron, steel and the 'mechanical' trades — and agriculture was also favoured. A tariff war occurred with France between 1888 and 1898 because of the seizure of Tunisia by the French but a negotiated settlement was sought when its harmful effect on both countries was realised. Both the high tariffs, and, on balance, the tariff war with France have been regarded, by most observers, as a source of positive encouragement for investment in Italian industry.[21]

4.2.3 Transportation

Following the political unification of Italy frantic efforts were being made to bind the country together. As a result the Italian State spent large sums in promoting the construction of Italy's railways, 50 per cent of the total during the entire period of construction activity. During 1860–1 it spent 100 million lira, and during 1862 20 per cent of the State budget was devoted to the railways. But in 1865 the poor condition of public finances forced the sale of State-owned lines to private buyers. The consolidation of Italian railways into four major networks was nevertheless achieved and State involvement continued. In 1868 the State found itself operating the lines completed by the Victor Emmanuel Company, which was in dire financial straits, and a new company was also formed to continue building the unfinished lines. It also took over the expensive lines of the Romana (Massa to the French frontier). In subsequent years economic setbacks in the industry were punctuated by the assumption of State ownership of more lines, e.g. the Alta Italia in 1873, 1882 and the remainder of the Romana and the Meridionali in 1884. By 1884 the State owned 6,971 km. and only 3,152 km. remained in private hands; a small distance (418 km.) of the railroads was owned jointly. Some co-operative arrangements were planned with private enterprise, but did not work satisfactorily, i.e. the convention of 1884-5. These agreements were abandoned and the State took over operation as well as ownership of the old and newly constructed lines. The State now owned 14,782 km., leaving only 2,296 km. in private hands.[22]

The involvement of the State in shipping was motivated by reasons similar to those evident in other latecomer countries in Europe. A successful shipping industry, both in construction and carrying, was considered '... crucial to the growth of a new nation'.[23] A well-developed merchant navy was also regarded as 'essential in order to provide a basis for a military marine';[24] the positive implications of the acquisition of a shipping industry for economic growth were, of course, also very much present in the thinking of Italian statesmen.

At the time of unification the founding-fathers assumed responsibility for paying subsidies agreed by the constituent States which had formed the modern Italian state, and also launched new governmental aid programmes; loans were provided without interest, for example. By 1870 40 new vessels had been acquired, and total tonnage rose to 1,012,164 and steam tonnage tripled. Other financial incentives were provided to shipping companies to establish certain carrying services. Later, tax advantages, bounties and rebates on imported materials for the construction of iron and steel ships were also made available but success proved elusive. The subsidy programme was expanded in 1874 and when this too proved inadequate another plan was adopted in 1885. The provision of aid by means of contracts was continued, and navigation and construction bounties were also given. The assistance was guaranteed for ten years in order to remove uncertainty, and the navigation bounties were designed to encourage the use of Italian ships. The bounties favoured iron vessels (four times higher than for wooden sailing ships) and special bounties were provided according to horsepower and weight of boilers. The bounties were also increased if ships were built '... to specifications which would allow the ships to be used in case of emergency for military purposes'.[25] The law, however, was not effective because the metallurgical and machine industries still could not compete with English prices. Additional laws were consequently passed in 1888 and 1889 raising the rates previously offered, and finally in 1893 lucrative contracts and generous subsidies were granted to shippers and shipbuilders. Again, Italian-built ships were favoured, and companies were required to meet certain specifications concerning steam and steel construction. It was hoped that the new services being promoted by these measures would open up new markets for Italian goods. The response to the law was favourable; construction in Italian yards rose from 7,113 tons per annum before 1896 to 62,294 tons per annum in 1900. A number of new companies also came into being (e.g. Societa Veneziana di Navigazione a Vapore in 1900, and the Lloyd Italiano in 1904, among others). By the end of 1900 13,842 million lira was paid out in navigation bounties — 3 million lira to sail ships and 8 million in construction bounties, and 2 million lira in customs rebates. Despite the imposition of limits to the subsidies later, a further 14 million lira was paid out between 1901-11 in subsidies and another 34,764,000 lira under other laws. From the founding of the Italian empire to 1914, the year before the abolition of the subsidy laws, State aid to shipping and ship-building amounted to 66.7 million lira, through contracts and subsidies.

4.2.4 *Iron and steel*

The relatively slow growth of the Italian economy between 1870 and 1914 has been attributed to the weakness of Italy's iron, steel and machine industries. These industries '... were not great enough to make the country a real industrial leader nor a major military power'.[26] Italian statesmen sought to remedy the situation, which was primarily due to a paucity of iron ore and coal and poor location. They realised that Elba ore could be used as an inducement for investment in the metallurgical industry. Before the unification of Italy 80-90 per cent of the Elba ore was exported, but in 1873 an agreement was reached that ore would not be exported without the consent of the State authorities; the leasor, however, got the ore which was owned by the State very cheaply. The arrangement was found unsatisfactory, however, and the Banca Generale took over the lease. The Banca subsequently set up the Ferriere Italiane in 1880, with works in several centres. When significant advances failed to occur high tariffs were imposed, up to 40 per cent on some items (on ferrous metals in the tariff of 1887, for example). The Ferriere Italiane was also given extremely generous subsidies. In 1890 it was paid 7.28 lira a ton for mined ore when the costs of mining and transportation were 6 lira a ton. But the leasor could only mine 200,000 tons of ore a year and only make the vastly profitable exports when 100,000 tons had been sold on the Italian market. The continuing failure to establish an industry resulted in two further take-overs, with the State finally abolishing restrictions on export in 1908, even encouraging maximum output from the mines, which reached 850,000 tons in 1916. The iron and steel industry eventually acquired a new lease of life through the introduction of new techniques (the Bessemer converter and the Martin Siemens furnace), high protective tariffs, rebates on imports of ore for ship-building, direct State assistance and the investments of large banks.

During the varied history of the Italian iron and steel industry the prices of its products remained at least a third above world market prices, and several layers of State intervention had to be introduced in order to establish the industry. Production at Terni, for example, encouraged by the Commission for the Navy because of its distance from the frontier, was aided financially by the Credito Mobiliare, the Banca Generale and naval orders at high prices.[27]

4.2.5 Machinery and engineering

In 1861 one of the largest plants in the 'mechanical' trade was the Pietrasa at Naples, which had been the main arsenal of the two Sicilies, and thus became the property of the State after the unification. It had equipment for the manufacture of arms, marine steam engines, locomotives, railway rolling stock, projectiles and construction iron and steel. This enterprise was transferred to private hands but ownership was restored to the State because of problems and failures. Another enterprise, the Ansaldo company of Genoa, had been originally established by an Englishman with the aid of Cavour. The objective had been to cater for Italy's railway building. The Ansaldo company later began making steam engines for ships and then went into ship-building; with orders from the merchant marine and the railways it flourished and achieved considerable fame. Finally, the other large company, Ernesto Breda, which was founded in 1886, initially manufactured locomotives and other railway rolling stock, moving later to allied fields and becoming one of the chief producers of steam boilers, tractors, agricultural and building equipment. During the First World War it had a large project building submarines. It also built electrical equipment and produced arms for the military and the sports industry.[28]

The links of the State in Italy with strategic industries is clear, differing from France and Germany only in style and degree of success; the latter is of course peripheral to the purpose of this assessment, which is to demonstrate State intervention rather than achievement of goals, as such.

4.3 Japan

The involvement of the Japanese State in industrialisation is the clearest and most graphic illustration of international political competition motivating strenuous efforts to industrialise. The effort to modernise the army and the police had begun under the Bakufu, fearful of foreign invasion and internal disturbances. After the Restoration the Meiji statesmen, 'with the fate of China before its eyes as an ever present warning of foreign menace'[29] and domestic agrarian and *samurai* unrest, continued the task in earnest. The question of national defence had been prominent in the last years of the Bakufu, and during the

first years of the Meiji era, the keenest minds were concerned
with such questions as the creation of trade and industry, not for
their own sake, but rather to establish those industries which one
might conveniently call strategic, as the *sine qua non* of a modern
army and navy, the creation of which was the central problem of
the day.[30]

It was their belief that heavy industries, engineering, mining, and
ship-building were essential for the maintenance of a modern army
and navy. It was this belief and the policies to which it gave rise that
determined the pattern of early industrialisation and its future
evolution. Thus it was the threat of foreign attack which had cast a
shadow over the country from the beginning of the nineteenth
century, punctuated by the bombardment of Kagoshima and
Shimonoseki in 1863, that instigated the desire for industry,
railways, the telegraph, etc., because of their strategic importance
for the political and military defence of Japan. Furthermore, it was a
safeguard 'against internal disturbances which might arise from the
excessive burdens laid upon the population in paying for this
modernization'.[31]

The expenditure of the State rose to approximately 10 per cent of
GNP in the 1880s, and the administration undertook about 40 per
cent of all capital formation in the economy; it also made large
transfer payments to ex-*samurai* and *daimio*. Among the specific
areas of involvement were the railways, telegraph and telephone
services, all considered directly relevant to military strategy. The
indemnity of $200 million extracted from China in 1895-6 permit-
ted the expansion of the army and navy.

Owing to the terms of the unequal treaties the Japanese State
could not initially resort to tariffs as a means of promoting industry.
Thus, it became much more directly involved in the economy than
in any other nineteenth-century country in the world, including
Tsarist Russia. It started enterprises in a number of fields, building
some of the railways and guaranteeing a return on capital on others
built privately. It also set up banks, insurance companies, as well as
factories. The State set up a cotton spinning mill, a silk reeling mill,
an agricultural machinery plant, a cement works, a glass factory, a
brick factory, nine modern mines, and shipyards, as well as military
installations. Most of these enterprises were initially run at a loss
and eventually sold to private entrepreneurs. But the Japanese
State remained active in heavy industries related to armaments,

both through the direct ownership and operation of armouries and naval shipyards and intimate collaboration with big business — the so-called Zaibatsu.

There was no very considered policy on the division of responsibility between public and private enterprise; the early decisions occurred on an *ad hoc* basis from military, political and fiscal motives. In practice, public policy aided the concentration of industrial and financial control in the hands of government ministries or business groups close to the authorities. The growth of great business combines in the large-scale corporate sector was facilitated by the use of political authority. And the influence of the State was supreme: in industries like shipping, railways, mining and metallurgy 'new entrepreneurs continued to be heavily influenced by favors extended or withheld by the Army and Navy, other government ministries, and the official banks'.[32] The big combines — the Zaibatsu — were therefore virtual partners of the State in establishing industries essential for national power. Indeed the senior personnel of the Zaibatsu were usually former employees of the State.

The attitude of the Japanese State towards the organisation of industrial development and its control was importantly affected by the immediacy of the political dangers perceived. The Zaibatsu grew to power as 'instruments of national policy'.[33] The concentration of capital was also encouraged and aided because the general level of capital accumulation was low and the need for large amounts of capital in the high technology industries, which had to be established on the most recent western scale. It was also felt that the market would not be able to accommodate duplicated facilities, especially because competitive enterprises already existed in advanced foreign countries.[34]

4.3.1 Banking, finance and education

The State provided medium- and long-term finance for industry through specialised institutions: a function of great importance in a country without a capital market. Between 1897 and 1900 a network of banks was created for industry and agriculture in the forty-six prefectures. In addition there were some regional banks for Hokkaido and for Formosa, and Korea. The State also fostered savings banks, post office savings and insurance companies; the Yokohama Specie Bank (founded in 1880) provided short-term credits for export. The Japan Industrial Bank was founded in 1902 for the purpose of specialising in the finance of industry.

[Thus] in Japan, banking and loan capital, leaning heavily upon the state for support, was used in turn by government to create those branches of industry requiring a greater capital investment;[35]

namely, the heavy industries considered more important for national defence and economic autonomy.[36]

The Meiji regime was eager to Westernise Japanese technology and education. A Ministry of Education was established in 1871, and the law concerning schooling was passed in 1872; in 1886 four years' schooling became compulsory. The introduction of mass education was successful in producing literacy and helped to diffuse technology. With admirable perspicacity vocational training was emphasised, and universities also created. In addition there were advanced technical institutions for medicine, military science, navigation, commerce, and fisheries.

The Meiji reformers dispatched people to study in various European countries. They also employed foreigners directly, at all levels, to help Japan modernise — in public health, the legal system, or the army and navy. These advisors were paid ten times more than any Japanese, and nearly half the budget of the Ministry of Industry was expended on foreign technicians during the entire period of its existence. They were also employed in industry and, particularly in the merchant navy as officers.[37]

4.3.2 *Tariffs*

The treaties imposed by Britain and the USA on Japan in 1858 and 1866 limited tariffs until the end of the century. Thus Japan came to rely more on direct State aid to industry, and tariff rates were no higher than 10-15 per cent until 1911. However, after 1891 a policy of protection was instituted, with revisions in 1911 and 1926 which announced a definite policy of tariff protection. The tariff of 1911 afforded particular protection to iron, steel and dyestuffs. Not surprisingly, most of Japan's industries were protectionist in sentiment, except for the successful cotton and silk industries which had important export markets. In the tariff of 1926 substantial aid was provided to industries considered to have a promising future: wool, rayon, machinery, chemicals, etc.; duties ranging from 5 to 15 per cent were imposed on 647 classes of goods. Already by 1924 a 100 per cent luxury duty had been imposed on 123 items and in the subsequent tariff of 1926, in instances where they were imposed on an *ad valorem* basis and not superseded by the 100 per cent tariff, they ranged from 30 to 50 per cent on such items as piece goods, copper, metal manufactures, autos, etc. As a rule the more advanced the stage of manufacture the greater the degree of protection provided. During the next decade the level and range of tariff protection was expanded, as the economic difficulties of the late 1920s and 1930s affected Japan's industries. It may also be recorded that an element of protection was certainly provided by Japan's geographical location and the distinctiveness of its socio-cultural identity, which is likely to have made the export of goods to Japan problematic — a situation of which Western traders complain even today.

4.3.3 Textiles

The first modern mill in Japan was founded by the Lord of Satsuma, and was managed by an Englishman and six English assistants; subsequently he built another mill in 1870, three years after the first one. The State also set up two modern mills in Hiroshima and Aichi in 1881 with the most up-to-date English machinery, and later sold them to private buyers. Spinning machinery was also imported and sold on extremely favourable terms to private buyers, and loans were made to others for the same purpose.

It was in the mid-1880s that the remarkable expansion of the spinning industry began, aided by several fctors, including the capture of the Korean market, sponsored by the State; the Chinese market also became fortuitously available to the Japanese because of the oubreak of an epidemic in Bombay, prompting the ban on Indian goods. Japan, of course, enjoyed some important natural advantages like the availability of cheap female labour, which provided a competitive edge. The progress of the cotton-weaving industry was also ultimately predetermined by the rise of mechanised spinning.

The fortunes of the woollen and worsted industry were primarily dependent on the needs of the armed forces. The Government had set up a factory in 1877 to make cloth for the army. Some private undertakings also came into existence, supplying the army with cloth, blankets and flannels but the State mill remained by far the most important. The output of these concerns fluctuated widely, rising substantially during the Sino–Japanese and Russo–Japanese wars; at other times it was unable to compete against foreign competition despite a 25 per cent *ad valorem* tariff on foreign woollens. Similarly, the heavy woollen branch of the industry was dependent on government orders for standardised fabrics. The less significant hemp industry was also stimulated by orders from the government, but decayed in the interval between the Sino–Japanese and Russo–Japanese wars. In fact the first hemp factory had been founded by the State in 1886, encouraging others to follow suit.

In conclusion it is evident that the State played an important role in the early Meiji years, although in later years the natural advantages of Japanese textile production reduced that to a regulatory one.[38]

4.3.4 Iron and steel

The history of iron and steel production in Japan predates the Meiji restoration. The first reverberatory furnace was established in 1850 by the Saga clan for the making of cannon. The earliest efforts of this clan to manufacture cannon were in 1842. More reverberatory furnaces had been built by other clans in 1853 (Satsuma) and 1855 (Mito), and for the Shogunate in 1853 by its great military reformer, Egawa Tarozaemon. In Choshu an iron foundry was built in 1854, but the first was built in Kanzaki in 1840 under Dutch supervision. In 1855 the Bakufu sponsored an iron foundry which was completed in 1861.[39]

With the restoration in 1867 the future of the Japanese iron industry came to be viewed with greater urgency. The Meiji State confiscated mines formerly operated by the Bakufu and also employed foreign experts to enhance their performance. These mines (including both iron ore and coal) were transferred to private hands following an initial period of State ownership. But even in 1896 the domestic output of pig iron was a mere 26,000 tons, approximately 40 per cent of total consumption. The production of steel was miniscule, virtually the entire consumption of 222,000 tons per annum being imported. The State then resolved to commence large-scale production in Japan of both iron and steel. The Yawata Iron Works, conceived in 1896, began operating in 1901. In subsequent years private interests founded more plants, and by 1913 the output of pig iron and steel reached 243,000 tons and 255,000 tons per annum, respectively: the former comprising 48 per cent of home consumption, the latter 34 per cent. The share of the single State undertaking constituted two-thirds of pig iron output and 85 per cent of steel output in 1913.[40]

4.3.5 Railways

In the early years after the restoration, up to the early 1880s, the State was responsible for almost all railway construction. This initial railway construction was financed by a loan of £913,000 from London. In subsequent decades private enterprise joined with the State in the construction of the growing railway network of Japan, and by the end of the century private capital exceeded the contribution of the State. However, all but the narrow-gauge lines were nationalised in 1906. The total mileage then stood at 6,000, rising to 7,000 in 1913. The total tonnage of freight traffic grew from 850,000 in 1888 to an impressive 40 million in 1913.

The importance of the railways in unifying the country and reducing the high costs of transport was of course recognised by the leaders of Japan; in particular, the latter was considered imperative for economic growth. But the military dimension loomed large. To quote one observer:

> . . . in 1892 when the law of railway construction was passed establishing the principle of government ownership, a supervisory council was set up . . . composed of twenty men, several of whom were military men, and its first president, General Kawakami Soroku, was perhaps the greatest strategist of the day.[41]

The building of the Nakasendo line through thinly populated mountainous terrain, for example, was dictated by strategic rather than commercial reasons.[42]

4.3.6 Shipping and ship-building

The progress of Japan's shipping and ship-building industry occurred under the impetus of trade, wars and 'the unremitting patronage of the government'.[43] After the restoration vessels were required for internal and external commerce, and for internal military transport and overseas conquests; the first of these excursions was to Formosa in 1874.

The traditions of seamanship and her geographical position and structure were factors favourable to the development of a mercantile marine in Japan. But owing to the restrictions of the Tokugawa period experience was lacking in ocean-going ships. In order to overcome this handicap the State set up schools of navigation and marine engineering, staffed with experts from Britain. Until the beginning of the twentieth century foreigners formed a high proportion of the officers in the mercantile marine and remained a significant number until 1914.

In 1870 the Kaiso Kaisha (Transport Company) was established with ships formerly owned by one of the clans and was financed jointly by the State and private entrepreneurs. Two years later this company was reorganised and operated a service between Tokyo and Osaka which was subsidised by the State. Another private company which was later to reach eminence was the Mitsubishi Shokai established by a *samurai*. When the State required ships in 1874 for the expedition to Formosa it bought them abroad and entrusted them to Mitsubishi, which organised the military transport. A year later Mitsubishi absorbed the Kaiso Kaisha, owning by then some 37 vessels with a tonnage of 23,000. It also opened a marine school with State aid and began operating a service to Shanghai. The Mitsubishi company's ships were used again during the Satsuma rebellion of 1877, and it was consequently able to extend its fleet with State finance. During this decade the activities of the Mitsubishi were thus intimately linked to the requirements of the State.

In the next five years Mitsubishi faced strong competition from the Kyodo Unyu Kaisha which had been established in 1882 by a merger of smaller concerns. Under pressure from the Government the competing companies were amalgamated to form the chief Japanese shipping line, the Nippon Yusen Kaisha. At this stage the company had 58 ships and a total tonnage of 65,000 tons, in addition to sailing ships. The Nippon Yusen Kaisha's association with the State remained close, with its dividends guaranteed at 8 per cent for 15 years. The business of the company was also supervised by State agencies and its routes designated. The second biggest shipping line of Japan, the Osaka Shoshen Kaisha, was also the result of the consolidation of small firms operating at a loss, at the instigation of the State in 1883. By this time a definite decision against public ownership had been taken.

During the Sino–Japanese War many new ships were added to the mercantile marine since more carrying capacity was needed. After the war State policy crystallised in the Navigation Subsidy Act of 1896, providing subsidies to Japanese shipowners on ships of 1,000 tons and over and 10 knots' speed, engaged in foreign trade. The subsidies encouraged shipowners to acquire larger ships and extend operations to distant ports. The impact of the Russo-Japanese War had a similar favourable influence on the fortunes of the shipping industry. There was a rapid increase in tonnage with the acquisition of ships for the war effort. These ships were employed on new routes following the war and a number of new companies came into existence. Further legislation in 1909 replaced the acts of 1896 and 1899, empowering the State to subsidise selected mail routes. The navigation subsidies also encouraged larger and faster ships, being extended only to vessels of 3,000 tons and over and 15 knots, and less than 15 years old.

Between 1900 and 1914 State subsidies provided 77 per cent of the earnings of Japanese shipping companies with an authorised capital of over 300,000 yen; of 158 million yen in total earnings 122 million yen comprised subsidy. The war eliminated the need for subsidies, but it was subsequently revived at the rate of 12 million to 15 million yen per annum.[44]

The success of the Japanese shipping industry can be observed from the changes which occurred in the amount of trade carried in Japanese ships and the number of Japanese ships entering Japanese ports. In 1893 the proportion of Japanese trade carried in Japanese bottoms amounted to 8 per cent and only 14 per cent of the ships entering ports were Japanese; by 1913 these figures had changed to approximately 50 per cent and 51 per cent, respectively.[45]

The Japanese ship-building industry began under the Meiji regime with yards confiscated from the Shogunate and the *daimyo*, e.g. Nagasaki, Kobe Uraga, Ishikawa. The largest yard, the Yokosuka, in which foreign instructors had been contracted even under the Bakufu employed 1,861 Japanese personnel in 1881, making it one of the largest factories in Japan. The Kagoshima ship-building yard, originally owned by the Lord of Satsuma, was adapted for the building of warships. The State subsequently transferred most of the yards to private hands. But the first steel ship was not launched until the nineties and only one steamship was launched before 1895. With the enactment of the Shipbuilding Encouragement Act in 1896 a new phase began. This act made available bounties for iron and steel ships over 700 gross tons. The bounty on ships below 1,000 tons was 12 yen a ton, whereas ships over 1,000 tons were given a bounty of 20 yen per ton; another 5 yen per horse-power was payable for marine engines built in Japan. But these measures were insufficient to overcome the lack of local materials and skilled manpower, although a number of companies had come into existence because of the law. Additional stimulus was provided in 1899 by the amendment of the Navigation Subsidy Law of 1896, entitling owners of Japanese-built ships to claim double the amount given to those who purchased ships abroad. As a consequence orders were placed with Japanese yards for a number of large ocean-going steamships. The revised subsidy law of 1909 provided another stimulus. In 1913 there were six yards capable of building vessels of over 1,000 tons and the number of workers in the industry was 26,000. The annual average gross tonnage of steamships launched rose from 10,000 per annum in the late 1890s to some 50,000 tons between 1909-13.[46]

4.3.7 Machinery and engineering

As Professor Allen has observed, the output of ship-building and engineering goods in Japan before 1913 was unimpressive compared to most leading Western countries, but the involvement of the State is nonetheless clear.[47] In the pre-Meiji days there were a number of enterprises engaged in the production of military equipment like cannon, e.g. in Satsuma. The Meiji Government took over these enterprises 'and came forward as the chief entrepreneur in mining and heavy industrial production'.[48] Among the undertakings it operated were the Tokyo and Osaka arsenals. In 1880 the State is reputed to have owned some fifty-two factories in all.

In later years, despite the progress of the railways, ship-building and power stations, much of the essential equipment was imported. There were a number of significant enterprises like the Shibaura Engineering Works. But again, the fortunes of these industries were constricted by lack of skills and foreign competition. However, the State itself discriminated in its purchasing policies and granted subsidies. According to Kobayashi, after the Restoration the government issued instructions to the military and naval authorities that locally produced goods should be used even if their quality (and appearance) were inferior to that of foreign goods, except when the price differential was very substantial. After the railways were nationalised in 1906 the State bought preferentially from domestic producers, and this branch of engineering expanded; for example, the Kawasaki Dockyard Company started its railway workshops in 1908.[49]

Much of the heavy engineering industry was concentrated in a few large firms closely dependent on government patronage and orders. For example, the subsidy granted to builders of marine engines prompted the creation of manufacturing plants by Mitsubishi and Kawasaki. Other branches were dependent on government orders, e.g. firms producing telegraphic apparatus and rolling stock.

> [Thus] the heavy engineering industry fell almost entirely within the second branch of Japan's economy which was distinguished by a concentration of control in a few capital groups and was moulded and governed by State policy.[50]

It was not until the 1930s that the heavy industries (metallurgy, machinery and chemicals) mushroomed under the stimulus of armament spending, growing in output by 83 per cent between 1930-6, in contrast to only 33 per cent in consumer goods' output.[51]

4.4 The USA

An analysis attempting to highlight State intervention in the USA to promote industrialisation may seem somewhat anomalous since the dominant perception of the US economy is that of a *laissez-faire* system *par excellence*, in which the role of the State has been peripheral. This perception is incomplete. State intervention in the US economy to promote industrialisation was less extensive and direct in comparison to Western Europe and Japan and other latecomer countries of the postwar period but in absolute terms its significance cannot be doubted. A brief survey is provided below to indicate the areas of State intervention which were of importance in promoting industrialisation in the USA.

Before proceeding to an analysis of this phenomenon, however, it would be appropriate to discuss a number of unique features which defined the form and limited the extent of State intervention in the US industrialisation process, in contrast to the experience of other countries.

The strong State in Britain, Western Europe and Japan, which in different ways created the conditions for industrialisation (in the case of Britain, in particular) and ensured its success by vigorous direct and indirect involvement in the economy (as detailed earlier), was the product of two basic interrelated factors: the socio-economic backwardness of agriculture (i.e. remnants of feudalism) and the interplay of international rivalry of the mercantilist period.

The modern State in Western Europe, for instance, was the product of struggles between the declining feudal aristocracy and the rising urban bourgeoisie. The overcoming of feudalism and its residual political pre-eminence was a pre-condition for industrialisation and the modern State pushed forward and symbolised this process. The USA, by contrast, as is often remarked, was 'born free' — traditional agriculture and the deep-seated socio-economic constraints to industrialisation which accompany it were absent; although conflicts between agricultural and industrial interests did take place and were only largely resolved with the outcome of the Civil War. But the fundamental pre-conditions for industrial transformation were not the cause for bitter and prolonged conflicts in comparison to the countries of Western Europe, Japan and elsewhere. Thus the State did not acquire the pervasive salience which is associated with these types of conflict.

The USA was also exempted from the mercantilist rivalries which were inextricably woven with the decline and eventual collapse of feudalism that stamped the modern European State indelibly. Indeed, the discovery of the Americas and struggles over its political control were part of this phenomenon.

There are two other conjunctural features which distinguish the US experience and partly explain the extent of State intervention in industrialisation, i.e. the absence of widespread initial public ownership of enterprises as compared to other latecomer countries of the nineteenth century.

The inflow of private foreign capital from Western Europe, particularly Britain, was substantial. The British preferred to invest in the USA because of historical and cultural links and, of course, the high returns to be earned in a rapidly growing economy. Foreign long-term investment in the US was $1.4 billion before the Civil War, rising to $3.150 billion by 1897. However, by then the USA had become an investor itself. In 1898 the total net investment abroad had reached $2.7 billion, most of it long term (2.5 billion). The rapid increase in foreign investment in the US coincided with the period of rapid economic expansion between 1897–1914. During this period, when the impact of foreign investment was at its most pronounced, US foreign debts reached $7.2 billion.[52]

In this instance, the presence of other industrialised countries with relatively abundant capital resources fulfilled a positive role since the role of the State in mobilising capital, common elsewhere, did not prove crucial in the US. Thus private entrepreneurs were able to take advantage of the larger pool of funds available in the economy without the necessity of the State being obliged to assume an entrepreneurial role to ensure the establishment of the strategic industries.

The second factor, though unamenable to quantification was nevertheless of considerable importance but is not taken into account in discussions about US industrialisation. The economies of nineteenth-century Western Europe and elsewhere encountered the profound problem of transforming a rural population into an urban citizenry with the attitudes and habits conducive to entre-preneurial activities and the role of proletariat indispensable to industrial revolution: an issue which is not without significance for countries attempting to industrialise in the contemporary period. The USA, however, enjoyed the advantage of receiving the great mass of its population from countries which had already crossed the preliminary threshold of industrialisation and therefore benefited from the slow process of change experienced in their countries of origin.

Between 1820 and 1930 recorded gross inter-continental migra-tion amounted to 62 million although this figure is much higher than the number of permanent transfers. Around three-fourths of this migration occurred during the 50 years before the First World War. Over the period 1861–1920 the total migration to the US totalled 45.525 million. Out of this total 38.765 million migrated in the period 1881–1920 and 31.110 million between 1891–1920, by when most of the European countries which were the source of this migration were industrialising rapidly. In terms of numbers the largest groups were from Germany, followed by Italy, Ireland, Austro–Hungary, Russia, Canada, England and Sweden during this latter period.[53]

The people who migrated were also disproportionately young and the more enterprising even when they came from countries like Ireland and Russia, which were still industrially backward. In the case of Italy it was only after 1897, during a period of rapid economic advance that large numbers migrated to the USA. This phenomenon of disproportionate migration of the enterprising is of course common to such migrations.

4.4.1 The Civil War

The positive impact of the Civil War on the US economy was the orthodox view, propounded by Hacker and the Beards, until recently. According to them, the war economy with its inflation, lucrative government contracts and contract immigration stimulated the reorganization of industrial labour processes and vastly increased the volume of production. On the other hand, the war allowed the political representatives of the rising industrial bourgeoisie to secure hegemony within the state apparatus and to pass a series of polices — tariff and monetary reform, unrestricted immigration, the Homestead Act and so on — which secured the conditions for untrammelled industrial expansion.[54]

This view was subsequently challenged by Cochran who provided evidence to argue that production in textiles, pig iron, and railroad production fell during the Civil War years, although the disruptions of war perhaps made it inevitable in the short run. However, it seems clear that the consolidation of the bourgeois state through the Civil War created the conditions for the subsequent phase of capitalist industrialisation. As compared to the decade 1850–60, the rate of growth of production in iron, coal and railroad lines was considerably higher during 1865–75.[55]

4.4.2 Tariffs

It was in 1791 that Hamilton presented his famous report to Congress on the principles of customs policy in order to transform the USA into an industrial nation like England; significantly, the report was titled 'Report on Manufactures'. Hamilton advocated the highest duties on articles which could be manufactured in the USA.

Between 1792–1816 some 25 tariff acts were passed; for a time the USA had found itself protected from European competition because of the Napoleonic Wars. The resumption of foreign trade threatened northern industries and despite opposition from the south the Tariff Act of 1816 was passed; this act was for protective rather than fiscal reasons. This was followed by two strongly protectionist tariffs in 1824 and 1828 but amended in 1837 because southern opponents threatened to withdraw from the Union. Protectionism was revived in 1842 but reductions were made in 1846 although *ad valorem* duties still ranged from 5 to 40 per cent; and further liberalisation was enacted in 1857. In 1861 slight increases were made and *ad valorem* rates were replaced by specific duties.

The Civil War and the consolidation of northern power marked a turning point. Tariffs were raised in 1862, and in 1864 became highly protectionist; special protection was provided for wool and copper. In 1867 wool and fabrics were given high specific and *ad valorem* duties; duties were revised upwards on flax, nickel, marble and steel rails in 1870. A 10 per cent reduction made in 1872 was repealed in 1875. A new tariff was introduced in 1883, primarily to mollify oppontents of high tariffs but without any real impact.

This period of tariff history concluded with the highly protectionist McKinley Act of 1890, coinciding with the phase of rapid US economic expansion. In 1897 tariffs were raised to an unprecedented level and remained in force till 1909, by which time the USA had become an established industrial nation.[56]

4.4.3 Transportation

The transport sector was one of the few beneficiaries of significant and direct State sponsorship in the USA.

In the shipping industry the involvement of the State was extensive and clearly motivated by awareness of its significance for national security. The US Congress justified its policy of fostering the development and ensuring the maintenance of a merchant marine because national interest required

> a shipping fleet (1) which is adequate to carry all the domestic and 'a substantial portion' of the foreign commerce of the United States on all 'essential' routes, and (2) which is 'capable of serving as a naval and military auxiliary in time of war or national emergency'.[57]

The US merchant marine grew from the seventeenth century onwards, with short periods of decline such as the American Revolution and the War of 1812. Between 1789 and 1855 US shipping engaged in carrying national foreign commerce rose from 123,893 tons to 2,348,000 tons.

During this period the State intervened with protection, financial assistance and regulation. In 1789 legislation was passed allowing only vessels built in US shipyards to be registered under the American flag. Foreign vessels were barred from coastal trade and subjected to discriminatory taxation at US ports. This legislation was crucial in promoting local construction and expanding the American merchant marine.

Following the Civil War the US merchant marine began to

decline in the face of competition from cheaper British iron ships. Protection remained effective only for the coastal fleet since it enjoyed the monopoly granted by Congress. Ships built in the US were more expensive owing to the higher cost of US steel.

The British government had also granted financial assistance for the establishment of a British passenger service to the US. The US Congress had authorised a mail subsidy in 1845 in the form of payments by the Post Office to carriers who contracted to carry mail. By 1858 the subsidy totalled $14 million, but the subsidy was terminated. Another similar subsidy was granted in 1865, and in 1891; the latter cost $29 million. The experiment with subsidies proved disappointing, however, and the fleet declined. By 1910 only 8.7 per cent of US commerce was being carried in US ships.

It was during the First World War that the consequences of the decline of the US merchant marine were felt. US farmers and manufacturers were unable to take advantage of the lucrative business which was available because of European wartime requirements. And when the US joined the war its troops were carried in the ships of allies because of the shortage of ships.

The government responded by creating a Shipping Board and Emergency Fleet Corporation. The shipbuilding programme cost $3 billion and greatly benefited the shipping industry and allied suppliers. Later, the ships built for the government during the war were sold to private shipowners at less than 10 per cent of their original value. Thus the basis for the future of the US merchant marine had been established. Despite subsequent setbacks, e.g. during the 1920s, the responsibility of the State for the existence of a national merchant marine able to serve security needs, first recognised in the seventeenth century, continued to be upheld.[58]

The involvement of the State in railroads has also been of considerable importance. According to the Association of American Railroads government had an influence on virtually every important aspect of the railway business.[59]

During the era of railroad construction between 1830–1900, 200,000 miles of trackage were constructed. The impact of the State and other public agencies on the vast expansion was of two types. The State and these agencies — like municipal and county government — provided outright subsidies, subscribed to railroad stocks, lent public money in the form of cash or government bonds, guaranteed the security of corporate bonds and the interest. In some cases railroads were laid at no cost to the private companies by local governments;

tax exemptions were also provided for varying periods. The full value of such assistance has been estimated at several million dollars.

The other more important subsidy given to railroad companies was in the form of land grants. The total grant given by the Federal Government has been estimated at 127 million acres; plus another 48 million acres provided by the state authorities. The net value of this land to the railroad companies has been placed at around $516 million, although its value to the State authorities was less since prices were lower at the time they could have been sold, and its value appreciated enormously over time.[60]

The railroad expansion aided by the State was of indirect benefit to other industries like iron and steel, machinery coal, etc., since it was the 'leading sector' in the economy.

The US government has played a much more significant role in industrialisation than is commonly recognised. The particular advantages it enjoyed, highlighted earlier, qualified the magnitude of intervention and influenced its form but did not make it unnecessary.

4.5 The Second Round

The importance of State intervention in the process of industrialisation in the latecomer west European countries, Japan, and to a limited degree, the USA, during the third quarter of the nineteenth and early twentieth centuries has been discussed. The creation of the group of strategic industries was, by and large, predicated on some form of direct and/or indirect State intervention prompted by political insecurity stemming from the emergence of other industrial nations in the international political system.

In this period the spread of industrialisation transformed the international political system, leading to the rise of new centres of power. Nevertheless, the distribution of military and political power in the international political system remained stratified despite the spread of industrialisation.[61] But even the relatively weaker latecomer industrial countries (e.g. Italy) achieved a measure of national autonomy which distinguished them from non-industrial nations. It was also possible for them to improve their relative regional status although remaining weak in global terms. But as it has been noted above, weaker countries strive to industrialise in order to achieve, at minimum, a reasonable measure of economic security, even if the politico-military goals are of circumscribed relevance to them, in contrast to larger powers, particularly of the 'first round'.[62]

During the second-half of the twentieth century a number of countries in the so-called Third World have appeared to embark on industrialisation, following the path of the 'first comer' industrial nations. Some of these countries only acquired political independence immediately after the Second World War, others even later. Of this group of countries only Argentina had experienced significant economic activity prior to 1950.[63] This chapter deals with the attempt of the State in two Third World countries to establish the group of strategic industries and thereby promote industralisation.

It should be reiterated that what has to be established is whether the State in these countries is actually attempting to industrialise by ensuring the creation of the group of strategic industries. It is the attempt to industrialise which requires to be demonstrated for the purposes of the hypothesis since the presumption, which will be analysed later, is that having once ensured the creation of the group of strategic industries for reasons of politico-military security, including a significant degree of economic independence in key intermediate inputs, the State will defend it against the competitive pressures of international trade. It has already been argued in an earlier chapter that industrialisation and the possession of the group of strategic industries which it automatically implies is a necessary pre-condition for political influence, even survival, in the modern international political system. Both Brazil and India are, at the very least, potential regional powers and the pursuit of international politico-military goals, in addition to economic security, is therefore not excluded for them. This is in contrast to the situation of most Third World countries for whom the achievement of economic security, rather than politico-military prominence, is the feasible option.

There is of course no guarantee that industrialisation will succeed in these countries although some efforts are evident. Indeed in much of the Third World significant efforts in this direction have been absent. For many of them their size alone precludes the possibility of the type of diversified economy in question. In numerous other instances local élites in control of the State apparatus have not sought to achieve economic, or even political self-reliance because of their subordination to foreign powers. In significant areas of Latin America, for example, efforts to industrialise are rather half-hearted because of economic and political dependence on the USA. The subordinate status of such countries in the international political system will continue to persist.

In the two countries to be examined below the State has made efforts to initiate industrialisation although the outcome cannot be considered a foregone conclusion. The presence of a large number of industrialised countries in the system has affected their course of economic development. Their economic relations with the advanced industrial nations in many instances clearly qualify their autonomy in a way which did not occur for the latecomer countries of the first period. The emergence of strategic industries under foreign ownership, for example, is a novel phenomenon. Thus their political destiny and the precise economic impact of their participation in the international economy are not yet wholly apparent: in the sense that only with the progress of industrialisation the participation of countries in international trade in manufactures intensifies competition over markets.[54]

4.6 Brazil

Beginning with the 1950s the history of State intervention in the process of industrialisation in Brazil can be divided into two periods. During the first period, including much of the 1960s, the role of the State in the economy was more direct. Following the military coup in 1964 there was a brief downgrading of the role of public capital but the declared ideological preferences of the military dictatorship were reversed in practice by 1966, underlining the unity of certain basic economic objectives of the Brazilian State despite the change in regime. Of course, socio-economic inequality in Brazilian society remained a constant feature and widened under the military dictatorship.

The two sectors in which State participation predates the 1950s are steel and petroleum. Iron and steel making were in private hands until the 1940s when the government intervened to expand the industry by establishing modern, larger, more capital-intensive integrated plants. At present government firms provide more than half the output of steel. Three large companies — CSN, COSIPA, and USIMINAS — of which the first is wholly owned by the State, and the others within its control, dominate steel production in Brazil.

The petroleum sector is dominated by Petrobas, a government enterprise founded in 1953. Of more direct interest to this discussion, since 1968 the government has entered the petro-chemical sector by creating a subsidiary of Petrobas — Petroquisa.[65] The decision of the State to establish these sectors was clearly dictated by nationalist impulses to promote economic self-sufficiency.[66]

4.6.1 Banking and credit

Apart from direct public ownership and control of these sectors, industrial priorities were powerfully influenced by credit and financial policies, especially through the National Economic Development Bank (Banco Nacional de Desenvolvimento Economico — BNDE).

During 1952–64 almost 60 per cent of the resources of the BNDE were devoted to energy and transport. A further 25 per cent was directed toward the steel sector and 4 per cent to chemicals. Around 8 per cent was distributed among motor vehicles, non-ferrous metals, ship-building, pulp and paper, and other metal products. After 1964 the BNDE disbursed its funds more widely, assisting particular buyers of Brazilian-made capital goods.

Between 1966–9 one-third of the resources of the BNDE, rising to one-half, was devoted to industrial sectors other than steel. Infrastructural activities like electricity, transport and communications received a third of its disbursements, a policy of direct and indirect benefit to the domestic capital goods sector.[67]

Other sectors of manufacturing activity, however, were not markedly affected by public investment. The policy of the government favoured steel and petroleum, and to a lesser extent chemicals. But private investment has been influenced by heavy public investment in electricity, transport and certain public utilities. Indeed the form of public investment has been an important component of the Brazilian 'miracle' in 1966–74.

4.6.2 Tariffs and related measures

Apart from the impact of publicly financed infrastructure and the key inputs provided by government enterprise, the State has used other instruments to mould private industry. These instruments include tariff policy, export incentives, tax exemptions and concessionary finance; price control and administrative procedures have also been employed with effect.

Protectionist measures, both taxes and the price effect of other policies, are crucial in Brazil and their varying incidence is reflected in the performance of the manufacturing sector. An analysis of 43 sectors by Bergsman showed that protection ranged from — 25 per cent to +158 per cent, with the weighted mean at 36 per cent;[68] Bergsman suggests that the mean has increased in recent years. A further quantitative analysis of 20 sectors showed that during the

period 1949–62 10 sectors had significant imports at the beginning
of the period. At the end of the period, 3 sectors within this group of
10 which had the highest protection — electrical equipment,
transport equipment and plastics — experienced the highest
import substitution. The other 7 sectors with lower levels of
protection — non-metallic mineral products, metals, machinery,
paper, chemicals, pharmaceuticals and miscellaneous goods — also
made progress. During the ten years preceding 1975 imports had
ceased to be a significant part of total supply of manufactured
goods, except in heavy equipment and certain chemicals.[69]

By the mid 1970s the tax system had become the most important
instrument of government policy to affect industrial priorities. In
addition to import duties and duty exemptions, export incentives
consisting of tax exemptions, were also available; non-tax import
regulations also had an important effect. The exemptions and
credits designed to promote exports were originally introduced in
1968 and have been strengthened since. These incentives vary
considerably between sectors, by as much as a factor of 4 — i.e. the
profitability of exports in some sectors can be four times as high
compared to others. The most favoured sectors were tobacco
products, non-ferrous metals, food products, thread and yarn,
textiles, metal products, ship-building and railroad vehicles. Some
of these sectors are promoted to increase foreign exchange
earnings for the import of essential inputs.

4.6.3 *Other administrative measures*

Investment decisions in industry formally remain largely in private
hands but in practice the influence of the government is compelling
because of its control over credit. More than 50 per cent of
commercial loans are provided by government sources. Other
sources of credit are public institutions like the BNDE, the Federal
Development Bank for the Northeast (Banco de Nordeste, BNB),
and the state development banks. An application for the importation of duty-free equipment also has to be approved by the Foreign
Trade Office of the Bank of Brazil (Carterio de Comercio Exterior —
CACEX). The prices to be charged for the product are reviewed by
government agencies. Thus, as Bergsman puts it '. . . the
government has the power to make, shape, or break any industrial
venture in the country'.[70]

In the 1950s the government exercised its influence through
formal consultative bodies called 'executive groups' (*grupos*

executivos) which co-ordinated policies relevant to investment decisions in close conjunction with representatives of private industry. These high-level bodies composed of personnel with authority from relevant ministries, the BNDE etc., functioned in the automotive, ship-building, capital goods, chemicals and iron-ore mining sectors.

The purpose of the 'executive group' was to co-ordinate government-sponsored benefits like credit, tax and import duty exemptions. The private investor was expected to respond by making the investments desired by the government. The assembling of the powerful package of instruments would then lead to the establishment of the industry. The anticipated financial rewards of such ventures were more an outcome of the decisions reached than the product of market conditions.[71]

The significance of the 'executive groups' diminished during the 1960s. Since then new institutions, originally created in 1970 under the aegis of the Industrial Development Council (the Conselho de Desenvolvimento Industrial — CDI) in the Ministry of Commerce and Industry, have fulfilled similar functions. Most important manufacturing sectors now have a CDI group. Such groups oversee more than half of manufacturing investment in Brazil.

In sum, during the past 30 years the State in Brazil has been impelled by the nationalist urge to produce domestically what was previously imported, to follow the path of other industrial countries and modernise. The creation of a self-sufficient national economy did not pay obeisance to the logic of static comparative advantage theory. As Bergsman has asserted, 'formal economic analysis seems to have played a small role, if any, in setting industrial priorities'.[72] In concluding it should nevertheless be recognised that foreign enterprises play a disproportionately large role in strategic sectors of the Brazilian economy, in marked contrast to the experience of latecomers of the 'first round'. In 1973 foreign enterprises were responsible for 51.4 per cent of exports of 318 leading enterprises. This included 74.3 per cent of non-metallic minerals, 80.1 per cent of non-electrical machinery, 91.8 per cent of electrical equipment, 85.6 per cent of transport equipment, and 84.1 per cent of chemicals. Similar levels of dominance are also evident in a number of other sectors like food, beverages, tobacco; in pharmaceuticals and printing and publishing 100 per cent of exports are undertaken by foreign firms.[73]

4.7 India

The drive for industrialisation in India has been uniquely dominated by the State apparatus among Third World countries. More surprisingly, at first sight, from a conventional perspective, the rise of several in the group of strategic industries has been intimately connected with the national defence effort.[74] However, while the State has been successful in installing a diversified industrial base the wider task of industrialisation, as reflected in sectoral shifts between agriculture and industry, and rising per capita incomes and industrial output, is yet to be achieved. The reasons for this failure are only of indirect concern for the purposes of this book since it is the attempt by the State to establish the group of strategic industries which demonstrates the underlying theme of politico-military motivation. Nevertheless some reasons for this failure will be discussed briefly because of the importance of per capita industrial output for national military potential.

4.7.1 Defence and industrialisation

The links between defence needs and the civilian economy have been direct in India because of the circumstances of its independence. The partition of India and ensuing disputes with the new nation of Pakistan introduced defence considerations into economic policies with an immediacy which prompted specific measures regarding defence production.

The two areas affected were transportation equipment, and engineering, which constitutes an important part of machinery.

In 1960 the Marazon Docks and the Garden Reach Workshops in eastern India were purchased from its British owners by the Department of Defence Production. It was primarily intended for the manufacture of Indian Navy warships but found itself heavily involved in the production and repair of civilian vessels, beginning with an order for two large liners. The complex and workshops also became involved in small-scale projects, manufacturing tugs and barges. The increased revenues allowed the workshops to diversify and establish new units for the manufacture of diesel engines, compressors, cranes and pumps.[75]

The domestic manufacture of aircraft had similar beginnings. In 1943 the Ministry of Defence had taken over the Hindustan Aeronautics Company. However, by 1959 it had become apparent that the possibility for manufacturing of civilian aircraft also existed.

The desire to achieve self-sufficiency in the manufacture of aeroplanes within twenty years of independence (1967) was not fulfilled, but India is virtually alone among Third World countries to have acquired a domestic capability in the manufacture of aircraft. Initially, the Hindustan Aeronautics Company (HAL) converted war-surplus machines but subsequently developed into the assembly of British aircraft. In recent decades HAL has manufactured supersonic fighters of indigenous design and under license. The first 'low cost' fighter of local design was a failure but the Gnat Folland proved a success; 85 per cent of its components were of local manufacture, including 60 per cent of its British Orpheus turbo-jet engine. The Russian Mig 21s, and more recently the advanced Mig 23, have been produced under license. HAL also manufactures helicopters, light aircraft and civil/military transports. It produced the HS 748 for military transport and successfully sold it to India's civil airlines.[76]

According to Whynes, India's electronics industry was also initiated for the supply of defence requirements and then expanded into the civilian market, providing radio components, transmitters and receivers, and navigational aids for shipping.[77] In recent years the Indian Government has established facilities for the manufacture of computers because of its importance to defence. Other military hardware like tanks, vehicles, armaments and ammunition requiring extensive engineering facilities is produced within the country.

However the bulk of India's defence equipment is still imported because the level of sophistication needed is dictated by the quality of weapons possessed by potential opponents, and large quantities of such equipment cannot be supplied by the restricted facilities at home, except in a few categories.[78]

Industrialisation, and the installation of the group of strategic industries which it entails, underlines the politico-military aspect of relative economic self-sufficiency, both as a potential input for defence production and insurance against insuperable external dependence. However it is actual involvement in conflict which vindicates this strategy, although there may be specific exceptions.[79] The linkage between defence production and industrialisation need not be a direct one, but in the case of India, as with Japan in the nineteenth century, the intimacy between the former and the latter was fairly immediate owing to the political circumstances encountered by them. India felt threatened by the new state of Pakistan and Japan feared western imperialism.

4.7.2 Industrialisation and the Indian State

The role of the State in industrialisation in India can be broadly understood in terms of Gerschenkron's hypothesis, which predicts a positive correlation between the degree of backwardness and the magnitude of State intervention. But the particular form of State intervention in India, with its emphasis on direct investment and economic planning, derived substantially from the favourable impression created on India's first Prime Minister, Nehru, by the Soviet example, despite the obvious contrasts between Bolshevik Russia and post-independence India.

4.7.2.1 Economic planning in India

The establishment of the Planning Commission in 1950 indicated the strategy of the Indian State for the future direction of the economy. The Planning Commission has produced six five-year plans since its inception, the first in 1951. The State has attempted to channel investment into 'socially desirable industries' and control the development of the private sector. The legal basis for these twin goals was the Industries Act of 1951 and the Industrial Policy Resolution of 1956.[80]

The Industrial Policy Resolution of 1956 demarcated the spheres of economic activity between the public and private sector. Industry was divided into three categories: Schedule A was the exclusive domain of the State, the expansion of capacity in Schedule B was reserved for the State. Remaining industries were to be consigned to the private sector under license although, again, the State could enter these sectors if it desired. However as the document stated:

> the division of industries into separate categories does not imply that they are being placed in watertight compartments . . . . In appropriate cases privately owned units may be permitted to produce an item falling within Schedule A or meeting their own requirements or as by-products.[81]

But by 1966 the government found it difficult to perpetuate control in conformity with the original divisions owing to a variety of economic and political pressures. The fourth five-year plan declared that 'within the broad framework of control in strategic areas there is advantage in allowing the market much fuller play'.[82]

Industrial licensing was phased out for more than forty industries. A further relaxation occurred in March 1970 when licensing was declared unnecessary for the construction or expansion of enterprises valued at less than Rs. 10 million, an increase by a factor of four over the previous figure, if certain foreign exchange, national ownership and monopoly criteria were satisfied.

The industrial programme of the first plan largely consisted of projects that were already in the process of implementation or due to start. Around two-thirds of its total industrial investment was for public sector projects, the remainder was allocated to the private sector. The finance made available to the latter was for the increase of output in existing capacity rather than the creation of new capacity. The second plan (1956/7 – 1960/1) was biased towards import substitution in heavy industry. The third plan continued the expansion of heavy industry, which according to scholars was concerned with choices about magnitudes and the pattern of such investments 'without reference to notions of economic calculus'.[83] By the end of the third five-year plan period, industrial output and investment had stagnated and observers increasingly attributed the situation to shortcomings in planning. A fourth plan was drawn up but by then the planners had already lost much of their political influence; by 1975 planning was largely discredited and the draft of the fifth plan was not finalised.[84]

4.7.2.2 *The public sector*

The importance of State investment in the group of strategic industries is readily apparent from the list of industries in Schedule A in the Annexure of the Industrial Policy Resolution of 1956 and Schedule B which contains the category, not automatically open to private investors. Since the formulation of these categories significant changes favouring private investors have occurred but the extent of public ownership remains formidable, judging from the number of State-owned corporations in key industrial sectors. These State-owned corporations are usually the dominant producer in the sector in which they operate, particularly in metals, electrical and non-electrical machinery, transport and transportation equipment.

The share of the public sector in total industrial investment in large-scale industry has risen sharply since the first five-year plan. From around 25 per cent at the beginning of the first plan period to roughly 50 per cent at the end of the third; and projected to reach over 60 per cent by the end of the fifth five-year plan.[85]

4.7.3 *The private sector*

The role of the private sector in the Indian economy was originally determined by the Industrial Development and Regulation Act of 1951 and the Industrial Policy Resolution of 1956 described earlier. The sphere of operation delineated by the IPR of 1956 has expanded since, during the mid 1960s and by the Janata Government a decade later. However, although 'decontrol' has been the trend the regulatory powers of the State remain compelling. The chief instruments of control wielded by the State are fiscal and administrative: taxes, subsidies, price and distributional controls, import and investment licensing and the pattern and volume of public expenditure. Some of these features are discussed briefly below.[86]

Licensing of investment and imports has been a crucial mechanism of direction since the inception of an industrial policy. Industrial licensing which regulates private investment is intended to enforce planned growth, combat monopolistic tendencies, ensure regional balance, protect small producers and encourage new entrepreneurs, and finally, foster optimum utilisation of capacity and the adoption of new technology. Thus the application for an industrial license is scrutinised by several official agencies before a decision is reached, allowing the State to retain maximum influence.

If imported inputs are required by a prospective producer a license has to be obtained from the appropriate agency. For example, the import of capital goods is cleared by an inter-departmental Capital Goods and Heavy Electrical Projects Committee. If a domestic input is available imports are prohibited. While industrial licensing does not apply to the public sector it is subject to the import procedures.[87]

4.7.4 *Protectionism*

The government proclaimed a three-year period of protection for sixty industries in 1947, after independence. In April 1949 the Fiscal Commission was set up to work out general principles for protection of industry. Its proposals were endorsed by the Act of 1951. Three recommendations were enumerated: the protection of defence and strategic industries regardless of economic considerations, guaranteed protection for heavy industries to be expanded under the five-year plans, with the forms, methods and obligations of the recipient industries subject to revision, and protection for infant industries unless the cost proved excessive. In 1952 a Tariff Commission was established to put the proposals into practice.

Up to the end of the 1950s customs duties were the primary method of protection. The level of duty was fixed to exceed the difference in cost between the price of the domestic product and the price of the article to be imported, thereby excluding the latter. By the mid 1960s customs duties constituted 38.1 per cent of the cost of imported commodities. Deterioration of the balance of payments also prompted the use of quantitative restrictions, which were subsequently to assume primary importance in regulating imports.[88]

4.7.5 Taxation and banking

The taxation policies reveal the same bias in favour of modern and heavy industry evident in the five-year plans, tariffs and choice of investment projects. The Taxation Enquiry Commission drafted the following principles: encouragement of industrial entrepreneurship in general, specific encouragement to modern industries — containing virtually all the group of strategic industries — expansion of the accumulation fund and accelerated renovation of fixed capital, and restriction of non-productive utilisation of profits.

In accordance with these aims indirect taxes, in particular excise-duties, were chosen. Since direct taxes were paid by a small minority and internal demand usually exceeded supply, producers were able to shift the burden of indirect taxation to the consumer; indirect taxation contributed more than 70 per cent of national revenue, rising from 50 per cent before independence. The Taxation Enquiry Commission also exempted from tax 6 per cent of profits on invested capital; in twenty-seven of the priority industries only 92 per cent of profits were subject to taxation.

From 1957 enterprises working two shifts were allowed 50 per cent increases in depreciation allowances, 100 per cent if three shifts were worked. Some modifications were introduced to take into account rising prices for equipment, building materials, etc. and different rates were fixed for industrial production assets established in different periods. Other changes were introduced following the devaluation of the rupee in 1966 for enterprises which imported equipment on credit or on an installment basis, allowing them to revalue their assets.

An innovation recommended by the Taxation Enquiry Commission introduced the concept of a development rebate, which enabled costs of new equipment (whatever the purpose: expansion or modernisation of existing capacity) to be treated as direct production costs, over eight years if it was very expensive or the enterprise operated at a loss. The ordinary depreciation deductions could continue to be made in the usual way.[89]

Credit policy to mobilise funds for planned economic growth was undertaken by a number of methods. The credit guarantee arrangements of the central bank, the Reserve Bank of India (RBI), encouraged medium-term loans to industry. More significant were the RBI credits to various industrial financing corporations. The State Bank of India, the biggest commercial bank, financed industry directly. In the mid 1960s industry accounted for approximately 80 per cent of its operations. Its credit policies also influenced the preferences of other smaller financial institutions.

During the early years of independence the central government extended long-term credits to large-scale industries which private sources were unable to finance or unwilling to risk. A number of substantial loans were made to chemicals, engineering, steel and textiles. However with the diversion of funds to planned sectors the importance of specialised credit agencies for the finance of private industry grew. The first such agency was founded in 1948, but by the end of the 1960s their number had risen to thirty. The most important are the Industrial Development Bank (founded in 1964), the Industrial Finance Corporation, the National Industries Development Corporation (the first such institution founded in 1954), the Industrial Credit and Investment Corporation (founded in 1955), and the Unit Trust of India (founded in 1964). Each state within the federal system also set up its own financial corporation.[90]

The role and functions of official credit agencies acquired growing importance with the expansion of industry. Their loans accounted for 5 per cent of total investments in the first plan period, around 10 per cent during the second, and 16 per cent in the private sector during the third.[91]

Notes

1. Rostow (1960) p. 26.
2. The present analysis suffers from the short-coming of being restricted to the limited number of secondary sources available in

English, in an area which is not particularly well researched. Thus some unevenness of scrutiny, as between the countries surveyed, may be evident. However, this does not detract, as will be evident, from the credibility of the conclusions which can be reached.

3. Hobsbawm (1969) p. 114-20; also see Fremdling (1977) pp. 583-604.
4. Detailed evidence concerning them is to be found in Sen (1982), chapter 4.
5. Knowles (1932) p. 112.
6. Clough (1939) p. 23.
7. Knowles (op. cit.) pp. 123-4.
8. Clough (op. cit.) p. 31.
9. Quoted in Ibid. p. 105.
10. Knowles (op. cit.) p. 163.
11. Henderson (1975) on luxuries, p. 127.
12. Knowles (op. cit.) p. 169.
13. Ibid. p. 165; and Howard (1907) p. 28.
14. Knowles)op. cit.) p. 169.
15. Fremdling (op. cit.).
16. Barker (1912) p. 68.
17. Clough (1964) pp. 19; 28-9.
18. Also see Lutz (1962), esp. Ch. XII pp. 268-84 for State participation.
19. Clough (op. cit.) pp. 128-9.
20. Ibid. pp. 124-31.
21. Ibid. pp. 63; 111-18.
22. Clough (op. cit.) pp. 67; 70-2.
23. Clough (op. cit.) pp. 71-2.
24. Ibid.
25. Ibid. p. 78.
26. Clough (op. cit.) p. 85.
27. Ibid. pp. 82; 86-7.
28. Ibid. pp. 86-92.
29. Norman (1975) p. 224.
30. Ibid. p. 225.
31. Norman (op. cit.) p. 230 and Kobayashi (1922) pp. 161-2.
32. Lockwood (1968) p. 562.
33. Ibid. p. 563.
34. Lockwood (op. cit.) pp. 561-3; Maddison (1969) pp. 14; 22-3; Norman (op. cit.) pp. 219-20.
35. Norman (op. cit.) p. 220.
36. Maddison (op. cit.) pp. 22–3; Norman (op. cit.) pp. 220–4.
37. Maddison (op. cit.) pp. 15-17.
38. Allen (1972) pp. 71-8; Norman (op. cit.) pp. 233-6.
39. Norman (op. cit.) p. 226.

40. Allen (op. cit.) pp. 79-80; Norman (op. cit.) pp. 226, 228.
41. Norman (op. cit.) p. 229.
42. Norman (op. cit.) pp. 90; 228-9.
43. Lockwood (op. cit.) p. 545.
44. Ibid. p. 546.
45. Allen (op. cit.) pp. 90-2; Lockwood, (op. cit.) pp. 528; 545-6.
46. Allen (op. cit.) pp. 34; 82-3, Lockwood (op. cit.) pp. 545-6; Norman (op. cit.) p. 227.
47. Allen (op. cit.) p. 83.
48. Norman (op. cit.) p. 227.
49. Allen (op. cit.) pp. 83-4; Kobayashi (op. cit.) p. 167.
50. Allen (op. cit.) p. 84.
51. Lockwood (op. cit.) pp. 70-1.
52. Woytinsky (1955) pp. 190-1.
53. Ashworth (1975) pp. 196-200; also see Kenwood & Lougheed (1971) on migration across the Atlantic.
54. In Post (1982) p. 49.
55. Salsbury in Nash (ed.) (1964).
56. Woytinsky (op. cit.) pp. 259-60; also see Ashley (1920) for a more detailed account; pp. 133-264.
57. Smead (1969) p. 228).
58. For a detailed account of US State intervention to promote the shipping industry see Smead (op. cit.) pp. 228-52.
59. Smead (op. cit.) p. 202.
60. Ibid. pp. 202-6.
61. The determinant parameter of this inequality between nations is the asymmetry of industrial strength, both GDP and per capita GDP, the latter determining the amount of resources which can be diverted for defence purposes. Obviously, there is no mechanically ordained hierarchy deriving from this criteria because a much more complex interaction occurs in reality, depending on the particular circumstances and issues involved, but any rank ordering of potential capacity, particularly military capacity, is likely to reflect industrial strength.
62. See chapter 2.
63. Maizels (1963) pp. 555 and 537.
64. It is only with the progress of industrialisation, as measured by per capita incomes and therefore diversified industrial structures, that international trade conflicts are precipitated. This industrial growth obviously also establishes the political stature of the nation.
65. As one of the group of strategic manufacturing sectors.
66. Bergsman in UNIDO (1979) p. 13.
67. Ibid.
68. Bergsman (1970) pp. 102-10.
69. Bergsman in UNIDO (1979) p. 16.

70.   Ibid. p. 14. According to Bach, Edmar, *et al* (quoted in Bergsman ibid. p. 19, footnote 20) '. . . the government has the power, overnight, to render profitable all investment projects that it wants to be implemented, and to make the ones it does not want to promote financially infeasible. . . . For all practical purposes, the private profitability of investment projects in Brazil is thus a by-product of the applications of the government's instruments of economic policy'.

71.   Bergsman in UNIDO (1979) p. 15.

72.   Ibid.

73.   Lal (1980) p. 2106.

74.   It has already been argued, in an earlier chapter, that there need not be a direct relationship between such defence production and the rise of the group of strategic industries since the latter are only a potential capability which can be deployed for the purposes of the former. The availability of domestic capacity in these industries also, of course, reduces economic vulnerability, a matter of politico-military significance.

75.   Whynes (1979) p. 45.

76.   Ibid. p. 47 and Kennedy (1974) pp 322-23.

77.   Whynes (1979) pp. 45-6.

78.   SIPRI (1971 and 1975).

79.   Military supplies can be provided by an ally or allies during a conflict but this will affect the manoeuvrability of the country concerned.

80.   Lal (1979) p. 24.

81.   Schedules A and B included virtually all the group of strategic industries; see Wadhva (1977), p. 28.

82.   Shirokov (1973) p. 85.

83.   Bhagwati and Desai, (1970) p. 111.

84.   Shirokov (op. cit.) and Frankel (1977).

85.   Lal (op. cit.) p. 29.

86.   Ibid. pp. 39-40. Bhagwati and Desai (op. cit.) pp. 231-80 and particularly pp. 249-73 for a detailed analysis.

87.   Lal (op. cit.) p. 27 and p. 29.

88.   Shirokov (op. cit.) pp. 90-2.

89.   Ibid. pp. 97-9.

90.   Ibid. pp. 103-5,

91.   Ibid. p. 113.

5 Changes in world market share and the response of the State

5.1 Introduction

This chapter analyses changes among major exporting countries in relative shares of world exports in strategic industries from the beginning of the twentieth century to the present. This analysis is situated in the context of the emergence of 'free trade' earlier in the nineteenth century. The strategic industries for which homogeneous data series are available from 1899 to 1971 are metals, machinery, textiles and clothing, transport equipment, and chemicals; paper and paper products for which similar data are unavailable are consequently excluded, but five strategic industries, out of the total of six, serve to depict the conflicts involved.[1] Data on metals are used instead of iron and steel alone. However, since iron and steel comprise the major component in metals, distortions owing to contrary movement of shares in the other components are not significant.

The major exporting countries are the UK, Germany, the USA, Japan, and one region, OWE (Other West European).

The concluding section of the chapter is devoted to an assessment of the responses of the State to losses in market shares during the post-war period. The responses of the State in the two countries, the USA and the UK, which have suffered a continuous decline of shares in all sectors, will be the main focus of attention. However, the experience of other countries will also be used to illustrate general features of State behaviour in this context.

The political impulses and outcome of conflicts over market shares in the preceding period are only sketched in broad terms, including an appraisal of the possible function fulfilled in this respect by the two world wars.

5.1.1 The argument so far

The inter-country similarities in the structure of production described earlier result from the attempt by States to pursue a relative economic self-sufficiency for politico-military reasons. The relative self-sufficiency in intermediate inputs which this creates provides the basis for the manufacture of defence hardware as well as instituting an important measure of economic autonomy, i.e. reducing dependence on other countries for key inputs used in the economy.

The evaluation of the role of the State in latecomer countries both in the nineteenth century and the post-Second World War period confirms the existence of a persistent impulse to achieve this kind of economic self-sufficiency.

The reproduction of similar structures of production introduces a secular tendency towards the creation of surplus capacity in substantial areas of manufacturing since internal and external economies of scale compel a level of production which most countries cannot sustain through domestic consumption alone. This phenomenon is, of course, observable from the outset as industrialisation progresses, since the process of economic growth is inextricably linked to participation in international trade. The latecomer countries thus unavoidably threaten the established positions of firstcomer countries. This threat provokes economic rivalry over markets in the latecomer country itself, in third markets, and in the domestic market of the firstcomer.

The post-war liberal international economic order on which the relatively free flow of goods and services across national boundaries is predicated is, by common consent, perceived to be threatened by protectionist pressures.[2] It has been argued in previous chapters that this threat derives, at bottom, from politico-military imperatives of the territorial state. The insecurity of participation in the international political system prompts the State to pursue the policies of relative economic self-sufficiency outlined earlier. These take the form of defensive tariff and non-tariff barriers to protect the strategic industries once they have been established through the process of industrialisation.

In the contemporary context, the principal focus of the present chapter, such defensive measures violate the principles of 'free trade' enshrined in GATT, and apparently threaten the whole post-war economic order.

It is contended that (a) 'free trade'[3] has been the exception rather than the norm in the international economic system since the late nineteenth century, and earlier, and (b) individual nation states have attempted to defend their strategic industries by resorting to the type of measures enumerated in chapter 3; the latter contention will be discussed primarily in terms of events which have occurred in the post-war period.[4]

5.1.2 *The origins of free trade*

Until the late eighteenth century mercantilist ideas and policy remained pre-eminent in Britain. Wars were fought to acquire markets in both east and west, and rivals were excluded from these markets, for instance the American continent, with the help of the Navigation Acts.[5] Indeed the preservation and expansion of the colonial market was considered 'axiomatic, for the colonies were regarded simply as an extension of the home market'.[6] In fact, 'in 1750 there was a heritage of controls, for protection for home manufactures was accepted policy'.[7] Industrial progress in other nations aroused gloom; even competition from India in the first quarter of the eighteenth century was 'stamped out'.[8]

Towards the end of the eighteenth century the growing strength of British manufacturing raised doubts about the efficacy of continuing such mercantilist policies. The free trade theories of Adam Smith began to gain adherents. In 1786 Pitt signed a treaty liberalising trade between France and Britain.

Britain's pre-eminence as a power and industrial nation was indisputable between the end of the Napoleonic Wars and the Crimean War, but other nations were beginning to compete. The home market was inadequate to absorb the growing output of factories and Britain pushed further into Africa, the Levant, and the Orient but these markets were insufficient. Europe and the USA remained markets but frequently protected by tariffs: European war-time protection had been extended after the war.[9]

In this situation it seemed wise to grant concessions and hence the abolition of the Corn Laws in 1846 and the Navigation Acts in 1849, as well as the Timber Duties — the chief objects of foreign hostility.[10]

> [Thus] step-by-step, often with a bitter struggle among opposing interests, free trade, the dream of the confident businessman of early Victorian England, was adopted as the policy of the nation.[11]

By then, the ideas of Smith, and later, Ricardo, had acquired the status of orthodoxy, a reflection of the supremacy of British industry, which politicians like Cobden recognised and were keen to translate into commercial advantage.[12]

Nevertheless, as it has already been shown, other European countries were unimpressed by Britain's 'free trade' policies and preferred to industrialise behind tariff barriers and other forms of State patronage. Between 1860 and the early 1870s, with the progress of industrialisation on the Continent, numerous treaties liberalising trading arrangements were signed betwen various countries. But such treaties did not habitually lead to freer trade since nations were unwilling to jeopardise their industries. For example, the most significant treaty of this period was the Cobden-Chevalier Treaty signed by Britain and France in 1860. This treaty was signed primarily for political reasons because the French Government felt isolated and thought that it might prevent war between the two countries.[13] In fact, the French government allocated 40 million francs as a subsidy to industry following the signing of the treaty. Out of this sizeable sum 9 million francs were devoted to metallurgy and 16 million francs to textiles.[14]

The spirit of the clauses in the treaties signed in Europe following the Cobden-Chevalier Treaty between France and Britain were apparently violated by 'administrative protection'.[15] According to Marshall the British response to protectionism in Europe was muted because her trading partners could turn elsewhere. In any case, the liberal treaties collapsed with the onset of economic depression in the late 1870s.[16] Thus, protectionism remained the norm in Europe, the USA and Japan despite the occasional contrary impulse.[17]

During the last quarter of the nineteenth century Britain encountered increasingly acute competition in export markets and the attractions of free trade diminished somewhat. Saul writes of the third quarter of the nineteenth century that

> one of the most important features of the new structure of multilateral trade was the growth of Britain's negative trade balance with countries such as Germany and the US, developing their manufacturing industries behind the shelter of high tariffs; at the same time there appeared more favourable balances within the empire and with other countries in the southern hemisphere, where tariff difficulties were much less formidable.[18]

Indeed, a third of Britain's deficit with Europe and the US was settled through India.[19]

The progress of industrialisation in Europe — in particular the rapid rise of Germany — and the USA intensified a debate in Britain about the merits of free trade — indeed such neo-mercantilist sentiments were never totally absent throughout the period of confluence between economic ascendancy and free trade policies. In the decade after 1903 Joseph Chamberlain called for imperial preference as a means of defending Britain's economic position but it did not become a reality until 1931.[20] However, Britain continued to attempt to maintain her position both through formal and informal empire, as it had done for much of the late nineteenth century.[21]

But, by the beginning of the twentieth century Britain had lost its lead as the dominant industrial nation.[22] It is the subsequent period which is of particular interest since this is the period which witnessed the 'cataclysmic' events which have been described as the culminant mode of change.[23] Relatively homogeneous data on trade are also available, allowing an assessment of changes in market shares to be made for the subsequent three-quarters of a century.

The remainder of the chapter is divided into two broad sections. The first briefly considers developments in international trade in manufactures until before the Second World War. The second section analyses similar changes in the post-war period until 1971 — when the homogeneous data series ends. However, some indication will be provided of conditions in the subsequent decade; these data are not comparable with the series beginning in 1899 and ending in 1971, although this series clearly highlights the dominant historical trend up to the 1980s.

A final section will offer more detailed consideration of the responses of declining countries in the post-Second World War period. Since such a long span of history is to be considered it is impossible to provide a comprehensive or systematic account of developments but the dominant thrust of events should become abundantly clear.

In this context it is important to clarify what is meant by the notion of decline. The decline of a country is the outcome of conflicts over markets whereby the relative share of that country in the world market is diminishing in some industry — in this case, in the group of strategic industries. This measure has been widely used by writers of differing persuasions to identify situations of conflict and rivalry between nations.[24] Nevertheless, it is necessary to answer the objection that a loss of relative market shares has no economic significance if production in the country concerned continues to grow in absolute terms; furthermore, such losses in relative shares are unavoidable as other countries industrialise. Indeed, Britain, which was considered the declining country in the post-1870s period, was experiencing growth in all the group of strategic industries despite the loss of relative shares in the world market.[25]

A relative loss of shares in the world market is significant under conditions of 'free trade' because it is invariably accompanied by competitive weakness. If a country's share of world trade is decreasing as a result of a loss in competitiveness, a decrease which is also likely to be reflected in domestic market penetration eventually, the process can become cumulative. Once a sector becomes uncompetitive in comparison to foreign producers there is no reason to suppose that the loss of shares in the world and home markets can be arrested in the normal course of events, even if growth in absolute terms continues for a time, with the country settling down to a lower but stable share of the market. Without exogenous intervention (e.g. from the State) the process is likely to become compelling, especially because the lower profits resulting from the initial losses in market shares will deter the new investment which might have restored the position.[26]

By contrast, successful countries with a rapidly growing market share and higher profits have the incentive to invest and innovate since demand for their product is more buoyant. In the process their competitive edge will widen, establishing a 'virtuous cycle' of larger market shares and higher profits, followed by investment and innovation leading to even larger market shares, etc.

Such an international competitive process under conditions of relatively 'free trade', assuming zero transport costs, is not dissimilar to the competition between firms within national economies, except that similarity of economic structures across countries entails competition on a whole range of goods between countries. Therefore, just as it is possible for weak firms within national economies to experience cumulative decline under free market conditions the same process of decline can occur internationally between countries under conditions of relatively 'free trade'.

From a political point of view, in terms of the response of the State towards international trade and other economic arrangements, the prevalence of the belief that the loss of relative market shares and consequent economic decline should be curbed makes it significant; such a belief is in fact widespread. This would be the case even if such a decline did not have economic significance. The principal underlying reason for the apparent belief that such a decline should be curbed can be deduced from the fact that more rapid growth of manufacturing production (in the group of strategic industries), which would accompany increasing market shares, has a military significance since it would be reflected in the enhanced productive capability of a war economy.

There is of course no inherent reason why firstcomer countries must inevitably decline with the appearance of latecomer countries. It might be possible to take appropriate corrective measures, for instance, by a particularly large and well-endowed country like the USA determined to maintain its position. Indeed since the beginning of the 1970s the USA has given every indication of reluctance to abandon its pre-eminence, and shown willingness to resort to 'unorthodox' measures. Of course, it is the size of the US economy which constitutes the basis for its potential resilience, a possibility precluded for Britain by virtue of its relative 'smallness'.[27]

5.2 The decline of Britain 1899-1937

The data show that during this period the first industrial nation, Britain, lost market shares in all industries belonging to the strategic group (excluding paper and paper products for which data is unavailable). Three distinctive phenomena are associated with the loss of relative market shares by Britain; firstly, the share of Britain's exports to industrialised areas decreased while the share of economically more backward regions, including countries in which she wielded political influence, increased; secondly, the First World War temporarily eliminated Germany, one of Britain's chief rivals, but aided other nations like the USA and to a lesser degree, Japan; thirdly, the world-wide cartelisation of nearly all types of production (i.e. including manufactures and raw materials) which had begun early in the twentieth century acquired further momentum in the 1930s owing to the economic depression.

Between 1899 and 1913 Britain's relative share of the world total in exports in five of the group of strategic industries declined.[28] The most significant decline occurred in transport equipment where a commanding position was nearly halved. Similar losses in market shares occurred in machinery, metals, chemicals, and to a certain degree in textiles and clothing (see Table 5.1).

The industrialisation of Europe and the USA also compelled the dominant imperial power to concentrate on markets in which it

Table 5.1   UK world trade shares in strategic industries (%)

	Machinery	Textiles/ Clothing	Chemicals	Transport	Metals
1899	37.6	46.5	23.3	60.0	36.1
1913	28.0	42.8	20.0	35.8	25.8
1929	16.9	34.4	16.1	15.0	16.8
1937	17.6	36.9	16.5	14.5	14.1
1950	25.0	33.0	18.8	38.4	16.7
1955	20.9	21.0	16.6	27.2	12.6
1963	16.1	13.3	13.7	19.8	11.2
1967	12.0	10.1	10.7	13.5	9.0
1971	11.9	9.0	9.4	10.1	8.1

Source: Based on Maizels (1963) *Industrial Growth and World Trade,* Cambridge, and
Batchelor *et al.* (1980) *Industrialisation and the Basis for Trade,* Cambridge.

held formal or informal sway, a feature already evident during the
third-quarter of the nineteenth century. In particular, the share of
exports of transport equipment, in which Britain remained the
dominant producer, to industrialised countries declined sharply
from 41.3 per cent to 32.5 per cent. The share of Continental Western Europe (CWE) only rose somewhat because industrialisation
had not reached a stage of sufficient maturity in all countries to
allow significant levels of output in transport equipment; the latter
industry is of course classified as a late industry, associated with a
mature stage of industrialisation (see Chapter 1). The relative share
of the Southern Dominions (SD) and India (I), where Britain's
political presence was prominent, and other semi-industrialised
countries (OSIC) rose sharply from 25.4 per cent to 42.9 per cent
(see Figure 5.1).

Between 1899 and 1913 a similar decline in relative world market
shares and increased reliance on markets in the SD, I, and OSIC
occurred for metals and machinery. Britain's relative share of the
world market for metals declined from 36.1 per cent to 25.8 per
cent; the proportion of British metal exports destined for industrialised countries fell from 50.4 per cent at the beginning of the
period to 33.9 per cent at the end; most of this loss is attributable to a
sharp fall in exports to CWE. By contrast, the SD, I, and OSIC
accounted for 43.9 per cent of British metal exports in 1913 as compared to 27.7 per cent in 1899 (see Figure 5.2).

Figure 5.1 Share (%) of each country subgroup in total UK exports (values) — Transport

KEY:

- - - = Continental Western Europe
——— = North America
—··— = Total Developed Countries (CWE + NA)
—·—· = Total Developing Countries (SD + I + OSIC)
········· = Rest of world

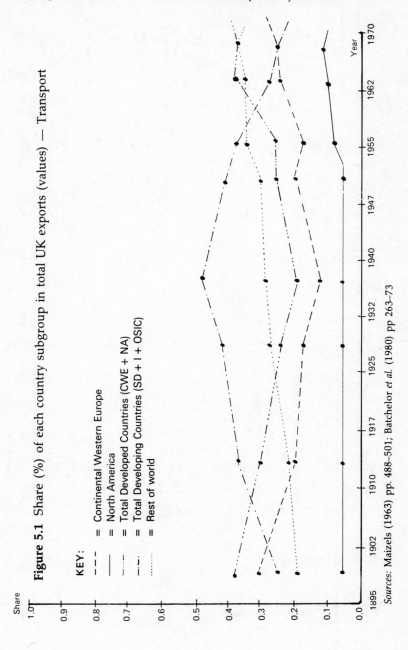

Sources: Maizels (1963) pp. 488–501; Batchelor *et al.* (1980) pp 263–73

Figure 5.2 Share (%) of each country subgroup in total UK exports (values) — Metals

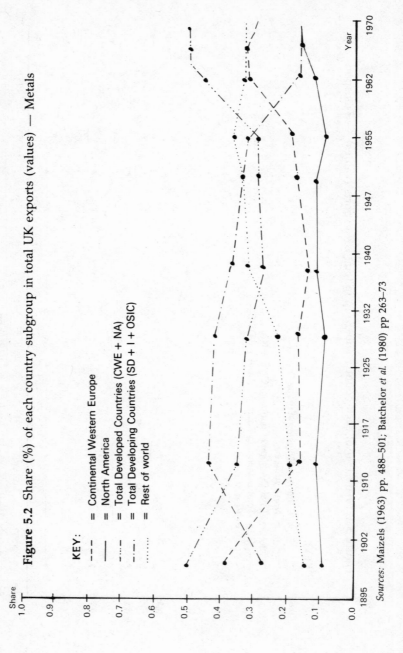

KEY:

- - -   = Continental Western Europe
———   = North America
— · · —   = Total Developed Countries (CWE + NA)
— · —   = Total Developing Countries (SD + I + OSIC)
· · · · ·   = Rest of world

Sources: Maizels (1963) pp. 488–501; Batchelor *et al.* (1980) pp 263–73

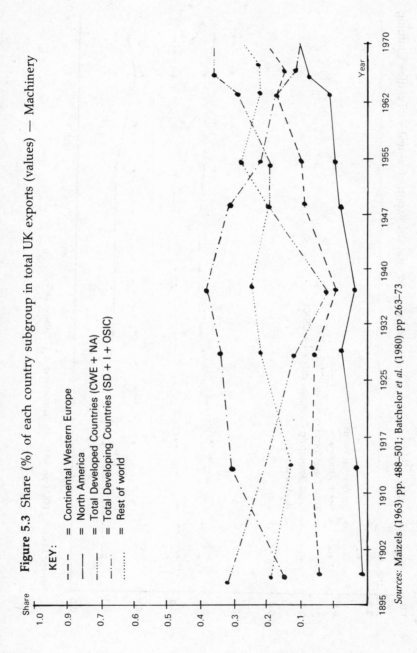

Figure 5.3 Share (%) of each country subgroup in total UK exports (values) — Machinery

KEY:

- - - = Continental Western Europe
——— = North America
········· = Total Developed Countries (CWE + NA)
—··—·· = Total Developing Countries (SD + I + OSIC)
········· = Rest of world

Sources: Maizels (1963) pp. 488–501; Batchelor et al. (1980) pp 263–73

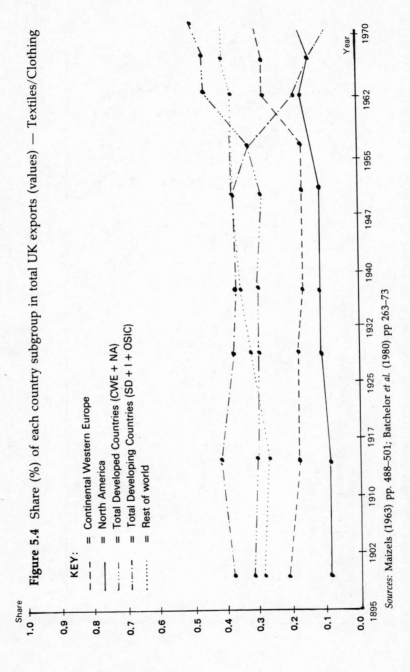

Figure 5.4 Share (%) of each country subgroup in total UK exports (values) — Textiles/Clothing

KEY:

- - - - = Continental Western Europe
———— = North America
-·-·-·- = Total Developed Countries (CWE + NA)
-··-··- = Total Developing Countries (SD + I + OSIC)
·········· = Rest of world

Sources: Maizels (1963) pp. 488–501; Batchelor *et al.* (1980) pp 263–73

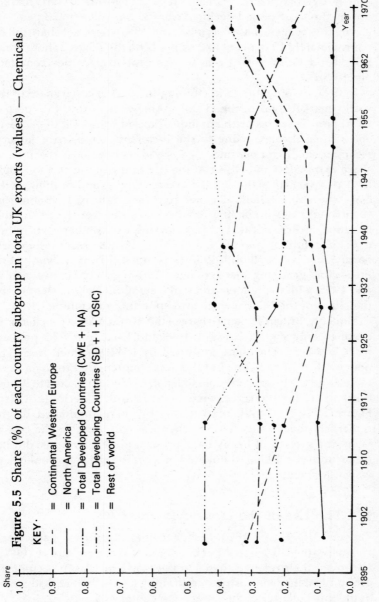

Figure 5.5 Share (%) of each country subgroup in total UK exports (values) — Chemicals

KEY:

- – – = Continental Western Europe
- ——— = North America
- –··– = Total Developed Countries (CWE + NA)
- –·–· = Total Developing Countries (SD + I + OSIC)
- ········ = Rest of world

Sources: Maizels (1963) pp. 488–501; Batchelor *et al.* (1980) pp 263–73

In the case of machinery Britain's relative share of the world market during the same period declined from 37.6 per cent to 28 per cent. Again, the steepest losses occurred in CWE, where the share fell by approximately 10 per cent to 20.5 per cent; the relative share of the SD, I, and OSIC rose from 26 per cent to 37.9 per cent (see Figure 5.3).

In the case of textiles and clothing Britain's relative share of the world market total declined only somewhat during this period, with some losses occurring in industrialised countries, the Far East and China; the latter due to the incipient incursion of Japan.[29] Again, a small compensatory gain was registered in the relative share of the SD, I and OSIC. At the beginning of the period Britain held 46.5 per cent of the world market in textiles and clothing; at the close she still retained 42.8 per cent (see Table 5.1). Somewhat surprisingly, despite falling relative world market shares the distribution of Britain's textile and clothing exports between industrialised countries, the SD, I, and OSIC, and the rest of the world hardly changed at all until 1955 (see Figure 5.4). However, within the second grouping sharp changes were registered between 1899 and 1955, with the relative share of I, and OSIC falling steeply and the share of the SD rising in corresponding magnitude.

Similarly, Britain's relative share of the world market for chemicals declined only slightly between 1899 and 1913, from 23.3 per cent to 20 per cent. The share imported by CWE declined from 31.3 per cent to 22.7 per cent, but this was compensated for by a rapid increase in the proportion sold to Japan (from 1.6 per cent to 9.2 per cent) and a slightly larger percentage to North America (NA) (see Figure 5.5). The CWE market was by then dominated by the remarkably successful German chemical industry.[30] In the case of Japan the growth of heavy industry, including chemicals, did not occur until the 1930s, stimulated, in part, by the requirements of war in Manchuria.[31]

5.3 The rise of the latecomer countries

Between 1899 and 1913 the latecomer countries, particularly Germany, the USA, and other countries of Western Europe (OWE) improved their relative shares in the world market in each of the group of strategic industries, continuing a trend which had begun in the third quarter of the nineteenth century (Tables 5.2, 5.3, 5.4). The competition not only affected Britain but undoubtedly

Table 5.2 German world trade shares in strategic industries (%)

	Machinery	Textiles/ Clothing	Chemicals	Transport	Metals
1899	23.6	16.2	27.0	8.6	19.0
1913	34.0	14.6	40.2	18.5	27.9
1929	26.0	7.3	27.5	8.1	24.3
1937	21.0	6.3	25.1	11.2	16.3
1950	7.9	2.5	9.7	5.1	11.3
1955	19.8	7.7	17.4	18.0	11.3
1963	20.9	10.7	22.0	22.9	17.8
1967	22.9	13.9	23.8	18.3	20.6
1971	20.6	18.1	22.3	18.4	17.8

Source: See Table 5.1

Table 5.3 US world trade shares in strategic industries (%)

	Machinery	Textiles/ Clothing	Chemicals	Transport	Metals
1899	25.0	2.5	17.1	15.2	23.2
1913	24.0	3.0	11.2	35.3	26.0
1929	29.7	4.8	16.7	54.5	23.8
1937	36.5	3.3	19.5	47.7	20.6
1950	42.0	11.0	38.4	34.8	18.3
1955	34.0	11.7	28.3	31.5	17.7
1963	28.5	9.3	25.5	23.0	12.2
1967	26.1	8.6	22.0	25.5	9.3
1971	20.8	5.6	19.0	20.8	7.3

Source: See Table 5.1.

provoked rivalry among the latecomer countries themselves.[32] This was the central reason for the world-wide cartelisation of industry which began at the start of the twentieth century. In view of the contemporary reluctance to recognise that 'free trade' has been an exceptional circumstance in the history of international economic relations it is worth quoting an impeccable authority at some length to illustrate the degree to which assumptions have been at variance with reality. According to Raymond Vernon

between 1900 and 1940, international cartel agreements were developed in practically every important processed metal, in most

Table 5.4 OWE* world trade shares in strategic industries (%)

	Machinery	Textiles/ Clothing	Chemicals	Transport	Metals
1899	8.3	12.8	13.5	6.7	11.3
1913	8.3	14.2	13.1	11.1	12.5
1929	17.3	16.0	15.5	12.4	17.1
1937	16.0	16.9	20.4	16.5	26.8
1950	15.0	21.2	17.9	9.6	22.1
1955	15.8	23.3	19.6	11.9	25.7
1963	20.2	35.2	22.6	16.4	26.3
1967	21.9	35.4	23.1	14.4	27.4
1971	23.4	36.1	26.4	13.8	26.5

* Other Western Europe

Source: See Table 5.1

important chemical products, in key pharmaceuticals, and in a variety of miscellaneous manufacturers running the alphabetical gamut from alkalis to zinc. The object of these agreements was generally the same as that of similar agreements in the raw-materials industries: to take the uncertainties out of the market. Practically all such agreements included some provision for the geographical division of markets among the participants. If the product was standardised and price-sensitive, as in the case of alkalis and steel, some arrangements were also made for the fixing of prices; if the product was technologically difficult, as in the case of advanced chemicals and machinery, there were measures to prevent any participant from stealing a technological march on the others. As a result of arrangements of this sort, US participants generally found their freedom of action curtailed in Europe, Africa, and the British Commonwealth; at the same time US firms usually gained some relief from competition in North America and Latin America.[33]

It was also during the early part of this period, before the outbreak of the First World War, that the debate on imperial preference divided political opinion in Britain. But the free traders continued to dominate government foreign economic policy, partly due to the backing of influential banking and financial interests. The war which economic rivalry encouraged constituted a watershed — the 'cataclysmic' mode of change described by Krasner.[34]

The First World War temporarily eliminated Germany as a serious economic competitor. Germany's share of world output of manufactured goods declined from 17 per cent in 1896/1900 to 12 per cent in 1926/29, and 11 per cent in 1936/38 (See Table 5.5). Her average annual rate of change in the volume of exports fell from 5.1 per cent in 1890/1913 to –2.5 per cent between 1913/50 (See Table 5.6). However, the war failed to arrest the inexorable decline of Britain as interested sections of domestic opinion had hoped. For example, the *Daily Telegraph* expressed the opinion of important industrial interests:

> This war provides our businessmen with such an opportunity as has never come their way before. . . . There is no reason why we should not permanently seize for this country a large proportion of Germany's export trade.[35]

Table 5.5 Shares of world output of manufactured goods (%)

	USA	Germany	UK	France	Japan
1870	23	13	32	10	—
1881-5	29	14	27	9	—
1896-1900	30	17	20	7	1
1906-10	35	15	15	6	1
1913	36	16	14	6	1
1926-9	42	12	9	7	3
1936-8*	32	11	9	5	3
1953	41	6**	6	3	2
1958	31	7	5	3	3
1963	28	6	4	2	4

* Sharp redistribution due to rapid growth of USSR economy
** Excluding GDR

Source: Glyn and Sutcliff (1972) *British Capitalism: Workers & the Profits Squeeze,* London, p. 17.

Unfortunately for Britain her share of world output of manufactured goods also declined from 20 per cent in 1896/1900 to 9 per cent in 1926/29 (see Table 5.5). Her average annual rate of change in the volume of exports was 2.1 per cent between 1890/1913, and stagnated at 0.2 per cent in 1913/50 (see Table 5.6). But it was Germany which suffered an actual loss in absolute terms.

The First World War aided other countries, in particular the USA, which raised its per capita manufactured production from $245 in

Table 5.6 Average annual percentage rate of change of volume
of exports

	1890-1913	1913-50	1950-60
Belgium	3.5	0.2	7.7
France	2.8	1.1	7.2
Germany	5.1	—2.5	15.8
Italy		1.4	11.8
Netherlands	4.6	1.2	10.0
United Kingdom	2.1	0.2	1.9
Western Europe	3.2	0.1	7.0
United States	3.8	2.3	5.0
Third World countries	3.5	1.8	6.4
World	3.5	1.3	6.4

Source: Maddison (1964) *Economic Growth in the West*, New York, p. 166.

1913 to $380 in 1929, at constant prices.[36] Her share of
world output of manufactured goods rose from 36 per cent in 1913 to
42 per cent in 1926/29 (see Table 5.5). At the same time the annual rate
of change in the volume of exports for the USA declined less, from
3.8 per cent in 1890/1913 to 2.3 per cent in 1913/50 (see Table 5.6).
Gains were also made by Japan and other countries outside Europe
unaffected by the war. According to Allen the economic historian of
Japan: 'In the early months of 1915 it became clear that the country
was on the threshold of a period of unexampled prosperity'.[37] This
situation was attributable to the inability of countries in Europe
involved in war to supply customers and their own additional war-
time requirements, e.g. for munitions and shipping services.

   In the immediate aftermath of the war there was a short-lived
boom beginning in the spring of 1919 both in western Europe and
the USA, while stocks were replenished and neglected maintenance
work revived. But by 1921 a severe depression was in progress in
Europe accompanied by protectionist trends.[38] Britain had passed
the McKenna Act in 1915 during the war to protect motor vehicle
and motor cycle production, and some other manufactures. In 1921
Britain introduced the Safeguarding of Industries Act and the
Dyestuffs Importation Act to protect the home market. The USA
passed the Fordney-McCumber Act in 1922 to protect domestic

producers, paradoxically, despite the relatively stronger position of the US economy.[39]

Another more sustained recovery occurred between 1925-29 but neither Britain nor Germany were able to regain their pre-war shares in the world market in the group of strategic industries. Indeed, Germany's relative share in each of the group of strategic industries remained significantly lower in 1929 compared to 1913; for example, her relative share of the world market for machinery fell from 18.5 per cent to 5.5 per cent over the period (see Table 5.2). The decline of Britain's relative shares also continued but at a slower pace: from 28 per cent to 16.9 per cent in machinery, for example (see Table 5.1). A similar picture is apparent in every sector for both countries. By contrast the USA and OWE increased their relative shares in every industry of the strategic group (see Tables 5.3 and 5.4). Thus the First World War resulted in economic and political setback for one of Britain's chief rivals, Germany, but failed to arrest the climb of others.

The history of the subsequent demise of the relatively open international economic order is too well known to require recounting here, except to summarise the crucial events which signalled its collapse.[40] The Hawley-Smoot Act passed in June 1930 by the USA and the imposition of Imperial Preference by Britain in 1931, which followed in its trail, constituted turning points for the open international economic system[41] And finally, the Import Duties Act passed in 1932 raised Britain's import tariffs to 33½ per cent on some manufactures.[42] This particular measure also symbolised the ending of almost three quarters of a century of 'free trade'.

In conjunction with protectionism, the world-wide cartelisation of manufacturing (and other) industry, which had begun early in the twentieth century, proceeded rapidly. Between the late 1920s and the 1930s a whole range of sectors including steel, chemicals and railway equipment were cartelised.[43] The critical problem as Ashworth has described it was surplus productive capacity, the outcome of 'expansion to meet temporary war-time needs, the spread of industrialization to new areas, and the failure of demand for some major items to expand as rapidly, as before. . . .'[44] This was a problem not overcome until the outbreak of the Second World War, until mid 1942 in the case of Germany, despite over two years of war[45] This problem in industrialised countries lends credence to the view expressed by Oskar Lange, among others, in another context, that such industrialised capitalist countries cannot benefit, in the long run, from the industrialisation of undeveloped areas — i.e.the Third World — since it would destroy their markets.[46]

5.4 War and economic rivalry

At this juncture it might be appropriate to address an issue which has been the source of considerable controversy: did economic rivalry, of which trade conflict is the principal manifestation, pre-cipitate the two major wars during the first half of the twentieth century?

It may be argued that the economic instability associated with the competition between firstcomer(s) and latecomer(s) undermined the conditions on which peace in Europe had rested during the cen-tury before the First World War. The collapse of 'co-existence' bet-ween the capitalist countries, particularly in Europe, which began in the late nineteenth century has been attributed by Lenin to the phenomenon of uneven development.[47] This uneven development of the individual elements of the world capitalist economy could be measured in terms of four indicators: GNP, per capita income, share of world trade and share of foreign investment. In all these indices the relative weakening of Britain's position towards the end of the nineteenth and early twentieth centuries is clearly apparent.

This development occurred because the latecomer(s) had certain advantages denied to an established economy like Britain. The for-mer were able to introduce advanced equipment and implement efficient location and lay-out of their plants. They sought and received bank participation, with the encouragement of the State, a feature notably absent in Britain. Bank participation enabled more rapid expansion because of the larger volume of available funds. On a subjective level, the latecomer(s) were compelled to compete more vigorously to enter established markets, having fewer reserves to cushion the initial delay. By contrast, Britain had the disadvan-tage of obsolescent equipment both in industry and infrastructure. The existence of older technologies limited the scope for applying new ones. As Kemp has put it,

> though it might be perfectly correct from an accounting point of view not to introduce certain technical improvements, in the long-run this might leave a whole industry with an unmanage-able proportion of old and obsolete machinery facing a well-equipped and technically progressive rival.[48]

In addition, an established Labour movement resisted changes in production methods which might have undermined its position. More intangibly, Britain had the difficulty of changing long-established habits in response to altering circumstances.

Why does the process of uneven development create a situation of potential conflict? Intuitively, it may be explained that the centre of gravity of the system shifts and a new equilibrium becomes necessary. In fact, several authors have reached a similar conclusion from different perspectives. Rosecrance concludes that '. . . it will be difficult to regulate a system which is equalitarian in one dimension and stratified in another. In particular, disproportions between influence and access to resources are likely to produce demands that cannot be moderated'.[49] The 'rank-disequilibrium' hypothesis of Galtung is similar to Rosecrance's 'influence-access discrepancy' theory. However, it should be pointed out that such systemic theories do not distinguish between types of internal arrangements within states; for example, Galtung predicts that the 'rank-disequilibrium' of China will cause instability in the future.[50]

Nevertheless, it may be argued that international economic relations comprise an important sub-system within the international system and any new equilibrium must also reflect a new balance of international economic relations. This is the starting point of Lenin's theory of rivalry between capitalist nations as a consequence of uneven development. He approvingly quotes the historian J.E. Driault, '. . . the relative power of the empires founded in the nineteenth century is totally out of proportion to the place occupied in Europe by the nations which founded them'.[51] As a consequence, according to the Leninist conception, a new equilibrium must emerge although it may not reflect a one-to-one correspondence of relative economic strength, since the equilibrium is conditioned by other contingent factors like geography, leadership, etc. However, the new equilibrium cannot be radically at variance with relative economic strength. In other words, the rise of the latecomers will result in a re-allocation of what Rosecrance describes as access to resources, including, and in particular, markets to reflect altered national economic power.

In the event, the two world wars fulfilled this objective function for the international system by re-ordering the economic bases which underpinned the balance of power. The defeat of Germany and the decline of Britain confirmed the ascendancy of the USA, at least temporarily; the defeat suffered by Japan also removed another contender. In addition, the rise of the Soviet system served to reconcile the former enemies. The presence of the Soviet system has continued to act as a powerful stimulus in preventing serious disputes between the former competitors despite the increasing divergence of interests, including acute economic rivalry.

5.5 The ascendancy of the USA and respite for the UK

At the end of the Second World War the balance of power among the capitalist powers had been altered decisively, with the US emerging as the leader. However, in terms of relative shares of the world market in each of the group of strategic industries the outcome was more ambiguous at the outset.

Between 1937 and 1950, the next year for which figures are available, the already dominant US improved its relative share of the world market in machinery, textiles and clothing (more than trebling its relative share from 3.3 per cent to 11 per cent), and chemicals. However, over this period its relative share of world exports of transport equipment and metals declined from 47.7 per cent to 34.8 per cent and 20.6 per cent to 18.3 per cent, respectively (see Table 5.3). Much of the loss of shares in this period occurred in CWE and the SD in the case of transport equipment, and the UK, CWE and to a lesser degree the SD in the case of metals. It should be borne in mind that during the decade and a half following the Second World War liberal trading arrangements did not prevail and import restrictions and non-convertibility of currencies was widespread, as a means of coping with postwar dislocation. Indeed, many European countries were specifically discriminatory against US exports, partly because of their inability to generate enough dollar earnings with which to pay for them.[52] The US chose rapid European reconstruction and political amity because of what it perceived to be the greater immediate threat of the Soviet Union.

The UK made distinct gains in every sector with the exception of textiles and clothing between 1937 and 1950. The relative share of the world market for transport equipment rose steeply from 14.5 per cent to 38.4 per cent; in machinery the relative share rose sharply from 17.6 per cent to 25 per cent (see Table 5.1). Most of the gains were made in CWE markets in which the relatively unscathed British economy enjoyed advantages denied to the US owing to discriminatory practices.[53]

By contrast, the relative shares of the devastated German and Japanese economies, not surprisingly, slumped. In the case of Germany there was a significant decline in the relative share of world exports of chemicals, from 25 per cent in 1937 to 9.7 per cent in 1950 (see Table 5.2).

In the case of Japan the sharpest decrease occurred in its relative share of world exports of textiles and clothing, from 21.8 per cent to 8 per cent between 1937 and 1950 (Table 5.7).

Table 5.7 Japanese world trade shares in strategic
industries (%)

	Machinery	Textiles/ Clothing	Chemicals	Transport	Metals
1899	0.00	2.5	0.01	0.000	2.1
1913	1.0	4.3	0.01	0.003	1.7
1929	0.5	9.7	2.2	0.004	0.1
1937	0.9	21.8	4.0	3.5	3.3
1950	0.5	8.0	0.2	1.4	5.9
1955	1.6	15.1	2.4	2.4	15.9
1963	6.8	16.3	5.4	5.9	10.5
1967	8.2	20.1	6.5	10.0	12.6
1971	13.9	19.7	9.2	15.7	21.6

Source: See Table 5.1.

5.6 The decline of Britain and the USA

In the twenty years after 1950, the two major countries which suffered a decline in relative shares in the world market for strategic industry exports were Britain and the USA.

Britain's relative share declined in every sector between 1950 and 1971. In machinery it fell from 25 per cent to 11.9 per cent, in textiles and clothing from 33 per cent to 9 per cent. The most significant reduction occurred in transport equipment in which the share dwindled to 10.1 per cent from 38.4 per cent (see Table 5.1).

The US also lost its commanding position, with its share in each group declining: from 42 per cent to 20.8 per cent in machinery, for instance, and 34.8 per cent to 20.8 per cent in transport equipment and 18.3 per cent to 7.3 per cent in metals; losses were also registered in other sectors. It should be noted that the US increased its relative share of the world market for transport equipment temporarily, between 1963 and 1967 (see Table 5.3). This increase was entirely due to the free trade in automotive parts agreed between the US and Canada at Ottawa in 1965.[54]

The relative shares of Britain and the USA in the group of strategic industries are negatively correlated with the growth of German and Japanese exports. Both Germany and Japan improved their relative shares in each of these industries, as did OWE countries.

Germany improved its relative share in machinery from 7.9 per cent in 1950 to 20.6 per cent in 1971; in textiles and clothing from 2.5 per cent to 18.1 per cent, in transport equipment from 5.1 per cent to 18.4 per cent etc. (see Tables 5.2). Similar though less spectacular improvements in relative shares were registered in each industry by OWE countries; for instance, in textile and clothing, in which the sharpest rise was recorded, OWE countries' relative share was 36.4 per cent in 1971 as compared to 21.2 per cent in 1950 (see Table 5.4).

Japan also increased its relative share in each industry between 1950 and 1971. For example, from 0.5 per cent in machinery to 13.9 per cent, and from 1.4 per cent in transport equipment to 15.7 per cent; similar changes were recorded in other industries (see Table 5.7).

British losses were incurred in part because of German competition in non-industrial markets (categorised as 'rest of the world') and the SD during the 1950s. Britain had also become more dependent on semi-industrial markets since the outset of the twentieth century because of industrialisation in Europe, and import-substitution policies in semi-industrial markets subsequently had a significant impact on British exports.[55] Britain also suffered losses in relative shares because of the US, and increasingly, Japan.[56]

A significant proportion of the US loss of relative shares in manufactured exports and the penetration of its domestic market was due to Japan. Between 1963 and 1971 almost half the US loss of relative shares in third markets was attributable to competition from Japan; severe competition was experienced by the US in iron and steel and electrical machinery in the initial period, extending to a whole range of products in the 1970s.[57] Japan's relative share improved in virtually every market but it was spectacular with respect to NA; for instance, the value of exports of transport equipment rose from $59 million in 1950 to approximately $1.2 billion in 1971, in constant prices, with the US taking 38.3 per cent of Japan's exports in this category, as compared to 7.7 per cent in 1950. In 1971 the US also took half of Japan's exports of machinery. Despite measures to curb the onslaught of Japanese exports to the US, between 1976 and 1980 its manufactured exports to the US rose from $13.4 billion to $30.6 billion (in current prices).[58]

In fact, the growth of Japan's exports in manufactured products inflicted losses on other countries as well. Japan secured 54 per cent of the total shift in market shares, comprising both established and new trade between 1963 and 1967.[59] And between 1967 and 1971 Japan gained 90 per cent of the $7.3 billion shift in market shares. An overwhelming percentage of this gain was in transport equipment, machinery, and to a lesser degree in intermediate metals and chemicals.[60] The rapid growth of intra-EEC trade (from a quarter to a third of world trade in manufactures between 1959 to 1977) enabled its members to maintain their relative share of the world market since non-members were at a disadvantage in the EEC market.[61]

5.7 Trends in market shares in manufactured exports after 1971

For the period after 1971 comparable data are unavailable owing to changes in product classification. Data for manufacturing as a whole (of which the group of strategic industries comprise a major part), however, indicate an unmistakable trend. The relative shares of the UK and the USA declined further. The relative share of the UK in world exports of manufactures fell from 10.8 per cent to 9.3 per cent and that of the US from 18.5 per cent to 15.9 per cent between 1970 and 1977.[62]

Germany's relative share of the world market in each of the group of strategic industries had peaked in 1967. Indeed, a modest decline had occurred in all categories, except textiles and clothing in 1971 (see Table 5.2). However, the figures for 1971 do not reflect the long-term trend for Germany accurately since the devaluation of the dollar in late 1971 undermined her export performance temporarily.[63] Germany's relative share of world exports of manufactures appears to have stabilised in 1960, and only showed a marginal increase by 1977 to 20.8 per cent from 19.3 per cent at the earlier date.[64] In part this was also attributable to Japanese competition, particularly in NA.

The competitive strength of Japan in manufactured products is highlighted by the rate of growth of productivity between 1967 and 1971.[65]During this period Japan managed to improve her relative share of the world market in each of the group of strategic industries despite the US devaluation because productivity gains more than compensated for the rise in prices (see Table 5.7). By 1977 Japan's relative share of world exports of manufactures had risen to 15.4 per cent, as compared to 11.7 per cent in 1970.

Finally, another indication of the weakening position of the UK and the USA is the rise of manufactured imports in relation to GNP (see Table 5.8). While it is apparent that the ratio of the volume of manufactured imports to GNP has also increased for EEC countries, in the case of the UK and the USA it has occurred in the context of declining world market shares. The EEC countries, by contrast, have increased their already substantial share of world exports of manufactures.[66] It should also be noted that the formation of the Common Market inevitably increased the ratio of

Table 5.8 Ratio of volume of manufactured imports to GNP

	1961	1969	1978
UK	4.6	8.0	14.2
Rest of EEC	6.1	10.1	15.8
USA	1.5	3.4	4.5
Japan	1.8	2.2	2.4

Source: DAE (1979) *Economic Policy Review*, Cambridge, No. 5, p. 5.

volume of manufactured imports of GNP for member countries because of the impetus it administered to intra-EEC trade. In fact Britain was a member of EFTA but trade among EFTA countries grew much more slowly and cannot account for the rapid increase in import penetration for Britain.[67] In addition, import penetration continued to increase for Britain despite a fall in GDP between 1973 and 1975.[68]

A useful comparison can be made between Germany and the UK to underline the extent to which the latter has suffered import penetration in particular industries of the strategic group. It should be reiterated that in the case of Germany it occurred in the context of a relatively high and stable share of the world market for manufactures. Indeed, in 1977 Germany remained the largest single exporter of manufactured products in the world.

In terms of the ratio of imports to gross output in the particular industry, as opposed to manufactured imports and GNP (i.e. a larger denominator) which would understate the magnitude of import penetration, a number of spectacular changes occurred for Britain. For example, in transport equipment the ratio rose from 7.8 per cent in 1970 to 34 per cent in 1978; similarly, in electrical machinery it increased from 9.6 per cent to 20 per cent. By comparison Germany appeared to have suffered a significant setback only in one industry: the ratio of textile imports to gross output rose from 27 per cent to 44 per cent over the same period (see Table 5.9). However, the rise in textile imports was primarily due to subcontracting (i.e. imports by German TNCs from their foreign subsidiaries), a conscious policy to maintain world market shares; an aim which succeeded (see Table 5.2).[69]

Table 5.9 Ratio of imports to gross output

| | Germany | | UK | |
	1970	1978	1970	1978
Textiles	27.0	44.0	12.7	27.9
Clothing/footwear	13.4	37.3	9.7	24.6
Paper	22.1	25.6	30.6	32.0
Printing	2.0	4.2	3.1	3.9
Chemicals	11.2	14.0	13.1	18.4
Basic metals	17.0	15.3	18.9	21.4
Metal products	8.2	12.8	6.0	12.3
Non-elect. mach.	11.4	12.6	17.0	25.9
Elect. mach.	8.1	12.0	9.0	20.0
Transp. equipment	10.1	14.1	7.8	34.0
Manufact. n.e.s.	26.4	32.3	19.6	40.1

Source: UN (1981) *Economic Survey of Europe in 1980*, New York, p. 235.

5.8 The role of developing market economies in international trade in manufactures

The role of developing market economies has been excluded because only competition among the major exporting countries and one region (i.e. OWE) has been taken into consideration. Manufacturing exports of the latter account for an overwhelming proportion of the international market for such traded goods, other than the trade of centrally planned economies. The share of developing market economies in the export of manufactures is not of major significance, although growth rates have been impressive, rising from 12 per cent per annum between 1963-7 to 20 per cent per annum between 1973-6.[70]

Table 5.10 OECD imports from LDCs, including NICs, as a percentage of total OECD imports

Industries and SITC code	Year	1 & 5 Total	1 All NICs	2 OECD NICs	3 Brazil Mexico	4 Far Eastern NICs	5 Other LDCs
Clothing (84)	1977	46.7	38.5	4.6	1.3	29.9	8.2
	1963	20.3	17.3	1.2	0.0	15.3	3.0
Electrical machinery (72)	1977	14.0	12.0	1.0	2.2	8.4	2.0
	1963	1.3	0.8	0.2	0.0	0.5	0.5
Misc. fin. mfg. (81, 82, 86, 89)	1977	12.6	11.2	1.3	0.7	8.7	1.4
	1963	5.0	4.2	0.7	0.2	2.7	0.8
Textiles (85)	1977	19.4	10.8	3.4	1.7	5.8	8.6
	1963	16.1	5.7	2.4	0.7	2.1	11.4
Metal mfg. (69)	1977	8.3	7.4	2.0	0.7	4.3	0.9
	1963	1.9	1.5	0.5	0.1	0.6	0.4
Iron & steel (67)	1977	6.5	4.8	2.4	1.0	1.0	1.7
	1963	2.1	1.3	0.5	0.4	0.0	0.8
Transport (73)	1977	3.2	2.8	1.7	0.4	0.5	0.4
	1963	1.8	1.0	0.5	0.0	0.1	0.8
Non-elec. machinery (71)	1977	3.2	2.8	1.0	0.8	0.8	0.4
	1963	0.6	0.3	0.2	0.0	0.0	0.3
Chemicals (5)	1977	7.5	2.5	1.1	0.6	0.6	3.2
	1963	5.6	2.1	0.9	0.8	0.2	3.5
Paper (64)	1977	2.3	2.2	1.0	0.5	0.5	0.1
	1963	0.6	0.3	0.1	0.0	0.0	0.3

Source: OECD (1978) *The Impact of Newly-Industrialising Countries on the Pattern of World Trade and Production in Manufactures*, Dept. of Economics & Statistics, Paris, p. 24.

Firstly, the share of this group of countries in world exports of manufactures was 7.6 per cent in 1975–6, growing from 6 per cent in 1970-1. However, it is to be recognised that around 30 per cent of the growth was concentrated in textiles and clothing.[71]

Secondly, although the share of developing market economies in the textile and clothing imports of OECD countries is high (19.4 per cent and 46.7 per cent, respectively, in 1977, it was still small in relation to domestic consumption. For instance, in 1974 it was only 2 per cent in France, 4 per cent in the USA and Japan, 5 per cent in Canada, 6 per cent in the UK and 8 per cent in Germany for both textiles and clothing.[72] Thus the 'miracle' of LDC textile and clothing exports seems to have been exaggerated.

Thirdly, as Table 5.10 indicates, their share in OECD imports is relatively small in the group of strategic industries. The comparatively larger share in electrical machinery (12 per cent) and manufactures of metal (7.4 per cent) is primarily due to subcontracting by TNCs. Nevertheless, the competitive threat does not emanate for LDCs; in 1971 imports of manufactures from developing countries only constituted 0.9 per cent of the US domestic market.[73]

5.9 The response of the State to losses in market shares

Below the responses of the State in the UK and the USA to the decline in market shares in the group of strategic industries will be considered in some detail. Before proceeding to this analysis some general remarks on State intervention and examples from other countries will be discussed to illustrate some points which are apposite.

At the outset it should be made clear that the aim of the State to preserve the group of strategic industries is not automatically translated into policy measures and implemented. Such aims may be viewed as common national interests but they are not overriding like the goal of defending territorial integrity in the face of physical threat. Unlike territorial defence, preserving the strategic industries provides the conditions for such defence, but lacks the immediate necessity which would raise it above significant domestic controversy. Thus, in common with other national interests which lack the urgency of immediate necessity, it is inevitably subject to differences of perception and opinion. It is therefore to be expected that although, over the long-run, the State will pursue relative economic self-sufficiency by preserving the industries of the strategic group, (1) the ability to pursue policies for its attainment in the short-run, and (2) the choice of instruments, will be affected by the cross-pressure of domestic politics. However, while the general thrust of State policy is in the direction of maintaining these industries, conflicts will habitually arise with its international obligations, i.e. commitment to the liberal international economic order and its key component, 'free trade', in the present context.

Evidence of the influence of domestic politics and interest groups on goals and the choice of instruments does not need to be cited extensively since its presence is not a matter of dispute. One significant example should suffice to illustrate its impact. Radical observers like Ernst Mandel who had predicted intensifying trade wars during the 1970s subsequently recognised that protectionism remained 'modest'.[74] In fact, the inference is not entirely correct since Mandel seems to be referring only to certain categories of protectionist measures like tariffs and not others (e.g. subsidy). The apparent quiescence of 'offensive' protectionist measures is primarily due to the influence of transnational corporations (TNCs). As it will be argued in the next chapter TNCs are opposed to such measures because it would disrupt their international production. Another important reason is undoubtedly the need to maintain western political unity in the presence of a powerful opposing group, i.e. the Warsaw Pact countries. However, while western governments have generally refrained from precipitating open trade warfare by indiscriminate resort to 'offensive measures' they have, as will be shown below, taken other measures to achieve the aim of protecting strategic industry, for example, through subsidy policies.

A second eventuality which should be recognised is that errors of policy-making which may have longer-term consequences can be observed periodically, usually with the benefit of hindsight. For example, in the late nineteenth century the French State, which was attempting to promote ship-building, mistakenly gave larger subsidies for the construction of sailing ships instead of the more modern steam ship, the vessels of the future, consequently failing to achieve the objective of creating a modern maritime force. Such errors are not uncommon and could be due, in part, to divergent perceptions and interests.

Finally, it should be borne in mind that efforts by the State to prevent the decline of industries of the stragegic group may fail because of factors beyond its control. However, the failure to defend these industries successfully should not be taken to indicate greater commitment to the liberal international economic order. Such failures may nevertheless be accompanied by vigorous and contentious efforts to prevent decline, efforts which still undermine the liberal international economic order. Indeed, Britain appears to have failed to arrest its decline since the late nineteenth century despite vigorous efforts, which included the attempt to eliminate Germany as an economic rival. This outcome can be attributed to the rise of the irresistibly powerful USA, and the re-emergence of other rivals like Germany and Japan as successful competitors on the international market and with a larger domestic manufacturing base, despite earlier setbacks.

5.10 The response of the State to competitive threat toward industries of the strategic group

The discussion below concentrates on the response of the State in the UK and the USA to the decline in market shares in the group of strategic industries. The UK and the USA are the two countries which have suffered continuing losses in each of these industries (see Table 5.1 and 5.3). However, as it has been noted above, competition for markets has also occurred between other countries and it will be illuminating to survey briefly responses of the State in these countries in order to situate the reaction of the State in the UK and the USA in a wider context.

The forms of State intervention are numerous (see Chapter 2). In the postwar period certain forms of intervention have assumed importance: outright nationalisation or public participation in threatened strategic industries, subsidies (both direct and indirect).[75] Other forms of intervention include preferential public procurement, tied aid, sponsorship of rationalisation programmes (through mergers, etc.), and finally, some form of control over imports (voluntary restraints, quotas etc.).

The forms of intervention identified above, as distinct from tariff barriers, seem to be predicated on the need to maintain at least an outward commitment to the liberal international economic order;[76] significantly, voluntary restraint is not an unilateral act but an agreement. In countries experiencing serious competitive threats the scale of the support required also compels the State to intervene directly. In addition, as it will be argued at length in the next chapter, it has been difficult to resort to tariff protection because of opposition from transnational corporations (TNCs) whose international production and trade would be adversely affected.

The form which State intervention takes also depends on contingent domestic political factors. For instance, domestic political constraints, both ideological and interest-group, may impede outright public ownership as a method of reversing the decline in an industry. However, it would seem that in dire circumstances the State does not flinch from adopting nationalisation as a solution, other imperatives notwithstanding. Indeed, even if nationalisation has occurred for ideological reasons, subsequent divestment of public ownership (e.g. Britain's steel industry during the 1950s and '60s) is perceived as a means of enhancing the performance of the industry rather than as a prelude to ending public losses regardless of the survival of the industry concerned. The controversy over the nationalisation of Britain's steel industry ceased as soon as it became apparent that it would not survive in private ownership; successive British governments subsequently provided huge financial subsidies irrespective of political preferences. Similarly, the present Conservative Government continues to underwrite the losses of the national car manufacturer, British Leyland, despite its apparent distaste for public participation. Thus, while political parties of different persuasions may have disagreements about the choice of instruments in defending national industries, the necessity of preventing collapse remains pre-eminent, regardless of the economic costs involved.

The brief summary here is intended to convey an impression of the various methods used by the State in western Europe and Japan to support strategic industries. One conclusion to emerge is that the State has intervened to support these industries in an effort to sponsor what Vernon terms 'national champions'.[77] The consensus of opinion vindicates the hypothesis that considerations of economic and military need have been prominent. However, it is also clear that industries and sectors which are not strategic have been provided assistance, e.g. leather goods, toys, etc. — if not to the same degree. It is obvious that the State in developed market economies is prepared to confront political allies and major economic partners if the strategic industries are threatened but it also does not hesitate to shelter other industries as well if the competitors are developing countries which have few options other than grudging acquiescence. The history of international trade in textiles and clothing, detailed below, underlines the ability of developed countries to dictate 'agreements' to developing countries without fear of retaliation. Despite modest levels of import penetration in textiles and clothing, developing countries have encountered the most persistent protectionism in the markets of developed countries. The situation is not very different if the State accedes to demands from leather and toy manufacturers for import relief, especially if employment considerations are also involved.

One observer has commented that very little of the contemporary protectionism of western economies has been directed against other OECD members, with the exception of Japan.[78] However, this presumption is not entirely accurate. It should be recognised that protectionist measures like subsidies, preferential public procurement, etc., which have become important affect all competitor countries; both these measures were the subject of negotiations at the Tokyo Round.[79] Of course members of the EEC can only resort to such measures to defend their industries from competitive threats within the European Community, since the absence of border impediments between themselves defines membership. But the formation of the EEC would not have been possible if membership had entailed the liquidation of national industries.[80]

Thus, while it is true that protectionist measures like 'voluntary' export restraints and quotas have been extracted almost exclusively from developing countries and Japan, disputes have increasingly arisen between the EEC and the USA as well.[81] In the case of Japan the hostility is not new as the controversy over Japan's membership of GATT during the initial stages confirms.[82]

Direct public ownership delineates one end of the spectrum of State intervention and constitutes a virtual guarantee of survival. This form of intervention is likeliest to occur in circumstances where the strategic industries and their sub-sectors encounter a serious threat to their survival. Of course, public ownership does not preclude other forms of State assistance as well. For example, nationalised industries also enjoy the protection of 'voluntary' export restraints.

Since the end of the Second World War State ownership of strategic manufacturing (and non-manufacturing, e.g. energy) industry, as the preferred form of intervention, has become common. Thus, most western European countries, including the major powers, have taken some of the strategic industries into public ownership.

The Federal Republic of Germany (FRG) has been one of the competitive countries and its major industries have not encountered serious threats to their viability.[83] Nevertheless, the State has acquired interests in iron and steel, the metal industry, transport (motor vehicles, and ship-building), and sub-sectors of the chemical industry. In 1974, the Federal Government could also influence 579 companies through 12 directly controlled companies because the latter held at least 25 per cent of the capital in the former.[84]

In France,

> first and foremost among the methods used to intervene in the economy is that of direct participation in the ownership of industrial and commercial companies . . . ranging from full-scale nationalisation to quite small holdings in a very large number of companies.[85]

Among the interests of the State are munitions, aircraft, motor vehicles and chemicals. The State has majority ownership in 500 industrial and commercial companies and minority holdings in a further 600; the State also owns 32 insurance companies and 4 deposit banks, which provide additional leverage through the provision of funds to industry.[86]

The degree of public ownership is considerable in other western European countries, e.g. Italy, Austria, Sweden but they are not important contenders for regional or global political prominence.[87]

In the case of Japan public ownership has not been a significant method of intervention since major Japanese industries have not faced the magnitude of problems which have led to widespread public ownership in other free enterprise economies like Britain. The State in Japan, however, owns the utilities (including transport, aircraft and communications) and the banks. The latter are of course important instruments for State intervention in the private sector.[88]

The State in western Europe and Japan has also intervened with a combination of other measures, short of outright ownership or limited participation. Such measures include direct and indirect subsidies (including regional aid and employment subsidy), preferential public procurement, various export promotion schemes like loans, tax concessions, tied aid, etc. In addition most governments are responsible for a substantial part of the national R & D effort and sponsor rationalisation programmes like mergers; the

State has also adopted an increasingly aggressive posture at international trade negotiations in recent years, e.g. actually reducing the export quota of developing countries in textiles and clothing.[89]

The strategic industries directly affected in all countries are steel, transportation equipment, plus of course, textiles and clothing. The demand for machinery is derivative and benefits from the injection of funds in other industries although some sub-sectors have also received direct aid (computers and electronics); chemicals are now facing growing competitive threats from east European and Third World producers and intervention is becoming common.[90]

It would be instructive to conclude with an examination of international trade policies of developed market economies towards the textile and clothing sector to illustrate future prospects for adjustment. As Keesing and Wolf argue in their thorough appraisal, the fortunes of international trade in this sector are a pointer towards the future of international trade in other sectors, as new entrants industrialise and acquire production capabilities in a wider range of products.[91]

The developed market economies responded to the shift in comparative advantage in textiles and clothing, particularly the latter which is more labour-intensive, by introducing the Long Term Agreement in Cotton Textiles (LTA) in 1962. This was preceded by 'voluntary' restraints by Japan in 1957. The US had failed to get similar agreements with Hong Kong and this increased the desire for a long-term global solution although Britain had already negotiated 'voluntary' restraints with Hong Kong (1959) and India (1960). The LTA initiative was crucial in winning the support of the textile and clothing industry for the US Trade Expansion Act of 1962. Thus textiles and clothing were excluded from the Kennedy Round of multilateral trade negotiations of 1963-7.

The rapid growth of exports of man-made fibre textiles from Japan and clothing from east Asian countries prompted the US to negotiate separate bilateral quotas setting limits to their exports to the US. Subsequently, the Multi-Fibre Agreement was negotiated with developing countries at the insistence of the US, as with the LTA in 1962, and came into effect in January 1974.[92]

Since then the conditions of the MFA have been made more restrictive because of pressure from the EEC; this was partly due to the recession which began early in 1974. The main objective, to lower exports from developing countries below the 6 per cent growth per annum agreed in the MFA, without having to provide proof of market disruption, was achieved. The new more restrictive MFA was thus agreed in December 1977 and renewed until 1981; the most recent re-negotiation of the MFA reduced the growth of exports from developing countries even further, to 1 per cent growth per annum.[93]

The significant feature of the LTA and the MFA was that they were not an attempt to impose orderly adjustment but to prevent the shift of these industries to other locations which might enjoy a comparative advantage. Indeed, this response of the State in firstcomer countries is in conformance with the behaviour predicted by the interpretation of this book: textiles and clothing are a strategic sector which countries will not abandon.

In this context, the argument put forward by Keesing and Wolf that if national security is the goal in protecting this sector it could be achieved by stockpiling, does not confront the issue fully.[94] Textiles and clothing are strategic not merely because they constitute an essential final product which can be stockpiled but because, like the other strategic industries, they provide intermediate inputs for other parts of the economy. The textile and clothing sector is also a source of external economies for other industries and therefore their long-run competitive strength.[95] Keesing and Wolf also contend that since most developed countries import raw cotton it is pointless to maintain capacity in textile and clothing for national security reasons. Firstly, petroleum is also imported by many countries but that would hardly suffice as an argument for the abandonment of refinery capacity; in the case of Japan, which imports an overwhelming proportion of its raw materials, including all its iron ore, the logical outcome of this argument would prove catastrophic. Secondly, like crude petroleum raw cotton can be more easily stockpiled if the capacity to turn it into intermediate and final products remains intact.

Another argument which is frequently put forward as an explanation for protectionism, particularly in the textile and clothing industry, is the need to preserve employment, or at least organise orderly retrenchment. Since 12 million people, or 17 per cent of the total employed in manufacturing, were in the textile and clothing industries in developed market economies in 1963 the argument merits serious consideration. However, it seems that while employment considerations may be a significant factor in the short-run, the desire to maintain output has been more important in the long-run.[96]

During the past two decades employment has fallen in the textile and clothing industry but output has remained stable, and in fact, risen in some instances; in the eight years preceding 1981, employment in this sector of the economy fell by 800,000 in Europe. Between 1960-70 output rose by 42 per cent in the US while both import penetration and employment remained virtually unchanged.[97] A similar situation is evident in the period between 1964-79 for industrialised countries; textile and clothing production did not suffer any decline, despite the recession, although employment continued to fall (see Table 5.11). Much of this change is attributable to rationalisation policies sponsored by the State, e.g. in Britain. Other European countries combined different strategies; for instance, the State in the FRG and the Netherlands also encouraged subcontracting as a means of maintaining profitability.[98]

Table 5.11 Index numbers of textile and apparel production in developed countries (1975 = 100)

	Year	All manufactures	Textiles	Apparel, leather and footwear
All Developed	1964	66	79	87
Market Economies	1979	126	114	117
North America	1964	70	74	96
	1979	133	121	119
Western Europe	1964	66	86	85
	1979	120	111	116

Source: Keesing and Wolf (1980) *Textile Quotas Against Developing Countries*, Trade Policy Research Centre, London, p. 111.

A number of economists argue that the decline in employment is due more to productivity gains than import penetration.[99] However, productivity gains and import penetration cannot be regarded as independent phenomena since the latter undoubtedly stimulates investment and technical change. The important point is that the State in the firstcomer countries has provided protection to enable the industry to become more competitive and maintain output while employment has fallen; import penetration from developing countries remains small. But enormous technological progress is being made to restore competitiveness. As the deputy chairman of ICI observed: 'even Britain's ailing textile industry has developed, technically, as fast as aerospace — Concorde and all'.[100] Similar developments are also in motion in the USA, Germany and Italy.[101] A Report by the ILO in Bangkok on the subject is worth quoting at some length to underline the significance of the technological changes now taking place:

> The developed countries are, for instance, currently investing heavily in automated equipment in certain industries. The introduction of computerised pattern-setting machines, electronically controlled laser cutting machines, micro-processor controlled sewing machines are . . . examples drawn from the textile sector, all dominated by fast developing microchip technologies. It is thus far from certain that the export-industries based on cheap labour that are now moving out of some of the NICs will be re-located to other developing countries where labour still is comparatively cheap; such industries may well be re-located back to the developed countries as a result of the changes in comparative advantage induced by technological change.[102]

The competition between developed market economies for export markets in textiles and clothing is, in fact, more acute. In particular, the US has increased its share of the EEC market, unlike developing country exporters. In 1979 US textile exports rose to 211 million tons, a 65 per cent rise over the previous year, as compared to the total export of 80 million by South Korea, a 3.7 per cent decline.[103] But the rules of competition between developed countries are refracted by stronger political considerations and a greater symmetry of economic bargaining power, thereby stopping short of the issuing of virtual ultimatums of the kind encountered by developing countries. Thus the latter group of countries, potential latecomers to the industrial elite, are hampered in their efforts to achieve the status enjoyed by the firstcomers. It is salutary to note, in conclusion, that the late H.G. Johnson, an apostle of free trade, succumbed to the logic of neo-mercantilism and argued against allowing developing countries to, what he also described as, disrupt western industry;[104] amen!

5.11 The USA

The US economy has lost its dominant position in the world export market for the strategic industries and also faces a challenge in its home market because of the appearance of competitive rival economies. A broad evaluation will be made below of the scope of the response of the State in the USA to this situation.

In evaluating the responses of the government a fundamental reality needs to be recognised: the US economy remains the world's largest market and enjoys considerable advantages of resilience (e.g. relative self-sufficiency in raw materials as compared to the EEC and Japan) and domestic purchasing power. It is also politically and militarily powerful; and this reality conditions the responses of the government to economic decline. For example, the outbreak of outright economic warfare with its economic partners would inflict far more economic and political damage on them than the US; an outcome the EEC sought to avoid in its dispute with the US over steel in July 1982. Thus, its strength permits a degree of manoeuverability and insouciance which make drastic action unnecessary. Obversely, the UK in its position of converse weaknesses is unable to respond with the decisiveness its situation demands. By contrast, powers like pre-war Japan and Germany responded dramatically to economic stalemate during the 1930s and 1940s precisely because they had sufficient military strength to entertain the possibility of changing the prevailing rules of the international system without being strong enough to dictate unless embarking dramatically on the use of force.

Unlike other developed coduntries the State in the USA has not used public ownership as an important method of intervention. The response of the government to contemporary economic decline can be analysed on six levels: firstly, US industry has always enjoyed an enormous indirect subsidy because of defence and government contracts (i.e. public procurement), which have cushioned the impact of deepening crisis, particularly since the early 1960s. Secondly, the State has provided direct subsidies which have been growing in importance. Thirdly, the State promotes industry and exports through cheap loans (including export credits) and tied aid. Fourthly, a variety of border impediments against imports have been brought into operation. Fifthly, exchange rate changes have lowered the prices of US exports; and aggressive negotiations with trading partners have increased US sales abroad. Finally, domestic economic policies have attempted to reduce production costs by lowering real wages and promoting economic rationalisation.

5.11.1 Defence and government contracts

Defence and other government contracts account for an important part of the sales of the strategic industries. Such contracts have been sheltered from competitive international bidding and are likely to continue to be so despite the agreements on public procurement policies at the Tokyo Round of GATT. It should be acknowledged that defence and other government purchases are not usually primarily motivated by the desire to subsidise industry although that is the effect; the question of objective economic compulsions asserted by Baran and Sweezy, to consume an economic surplus, need not be addressed here to establish the validity of the argument that such purchases have the effect of a subsidy.[105]

According to the Survey of Current Business, in 1958 the strategic industries and their various sub-sectors were dependent on federal purchases to a substantial degree: ranging from 12.8 per cent for iron and feralloy ores mining and 15.3 per cent for general industrial machinery and equipment to 86.7 per cent for aircraft and parts (see Table 5.12). Procurement for the space programme also constitutes a powerful stimulus to industry both in the form of research and development and purchases; for example, almost 80 per cent of computers were sold to the space and defence industry in 1955 and only fell to 47 per cent in 1963, by which time civilian sales had become important (see Table 5.13).[106]

A different classification of the Bureau of Census shows lower figures for a larger variety of industries (e.g. including chemicals) although in a more aggregate form (see Table 5.14); it might be noted that the Bureau of Census describes these industries as being 'defence-oriented' (only defence purchases are recorded in this census). Federal procurement in 1979 for a selected group of industries, as opposed to defence industries alone, reaffirms the overall trend of purchases by the State highlighted by the figures for 1958 (see Table 5.15).

These figures, however, understate the true impact of such purchases significantly for two reasons: firstly, defence sales, unlike commercial sales, involve little risk and provide guaranteed profits. The federal government allows contractors to write off R & D costs and calculate prices on the basis of total production costs, plus a percentage mark-up for profits. In turn, this system of costing has a beneficial impact on civilian sales through both lower unit costs deriving from the larger volume of production and the method

Table 5.12 Percentage of total output attributable to federal purchases, 1958.

Industry	Percent of Output
Iron & feralloy ores mining	12.8
Ordinance and accessories	86.7
Primary iron and steel manufacturing	12.5
Stamping, screw machine products	18.2
Other fabricated metal products	11.9
Engines and turbines	19.7
Farm machinery and equipment	2.9
Construction, mining and oil field machinery	6.1
Materials handling machinery and equipment	17.2
Metal working machinery and equipment	20.6
Special industry machinery and equipment	4.3
General industrial machinery and equipment	15.3
Machine shop products	39.0
Electrical industrial equipment and apparatus	17.0
Electrical lighting and wiring equipment	14.5
Radio, TV and communication equipment	40.7
Electronic components and accessories	38.9
Misc. electrical mach., equipment and supplies	15.1
Aircraft and parts	86.7
Other transportation equipment (excl. autos)	20.9
Scientific and controlling instruments	30.2

Source: Magdoff (1962) *The Age of Imperialism*, New York, p. 188.

Table 5.13 Federal government and space/defence industry purchases of US computers and semiconductors as percentage of all sales

	Semiconductors purchased by the Federal government	Computers purchased by the space/defence industry
Year	%	%
1955	38	79
1957	36	60
1959	45	72
1961	39	55
1963	35	47

Source: (1982) *Harvard Business Review*, (January-February), pp. 76 and 80.

Table 5.14 Purchases by the US defence establishment 1978, percentage of total shipment.

Industry	Percentage
Chemicals and allied products	10.7
Gaskets, packing and sealing devices	2.3
Primary metal industries	3.2
Fabricated metal products	9.1
Machinery, except electrical	4.1
Electrical equipment and supplies	15.6
Transportation equipment	49.7
Instruments and related products	8.0

Source: US Dept. of Commerce, Bureau of the Census, *Statistical Abstract of the US 1980*, Washington DC, p. 373.

Table 5.15 Federal procurement as a percentage of sales of selected US industries, 1979

Industry	% Federal Procurement
Aircraft	56
Radio and TV communications equipment	57
Engineering and scientific instruments	23
Electronics tubes	33
Non-ferrous forgings	36
Optical instruments and lenses	12

Source: See Table 5.13.

of costing and 'free R & D'. The second reason for understatement is due to the method of measuring the extent of defence/federal purchases. An example will illustrate the importance of the underestimation. If the Pentagon places an order for ships or aircraft it also results in orders for a number of industries like steel, machinery, etc., but the latter transactions are classified under non-governmental purchases because they are sales and purchases between private corporations. Further, the steel industry buys from other sectors like machinery when the original order for aircraft results in an order for steel, and so on. Thus the multiplier effect stimulates a much larger volume of inter-industry transactions which are not classified as federal purchases although they result from them; this of course does not include the impact further along the line through increased wages and salaries. The precise impact of such inter-industry transactions would be difficult to estimate but it must be considerable.

The present Reagan administration has been expressing vocal concern about the Soviet military threat to justify vastly increased military expenditure. However, it has an admirable grasp over the likely positive economic effects of this expenditure on US industry, particularly the sectors classified as 'defence-oriented'.

Defence spending is considered a 'key area of rebound' which will 'lead the expansion in 1982-83'.[107] The planned expenditure, as Rothschild comments, 'will differ from earlier booms in that it is highly concentrated in certain kinds of military spending, namely weapons procurement and research and development'.[108] It is estimated that such spending will increase by 16 per cent per annum in real terms between 1981-5; this will exceed the 14 per cent (real) annual real rate of increase that occurred during the three peak years of the Vietnam build-up. By contrast, payments to soldiers and civilian government employees will only increase 5 per cent a year.

5.11.2 Direct subsidies

Direct subsidies have played an unusually important role in industry for a country unwilling to intervene in the market. In 1980 such spending was of particular significance for cotton ($232 million), automobiles and highways ($1,394 million), aviation ($2,994 million) and textiles ($60 million), among the strategic industries.[109] But these subsidies also constituted an obvious stimulus to other industries through inter-industry linkages; for example, steel received only $45 million but was a beneficiary of aid to transport industries as was the machinery sector.

The US, in common with a number of other developed countries, also underwrites a substantial percentage of the national R & D effort. It is of course concentrated in certain industries, in particular industries which undertake government contracts (i.e. the strategic industries involved directly in the defence and space programmes). Thus although in relation to total national expenditure on research and development the State contributed approximately 65 per cent to 50 per cent between 1960 and 1979, the so-called defence industries benefited disproportionately in absolute terms. For instance, in 1961-2 and 1974-5 the percentages of R & D financed by the State devoted to defence and the space programme were 83 per cent and 64 per cent respectively (see Table 5.16).

Table 5.16   The contribution of the state to R & D expenditure as a percentage of total national R & D effort (I) and percentage of state-financed R & D in the defence/space section, in selected developed countries (II)

	I				II	
USA	1960	1970	1975	1979	1961-2	1974-5
	64.6	56.6	51.6	49.8	83	64
UK	1961	1964	1967			
	41	36	32	—	66	49
France	1961	1963	1967	1969		
	33	30	37	39	45	36
Germany	1964	1967	1969			
	14	17	13	—	22	15

Sources: Based on OECD reports for 1975, 1977 and 1972. Reproduced in Garfield and Choate (1980) *Being Number One: Rebuilding the U.S. Economy*, Lexington Mass., pp. 26-77; and in Pavitt and Warboys (1977) *Science, Technology and the Modern Industrial State*, London.

In 1969 an overwhelming proportion of the national research and development effort was devoted to six industries and sub-sectors, all members of the group of strategic industries; together, they accounted for 91 per cent of all research and development conducted in the US that year (see Table 5.17). These were also the industries and sub-sectors which benefited most from the contribution of the State towards R & D through expenditure on defence and space programmes.

Finally, it should be noted that the tax burden of major US corporations is minimal. According to one report 17 big companies in the US paid no tax in 1976 and 41 others paid less than 10 per cent [110]

5.11.3 Other measures: loans and export subsidies

The US government provides a variety of loans and guarantees (including export subsidies). In the fiscal year 1980 the maritime industry alone received $6,342 million, the railroad industry $2,064 million, aviation $558 million, steel $393 million and automobiles and highways $940 million.[111]

The US government also intervenes to promote foreign sales of

Table 5.17 The percentage distribution of national R & D effort by industry (I), and the percentage of R & D expenditure contributed by the state in each industry (II), 1969.

	US		UK		France		FRG	
	I	II	I	II	I	II	I	II
Electrical and electronic	23	54	23	33	25	34	28	10
Chemicals, drugs and petroleum	13	10	14	3	17	5	29	1
Aircraft	31	78	25	84	23	87	7	99
Motor vehicles, ships and other transport	9	—		6	9	38	15	1
Metals and metal products	2	5	4	4	3	6	5	2
Instruments and machinery	13	25	11	17	8	28	9	13

Source: See Table 5.16.

the 'defence-oriented' industries through tied aid and armament exports. For example, in 1965 a significant proportion of exports in these sectors were financed by US aid; ranging from 5.3 per cent in machinery and equipment and chemicals to between 25-30 per cent for iron and steel, fertilisers and railroad transportation equipment.[112] Such sales financed by tied aid are more important than the figures above suggest since once the buyer is locked into equipment and technology from a particular country further purchases are likely to be forthcoming.

The export of armaments, much of which is not conducted through normal commercial channels, also aids the strategic industries directly; in particular, steel, transportation equipment, machinery, and to a lesser degree, certain sub-sectors of the chemical industry. Between 1970-9 the value of military sales was approximately $85.5 billion, in 1979 alone it was over $13 billion.[113]

5.11.4 Border impediments

Border impediments in the form of quotas against textile and clothing imports have existed since the late 1950s in all developed countries, including the USA; one estimate puts the cost of import restrictions to consumers in this sector alone at $1.9 billion per annum.[114] Restrictions have also been placed on steel imports. In 1968 the Japanese were compelled to negotiate 'voluntary' limitations, which were renewed in 1971. In 1977 the 'trigger price' system came into opertion, covering sixty varieties of products.[115] The USA has also extracted agreements with Japan on automobiles. In fact 20 to 25 per cent of all Japanese exports to the USA face some kind of restriction.[116]

In July 1982 conflicts between the USA and the EEC over steel became acute; its closest ally, Britain, was threatened with a 40 per cent duty against its steel exports to the USA.[117]

Finally, it might be noted in conclusion that apart from textiles and clothing, steel and automobiles, another sub-sector of the transport industry, ships, faces direct limits. The Jones Act legally compels ships plying between US ports to be built in the USA.[118]

5.11.5 Exchange rates and foreign markets

The devaluation of August 1971 also had the effect of making US goods more competitive on world markets. Conversely, it had a detrimental effect on the exports of US rivals; manufactures also had a 10 per cent surcharge placed on most exports to the USA. Until the introduction of floating exchange rates the Japanese were frequently urged to revalue the yen, a goal achieved by the so-called 'Nixon shocks' of August 1971.

The US government continues to lobby the Japanese to import more US goods, including armaments, with a determination which can only be described as threats although evidence of unfair trading practices by Japan is less convincing than protestations by Western exporters imply.[119] Similar tactics have been used against other major trading partners with some success.[120]

The recent change in US domestic economic strategy has raised the value of the dollar but, as it will be argued below, despite the higher value of the dollar, which raises US export prices, policy-makers hope that in the long-term the strategy will make US goods more competitive.

5.11.6 Present US domestic economic policy and exports

One important goal of the incumbent Reagan administration's economic strategy is to reverse the lack of competitiveness which has now become a generalised phenomenon in the US economy, like that of the UK. A number of sectors may continue to enjoy competitive advantages but even in a sector like computers Japanese competition is beginning to pose a serious challenge.[121]

The US government is making an effort along a broad front, in addition to measures of the kind described above aimed at specific industries, to achieve a permanent improvement. The deflation engineered is a traditional capitalist solution to over-expansion. This policy has an interrelated two-fold purpose: the reduction of wage costs by undermining the trade union movement through mass unemployment and raising productivity through economic rationalisation by eliminating weak firms in an industry (i.e. by reducing 'overmanning' and by mergers). This strategy it is hoped will restore the competitiveness of the US economy as a whole. However, it should be recognised that despite some initial gains these policies cannot be guaranteed success since domestic opposition may not be sufficiently undermined to achieve a significant turn-around.

In conclusion, it need only be reaffirmed that in the USA the State has defended its strategic industries through a variety of overt and less observable measures despite its international obligations and apparent commitment to unfettered economic exchange. However, every action does not require to be analysed to substantiate the hypothesis that the State will strive to defend the strategic industries since other factors, like group interests, as noted earlier, have an influence in determining policies of the State.[122]

5.12 The UK

The circumstances encountered by the UK economy and its strategic industries are rather more stark, as compared to the US. The decline of UK market shares predates the end of the Second World War, underlining the gravity of the situation, despite a temporary improvement in its aftermath.

The response of the State in the UK has been affected by a number of general factors which have been touched upon earlier in the chapter, but could be usefully reiterated. The UK unlike the US, does not enjoy the basic strength of size and relative economic wealth (as measured by per capita income), nor does it occupy a position of military and political prominence in relation to its chief economic rivals. Its membership of the EEC also circumscribes its manoeuverability in dealings with partners in the Community, in particular its most important economic competitor, the FRG; the use of significant border impediments in defence of national industry are precluded, for instance. A further issue is the inability of the British State to provide the kind of political and military backing abroad for its weakened capitalist class as it did in the eighteenth and nineteenth centuries, and is now demanded by circumstances. The loyalty of the capitalist class to State institutions and the national economy is therefore qualified to the degree that the State is unable to defend their interests, given the changed fortunes of the British State in the international league of nation-states.

The responses of the State nevertheless follow the pattern evident elsewhere although the instruments chosen and the magnitude of the intervention it has engaged in reflect the seriousness of the situation. First, and foremost, some of the strategic industries have faced such intractable problems that outright public ownership has been common. Second, direct subsidies have been widespread and sometimes large (including subsidised R & D costs). Thirdly, preferential State procurement is used to bolster industry. Fourthly, a variety of border impediments have been instituted against imports. Fifth, and finally, like the US government, the State in the UK has used deflation to impose cost reductions and promote economic rationalisation.

5.12.1 Nationalisation

Although various ideological motives are adduced for British nationalisation policy, particularly of successive Labour governments, beginning with the Attlee administration, one feature most of the potential public industries have had in common has been severe economic difficulties. No doubt ideological impulses have been present, as was pressure from interest groups (e.g. employees) but it should be borne in mind that virtually no successful British industry has been nationalised — the limits of ideology have been clearly defined, to say the least. In addition, Tory governments with contrary impulses have also taken ailing industries into public ownership.

In Britain, the steel and the transport sector were successively patronised by the State as their survival was found to be in jeopardy. Steel was nationalised in 1951 by the Attlee government, denationalised in 1953 by the Conservatives, and renationalised in 1967 by the Wilson administration. The State appears to have virtually provided a blank cheque to guarantee the viability of the steel industry, although obviously more and more determined efforts to restore competitiveness and reduce losses are evident.

In 1971 a ten-year development strategy was elaborated, involving a public contribution of £3 billion.[123] A decade later the

State agreed to a £1.5 billion rescue package to prevent bank-ruptcy.[124] However, in 1980 losses amounted to £600 million, although they were lower in 1982 following ruthless rationalisation.[125]

Britain's rail network was nationalised in 1948 and successive governments, both Labour and Conservative, have underwritten losses and made available funds for modernisation — to the benefit of other industries as well, e.g. machinery (including communications) and steel. Other transport sub-sectors owned by the State are civil aviation and ship-building (from 1977) but excluding the profitable ship repairers. In 1974 the equity holding of the State in the national car manufacturer, British Leyland, was increased with a £200 million stake.

Earlier, in 1971, the Conservative government nationalised the aero-engine and gas-turbine engine divisions of Rolls Royce when it ran into financial difficulties, despite electoral commitments against bailing out so called 'lame ducks'. Again, as in the case of the shipping industry, the profitable car division was left in private hands.

5.12.2 *Subsidy policies*

The ship-building industry was nationalised in 1977 but large subsidies were provided from the early 1960s. In 1970-1 such direct and indirect subsidies amounted to over £76 million. Other assistance included operating subsidies, varying from 2 to 25 per cent, according to the financial situation of each of the major merchant ship-building firms.[126] In 1978 the subsidy for Royal Navy boats was estimated at £50 million per vessel.[127]

The aircraft industry has been the largest single recipient of subsidies, assistance designed to maintain a national champion. In 1974-5 it received £157 million. One large and growing component of expenditure has been the supersonic aircraft (Concorde) programme. During the two decades following 1950 the total assistance extended to the aircraft industry amounted to £1.2 billion.[128]

The automobile industry joined the lengthening queue of ailing industries and received two large infusions of aid. In 1974 British Leyland received a £700 million subsidy (apart from the £200 million equity stake) for its restructuring programme; and in the following year Chrysler, UK received £162.5 million (including a guarantee and low interest loan).[129]

Britain's computer industry received £40 million in aid between

1966-70 and a further £25 million in the period 1971-5. The State now owns a 25 per cent stake in International Computers Ltd., which was created in 1968.[130] The desire to create a national champion was clearly illustrated again in the sponsorship of the computer industry.[31]

During 1970-1 direct and indirect subsidies (including tax relief and government expenditure) to industry totalled £1,774.79 million; of this amount the six strategic industries — other than aircraft but including chemicals and paper and paper products — received £1,437.667 million[132] The total subsidy to privately-owned firms between 1974-5 and 1977-8 (at 1977 survey prices) was approximately £1,849 million.[133]

The participation of the State in R & D in the UK also illustrates the preponderant bias in favour of the group of strategic industries. Like a number of other developed countries (e.g. the USA and France) such R & D is also substantially for defence-related industries, including the space programme. Between 1961 and 1967 the State contributed around 32 to 41 per cent of the total national R & D effort (see Table 5.16). In 1969 the electrical and electronic, and aircraft sectors were responsible for 23 per cent and 25 per cent, respectively, of all R & D conducted in the country. The contribution of the State towards R & D in these two sectors was 33 per cent and 84 per cent, respectively. At the same time 66 per cent of the entire State contribution in 1961-2 and 49 per cent in 1974-5 was devoted to defence and space. Thus, the identity of the strategic industries for which the State contributed a significant percentage of R & D expenditure coincides with the defence sector; apart from the two sectors identified above the other strategic industries which benefited were motor vehicles, ships, other transport, metals, metal products, instruments and machinery (see Table 5.17).

Like other countries Britain also provides export subsidies and employs aid as an instrument to promote British Exports. As it has already been observed, the impact of such aid-financed exports is greater than the value of the sums of aid involved since current purchases lead to more orders in the future. In 1976-7 the cost of various trade promotion devices (other than aid) amounted to £804 million.[134]

5.12.3 Preferential procurement

Purchases by Britain's nationalised industries and public agencies are usually made from local manufacturers. The government also attempts to influence the buying policies of the private sector.

In 1970-1 90 per cent of central government computer orders were placed with ICL.[135] Recently, the State ensured the order for a replacement to the ship the *Atlantic Conveyor* for British ship-builders by providing financial assistance to bridge the cost difference between the domestic and international price.[136] The armed forces also discriminate in favour of local manufacturers in the procurement of hardware, except in the case of certain weapons which are too expensive to be underwritten by State aids.

5.12.4 Border impediments

These have been employed most directly in the case of textiles and clothing. Restrictions have also been placed on automobile imports from Japan through 'voluntary' agreements.

Since December 1977 the EEC, including the UK, has operated 'a basic import price scheme for steel imports from third countries. Any imports below this basic price are examined to see whether provisional anti-dumping duties should be imposed.'[137] Separate agreements covering volume and price affect imports from Japan and certain east European exporters and Spain. Some 20 to 25 per cent of all imports from Japan face limitations.[138] In 1978 the National Consumer Council estimated that 600 individual products encountered some kind of import restraint.[139]

5.12.5 Rationalisation of industry and cost reduction

The State in the UK has been involved in a number of rationalisation programmes, primarily aimed at the group of strategic industries. The turning point from an organisational perspective was the creation of the National Development Council (Neddy) in 1963 by the Conservative government. But the influence of Neddy was not discernibly great. In 1966 the Labour government set up the Industrial Reorganisation Corporation (IRC) 'with large funds to actively foster mergers';[140] most notably in the bid of GEC for AEI in 1967. Other significant mergers promoted by the IRC include the creation of ICL (1968), and the emergence of BL (1968). Loans were also made available to Marvins and Herbert-Ingersoll as well as Plessey, Airmec, Ferranti, and Kearney and Trecker for rationalisation programmes. Another loan of £10 million was made to BL for the purchase of machine tools to modernise and expand production.[141] Britain's industrial strategy was further developed with the Industrial Expansion Act of 1968.

In 1975 the Industry Act established the National Enterprise Board with access to funds of over £1 billion. The NEB was an expanded version of the IRC and like the IRC

> its main policy was to encourage mergers, especially in the automobile, computer and aircraft sectors . . . promoting 'national champions' in these branches. The penchant for merging so called 'strategic sectors' was prompted by the need to avoid an undue reliance on foreign suppliers.[142]

The election of the Thatcher government in 1979 in the context of continuing economic decline despite attempts to stem the tide introduced a new dynamic. The Thatcher government, like Reagan's administration, which came to office in the US later, has been attempting to reduce wage costs and implement a major industrial reorganisation through deflation. The economic malaise of UK industry is so deep that specific sectoral policies are no longer regarded as adequate. Already the mass unemployment caused by deflation has raised productivity by reducing 'over-manning' and caused a fall in real wages; recent wage settlements have been consistently below the rate of inflation.

However, unlike the US, the position of the UK is fundamentally weak, and dramatic incursions into the world market for strategic goods and the reconquest of the domestic market may prove elusive. Furthermore, the sharp rise in the outflow of capital from Britain, amounting to £10 billion in 1981 from £2.3 billion in 1977, highlights the difficulty of an economy in which demand is weak in competing for investment; in addition, relative profits abroad, with the high interest rates (e.g. in the US), and in speculation at home are higher than in British industry.[143]

Notes

1. Data on textiles alone are not available.
2. Information on this issue derives from numerous sources, in particular the *Financial Times*; *The Economist*, London; *Journal of the World Economy*; *Monthly Review*. See Dunkel (1982); Hieronymi (1980); Diebold Jr. (1980); Hanabusa (1979); Krauss (1979); Mandel (1978); Balassa (1978); Blackhurst *et al.* (1977; 1978); Tumlir (1978); Hudson (1977); Corden and Fels (1976); Bergsten (1975; 1973); Malmgren (1971); 'The Threat to World Trade' (16 March 1952) p. 18.

3. Free trade in this context refers to the relatively unhindered flow of goods and services which has characterised international economic relations during certain periods (e.g. during the two decades following the Cobden-Chevalier treaty of 1860 and the post-Kennedy round of GATT in 1962) rather than the pure conception of textbooks.

4. The responses of nation–States in the period before the end of World War II will also be sketched but a more detailed analysis will be carried out for the post-war period. The latter discussion will suffice to highlight the general tendencies involved.

5. Williams (1972) p. 16.

6. Ibid. pp. 439-40.

7. Ibid. pp. 439-40.

8. Davis (1979) p. 65.

9. Williams (op. cit.) pp. 447-8.

10. Ibid.

11. Williams (op. cit.) p. 449.

12. Semmel (1970) pp. 1-13; also see Ashley (1920); Saul (1960); Hobsbawm (1972).

13. Ashley (1920) pp. 298-9.

14. Pollard (1981).

15. Ibid. p. 136.

16. Ibid. pp. 257-60.

17. Ashley and Semmel (op. cit.); Allen (1972); Henderson (1961); Lockwood (1954).

18. Saul (op. cit.) p. 135.

19. Ibid. p. 56

20. Semmel (op. cit.) p. 226.

21. Gallagher and Robinson in Wolfe (ed.) (1972) pp. 53-5.

22. Kemp (1969) pp. 179-99; Mulhall (1892) and Mitchell and Deane (1962) provide an array of quantitative data in various chapters and sections.

23. Krasner (1976.

24. Maizels (1963); and *Cambridge Economic Policy Review* (April 1979) No. 5, p. 2. Also Schwartz and Choate (1980) p. 35.

25. Saul (op. cit.).

26. See, for example Kemp (1969) pp. 179-200 and Levine (1967); for the importance of labour resistance to industrial change see Zeitlin (1979); Elbaum and Wilkinson (1979) and Lazonick (1979).

27. The importance of size is reflected in two factors; the possibility of falling back on the national economy and also engaging in successful international political bargaining over economic positions because of the political and economic influence large size brings.

28. 'Metals', one of the six strategic industries, includes metals other than steel, although the latter remains the most significant component.

29.   Sugihara (1980); also see Lockwood (1954); and Allen (1972).
30.   Henderson (1975).
31.   See Allen (op. cit.) pp. 127-60.
32.   Lenin (1973); Hilferding (1981); Wehler in Owen and Sutcliffe (1972); Vernon (1973) pp. 86-7.
33.   Vernon (1973) p. 87.
34.   Krasner (op. cit.).
35.   Quoted in Glyn and Sutcliffe (1972) p. 20.
36.   At constant 1955 prices; Maizels (op. cit.).
37.   See Allen (op. cit.) p. 97 for fuller details.
38.   Ashworth (1975) p. 231.
39.   Kenwood and Lougheed (1971) pp. 185-88.
40.   See Chandler (1970); Kenwood and Lougheed (op. cit.); Kindleberger (1973 and Ashworth (1975).
41.   Kenwood and Lougheed (op. cit.) pp. 190-219.
42.   Ashworth (op. cit.) p. 250.
43.   Hexner (1946) *Passim*.
44.   Ashworth (op. cit.) p. 247.
45.   Brodie (1971) p. 110.
46.   See for example Lange. Quoted in Dobb (1963) pp. 18-19. Also Foreign and Commonwealth Office (1979); Cable (1979); Lal (1979).
47.   Lenin (op. cit.).
48.   Kemp (op. cit.) p. 186.
49.   Rosecrance (1973) pp. 113-14.
50.   In Pettman (1975) pp. 231-71.
51.   Lenin (op. cit.) p. 104.
52.   Patterson (1966) p. 32.
53.   Patterson (op. cit.) pp. 75-80; see also Diebold (1952).
54.   Batchelor *et al.* (1980) pp. 54-5.
55.   Maizels (1970) p. 231.
56.   For a detailed analysis see Batchelor *et al.* (op. cit.) p. 65.
57.   Roemer (1976) pp. 34-83 and 84-6.
58.   Calder (1982) p. 3.
59.   Gains in new trade represent a deviation of relative shares from the previous trend in growth of world trade.
60.   Batchelor *et al* (op. cit.) p. 53.
61.   Batchelor *et al.* (op. cit.) pp. 27-8.
62.   Blackaby (1978) p. 241.
63.   Batchelor *et al.* (op. cit.) p. 58.
64.   Blackaby (op. cit.).
65.   Blackaby (op. cit.) p. 249.
66.   *Cambridge Economic Policy Review* (1979) p. 2.
67.   Batchelor *et al.* (op. cit.) p. 57
68.   Blackaby (op. cit.) p. 228.

69. OECD (1979); Froebel *et al* (1980).
70. Blackhurst *et al*. quoted in Lal (1980) Part I.
71. UNIDO (1979) *World Industry since 1960: Progress and Prospects*, p. 156 and 160.
72. Batchelor (op. cit.); also *Financial Times* (8 May 1979) p. 16.
73. UNIDO (op. cit.) p. 156; also UN (1981).
74. Mandel (op. cit.) pp. 103-4.
75. The latter can be seen as a logical corollary of the former, indeed often leading to it.
76. Pestieau in Warnecke (ed.) (1978) p. 100.
77. Vernon (1974) pp. 3-24.
78. Cable (1979) esp. p. 2; also see F.T. 'South Korea's Shipbuilding Under Attack Again', (1 April 1982) p. 6.
79. Golt (1978); also see F.T. 'World Trade News' (12 December 1979).
80. Krauss in Ohlin *et al*. (eds.) (1977) p. 277.
81. See for example F.T. (5 July 1982); and *Guardian* (24 June 1982) p. 19.
82. Patterson (op. cit.) pp. 271-88 and 317.
83. Owen-Smith in Maunder (ed.) (1979) pp. 160-89; and Griffiths (1977) pp. 125-7.
84. Griffiths (op. cit.) p. 126.
85. Hough in Maunder (op. cit.) p. 191.
86. Ibid.
87. In Italy, for example, the State has nationalised virtually all textile and chemical firms on the verge of collapse through the ENI; also see Maunder and Vernon (op. cit.) and Shonfield (1977).
88. See Allen in Maunder (ed.) (op. cit.).
89. For such various measures see Hughes in Saunders (ed.) (1981) pp. 97-131 and Hughes and Singh (1979); Maunder, Warnecke, Vernon (eds.) (op. cit.); also, Reich HBR (1982); Johnson (1982); Donges (1980); OECD (1979); Franko (1979); Hayward and Narkiewicz (eds.) (1978); Curzon (1978); Corden and Fels (eds.) (1976); Miles in Whiting (ed.) (1976); *The Economist*, 'Industry in Trouble' (**265**, No. 7009, 31 December to 6 January 1977-8) pp. 75-95; and *The Economist*, 'Protectionism' (**282**, No. 7220, 6 January 1982) p. 34; also *The Guardian*, 'Japan Knows How to Get its Economic Priorities Right' (8 February 1980); and *Financial Times*, 'U.S. urged to act on Non-Tariff Barriers' (8 May 1979) p. 3, on Japanese Public Procurement Policies; Sayle, *New Statesman*, 'Japan's Miracle Turns Sour' **94**, No. 2434, (11 November 1977).
90. Diebold (1980) and Turner and Bedore (1978/79).
91. Keesing and Wolf (op. cit.) pp. 3-4.
92. Keesing and Wolf (op. cit.) pp. 16-38.
93. See the *Guardian* business page for details (17 June 1982).

94.   Keesing and Wolf (op. cit.) p. 173.
95.   Rosenberg (1976) pp. 141-72.
96.   Keesing and Wolf (op. cit.) p.111.
97.   Keesing and Wolf (op. cit.) pp. 117 and 120; and *Guardian*, 'No Justice in Cutting Quotas To Suit the Rich' (1 October 1981) p. 21.
98.   Shepherd in Saunders (ed.) (op. cit.) pp. 132-56; Froebel *et al.* (1980); Tharakan (1979); Evers in OECD (1979) pp. 139-80.
99.   See in particular Krueger in Black and Hindley (eds.) 1980 Ch. 5.
100.   *Guardian*, 'Hanging By a Thread' (20 May 1981) p. 9.
101.   Froebel *et al.* and Shepherd in Saunders (op. cit.); *Newsweek* (27 July 1981) p. 43.
102.   ILO (1982) p. 4.
103.   *Guardian* (20 May 1982) p. 9.
104.   Johnson quoted in Helleiner (1980) p. 97.
105.   Baran and Sweezy (1966).
106.   Also see *Newsweek* (27 April 1981) p. 19.
107.   Rothschild (1982) p. 19.
108.   Rothschild (op. cit.) p. 19; one significant planned expenditure is on the increase in the size of the US Navy from 450 to 600 ships.
109.   Reich, HBR (1982) p. 78.
110.   *Financial Times*, 'Seventeen Big Companies in the U.S. Paid No Tax in 1976' (30 January 1978) p. 2.
111.   Reich, HBR (1982) p. 78.
112.   Magdoff (1968) p. 130.
113.   Dept. of Commerce, Bureau of the Census (1980) p. 370.
114.   Reich, NYRB (1982) p. 37.
115.   Reich, NYRB (1982) p. 38; also *The Economist* 31 December – 6 January 1977-8); the *Guardian*, 'Subsidy Row Threatens EEC Steel Peace' (17 June 1982) p. 14.
116.   Allen (1967) p. 96; also see Roemer (op. cit.) and Saxonhouse in Taylor (ed.) (1973).
117.   The *Guardian*, 'Subsidy Row Threatens EEC Steel Peace' (17 June 1982) p. 14.
118.   *The Economist* (December-January 1977-8 op. cit.).
119.   Allen (1978) also *Financial Times*, 'U.S. — Japan Government Procurement Talks Fail' (30 March 1979) p. 6; and 'Gatt Negotiations Conclude Tokyo Round' (12 April 1979) p. 6.
120.   *Financial Times*, 'U.S. Pressed Over Threat to Trade' (17 November 1978) p. 5; *Guardian* 'U.S. Trade Attitude Spreads Dissent Through West', (31 October 1979) p. 19; *Guardian* 'U.S. Takes A Softer Line on Steel Imports', (19 February 1982) p. 19; *Observer* Business 'Steel Finale' (1 August 1982) p. 13.
121.   The *Guardian* 'Japan and U.S. Meet for Trade Dialogue' (3 August 1982) p. 16.

122. Reich, HBR (1982) pp. 80-1.
123. Carmoy in Warnecke (ed.) (1978) p. 39.
124. The *Guardian*, 'Government Throws BSC £1.5b Lifeline' (27 June 1980) p.1.
125. *Sunday Times Business News* 'State Steel Halves its Losses' (5 July 1982) p. 49.
126. Also see Corden and Fels (op. cit.) p. 123; Curzon (op. cit.) p. 64 and *Financial Times* (7 November 1978) p. 1.
127. Curzon ibid.
128. Carmoy in Warnecke (ed.) (op. cit.) and Maunder (1979) p. 151.
129. Carmoy in Warnecke (ed.) (op. cit.) p. 40 and Maunder (1979) p. 149.
130. Carmoy in Warnecke (ed.) (op. cit.) pp. 39-40.
131. Vernon (ed.) (1974) pp. 3-24 and the *Guardian* (29 July 1982) p. 1.
132. Corden and Fels (op. cit.).
133. Maunder (ed.) (op. cit.) p. 155.
134. Maunder (ed.) (op. cit.) p. 133; Also see the *Guardian* 'CBI Call to Buy British' (21 December 1981) p. 13.
135. Carmoy in Warnecke (ed.) (op. cit.) p. 40.
136. The *Guardian* (29 July 1982) p. 1.
137. Foreign Office (1979) p. 57.
138. The *Guardian* 'EEC Seeks Unity on Japan' (22 February 1982) p. 14.
139. National Consumer Council (September 1978) p. 55.
140. Maunder (ed.) (op. cit.) p. 145.
141. Blackaby (ed.) (op. cit.) p. 443.
142. Carmoy in Warnecke (ed.) (op. cit.) p. 37.
143. *Sunday Times Business News* 'Investment Drain Tops £10 billion' (20 June 1982) p. 49; *Financial Times*, 'Plugging Loopholes in the Employment Bill' (23 July 1982) p. 10; *The Economist* (24-30 July 1982) for further evidence on State policy towards unions.

6 Transnational corporations, the national economy and international trade

6.1 Introduction

The similarities in the structures of production and traditional flows of international trade (i.e. normal third-party trade) in an open world economy, which constitute the parameters for the hypothesis put forward on the relationship between State intervention in the economy and international political imperatives, need to be situated in the context of certain incipient structural changes in the world economy. These evident structural modifications are partly the outcome of the activities of transnational corporations (TNCs).[1]

Firstly, there has been a remarkable growth in direct foreign investment, particularly in the manufacturing sector — to which the group of strategic industries belong — owing to the TNCs. Secondly, it seems that such direct foreign investment has altered the nature of conventional international trade flows.

The incipient structural changes in the world economy coincide partly with the emerging new international division of labour (NIDL) discussed widely in recent years. The NIDL essentially refers to the appearance of the newly-industrialising countries (NICs) in the world economy, and the role of TNCs in the growth of manufacturing industry in these countries which this process implies. However, the significance of TNCs for the present analysis derives from their world-wide operations, both in developing and developed market economies, and the attendant consequences for the international allocation of resources. Therefore although the NIDL, which relates to the NICs, represents the most striking contemporary example of structural mutation in the world economy and the role of TNCs in this change, any assessment of the consequences of TNC operations for the relative economic autonomy of the State must necessarily consider the structural changes occuring in developed market economies as well; in any case the latter is quantitatively more significant, as the evidence below highlights. These structural changes in the developed market economies are also substantially due to the operations of TNCs.

Thus the discussion will evaluate the incipient structural changes inaugurated by TNCs in both developed and developing market economies, and their potential impact on the two concerns of this book: relative national economic self-sufficiency (as represented by similar structures of production), and international trading arrangements delimited by it.

6.1.1 *The influence of TNCs on the structure of production*

TNC operations have now made significant inroads into virtually all market economies, developed and developing, with the exception of the USA and Japan.[2] If the spread of TNCs leads to the globalisation of economic activities, especially manufacturing production, the national organisation of production apparent in the existence of similar structures of production described earlier would be correspondingly undermined.

It is perfectly plausible that the priorities of TNCs, based primarily on private economic considerations (profit maximisation, etc.), can diverge from the political objectives of the territorial-state. The rationalisation of production globally by TNCs can create economic structures which transcend national geopolitical boundaries, which are the crucial spatial economic horizon of the territorial-state. The latter, as it has been argued, seeks to institute and maintain a relative economic self-sufficiency in key intermediate inputs by reproducing the group of strategic industries within its territorial-political confines. Thus the outcome of these two dissonant pressures has important consequences for the character of the existing territorial-state system.

Foreign participation in the economy, however large, does not inherently undermine the economic autonomy of the State since it can only affect ownership rather than the structure of production within the economy, i.e. the same products can be manufactured in the country, maintaining the familiar structure of production even if the ownership is foreign. Of course secondary effects can ensue because foreign owners are less likely to be sympathetic to national objectives.

If instead the organisation of production became transnational — i.e. the allocation of economic activities is rationalised globally with the spread of TNC involvement in the manufacturing sector — it might affect the similar structures of production on two levels. Firstly, the existence of the TNCs' network might induce a modification of the sectoral distribution of economic activities such that imports rather than domestic production constitute at least a substantial portion of the local supplies of a particular industrial product. For example, one or more of the group of strategic industries, or one of its important sub-sectors may not exist in the country, imports providing local consumption requirements. Secondly, the finished product in a particular industry might not be manufactured in entirety locally, within one country, since different stages of the production process can be located in more than one country.

The evidence shows that the first potential development, the modification of the sectoral distribution of industry has not in fact occurred. In the main, TNC participation in the economy has affected ownership rather than the pattern of economic activities within the country concerned. It would seem that TNCs have largely adapted to the industrial structure preferred by the State in developed market economies and NICs. This finding cannot however be taken to imply that TNC policies and objectives have played no part in the failure of other developing countries to achieve meaningful levels of industrialisation. The latter issue requires separate consideration which is outside the scope of the present discussion.

The second feature, the location of different stages of the production process in different countries, is established by the empirical evidence. But its impact on the national organisation of production (i.e. the similar structures of production) is not yet significant. The total estimated value of transactions arising from the decomposition of the production process is small in relation to total manufacturing production in market economies. It is the impact of such transactions on the pattern of international trade flows, however, which is apparently of growing significance.

6.1.2 The impact of TNCs on the pattern of international trade

The location of different stages of the production process of a single product in different countries leads to trade across national geographical boundaries but within the same firm, i.e. intra-firm trade. This intra-firm trade straddling national boundaries occurs between plants owned wholly or (more usually) partly by the same organisation; evidently, between parent companies and their majority-owned or minority-owned affiliates, as opposed to inter-affiliate transactions.

The phenomenon of intra-firm trade occurs because of the internationalisation of the production process which has been taking place, 'sourcing' policy as Gygory Adam described it.[3] The location of different parts of the production process in more than one country is of special significance for contemporary trade disputes since its survival is predicated upon an open international trading system. Thus if TNCs rely on transnational transactions to produce finished goods previously manufactured nationally it will be opposed to protectionism. In the past, as will be posited later, the State, labour and industry interests converged towards protectionism to defend domestic markets whenever foreign competition became acute. Intra-firm trade alters the configuration of interests affected by contemporary international trade disputes in manufactured products. TNCs strongly favour an open international economic order, on which intra-firm trade is predicated.

The quantitative dimensions of this phenomenon and its economic importance to TNCs need to be analysed in order to assess the role of TNCs in the evolution of contemporary international trade relations, i.e. the potential influence of TNCs on the apparent disjuncture in progress.

6.1.3 *The organisation of the data and discussion*

The presentation of data and discussion are divided into two sections. The first section deals with the growth of foreign investment since the period before the First World War.

The data highlights the dominance of direct foreign investment (as opposed to portfolio investment or investment in government bonds), and therefore TNC involvement since the beginning of the post-war period. The importance of the manufacturing sector for direct foreign investment is noted. In addition, changes in the relative shares of leading investor countries in total foreign investment and the geographical distribution of such investment is outlined. The role of TNCs in the group of strategic industries is highlighted, and the crucial distinguishing feature between developed and developing market economies with respect to direct foreign investment is stressed.

The data on the growth, form, location, etc., of foreign investment by TNCs establish the context in which the potential transformation of similar structures of production, owing to the globalisation of economic activities, is to be viewed. The section is concluded with a theoretical and empirical evaluation of the impact of direct foreign investment in manufacturing on the similar structures of production and thus the strategic autonomy of the nation-state. It also highlights the issue of TNC salience in general, especially as a background to the impact of TNC operations on traditional international trade flows.

The second section is concerned with the relationship between TNCs and international trade flows. The evidence demonstrates the growing importance of TNCs in international trade, and the significant proportion comprised by intra-firm trade. The data on intra-firm trade are disaggregated to differentiate between unfinished and finished goods; intra-firm trade between affiliates, as opposed to parent-affiliate trade is distinguished, and the experiences in developed and developing market economies are noted. The section is concluded with a discussion about the economic importance of intra-firm trade for TNCs and their impact on trade policies in developed market economies.

6.2 Foreign investment: its growth, composition and shares

The total value of the stock of foreign investment amounted to $40 billion in 1919, declining somewhat to $37 billion in 1929.[4] In the subsequent decade the value of total foreign investment (both direct and portfolio) declined again in real terms. The position of the largest single foreign investor, the UK, improved slightly in nominal terms from $18.2 to $18.7 billion by 1939. But both wholesale prices and actual living costs were higher in 1929 than in 1937 so that the real value of British foreign assets in 1939 appears much higher than before the depression, i.e. in 1929. In the same period the value of foreign assets held by the US, the second largest investor, deteriorated from $4.8 billion in 1931 to $11.5 billion in 1939.[5]

According to rough estimates, the value of all outstanding long-term foreign investments — private, public, direct and portfolio — (excluding valueless debts in default) totalled $44 billion in 1944-5; this was equivalent to $25 billion at 1914 dollar prices.[6] Thus foreign investment activities of all types, not surprisingly, actually declined in the years demarcated by the beginning of the First World War and the end of the Second World War.

By contrast, foreign investment activity experienced a remarkable increase during the subsequent three decades, and showed no sign of abating. By 1967 the total stock of direct foreign investment alone (i.e. private investment in business enterprise), which accounted for the major part of all foreign investment (including portfolio investment), had risen to $105 billion. In 1976 such direct foreign investment amounted to $287 billion.[7] Thus, even allowing for price changes the growth of direct foreign investment has been substantial. It has been estimated that majority-owned foreign affiliates of TNCs currently produce 20 per cent of world output, underlining the importance of foreign economic involvement.[8]

An extensive UN survey provides further evidence on the continued expansion of foreign subsidiaries. According to the survey 'in constant terms, the sales of foreign affiliates and consolidated sales have grown at annual compound rates of 11.1 per cent and 6.2 per cent respectively.[9]

Finally, a further indication of the growth of direct foreign investment is the increase in the number of subsidiaries owned by US-based manufacturing TNCs. From a total of 47 in 1907, the number rose to 715 in 1939, and 3,646 in 1967.[10] A further 4,700 were added by the end of 1975 although 2,400 affiliates were liquidated, sold or nationalised (see Table 6.1).[11] Thus the growth of direct foreign investment in the post-war period has been remarkable. Indeed, it can be regarded as the most significant development in the history of twentieth-century capitalism.

Table 6.1 Number of foreign manufacturing subsidiaries of 187 US-controlled manufacturing enterprises, selected years, 1901-75

Year	Total	Latin America	Others*
1901	47	3	0
1913	116	10	1
1919	180	20	7
1929	467	56	23
1939	715	114	28
1950	988	259	42
1959	1,891	572	128
1967	3,646	950	454
1975	5,946**	—	—

*   Other than Canada, Europe, Latin America, and the Southern Dominions
** Only 180 of the largest US-based TNCs in the manufacturing sector

Source: Vaupel and Curhan (1969) *The Making of Multinational Enterprises*, Boston, p. 125; United Nations Economic and Social Council (1978) *Transnational Corporation in World Development*, Commission on Transnational Corporations, Fourth Session, E/C. 10/38, New York, p. 39.

Two features already apparent from the type of figures cited above to highlight the post-war expansion of foreign investment should be emphasised. Firstly, much of the foreign investment in the post-war period has been in the manufacturing sector as opposed to extractive ventures, services, banking and insurance. Secondly, long-term foreign investment has been overwhelmingly direct, rather than portfolio in form. These two features are relevant because the group of strategic industries is in the manufacturing sector (of which they comprise a large part), and the globalisation of economic activities (including sourcing policy) can occur through direct foreign investment, i.e. by TNCs.

In the 50 years ending in 1914, when foreign investment ceased to grow, 40 per cent of all British foreign investment was in railways, and a further 30 per cent in government and municipal securities. Similarly, French and German foreign investments were primarily in securities although loans might be used to finance manufacturing activities by the borrower. In 1900, 60 out of 107 affiliates of 187 US-controlled TNCs were in activities other than manufacturing.[12]

But even where the loans were invested in manufacturing activities by the borrower it was usually in portfolio form, e.g. British railway investments in the USA, French investments in Russia. In the period up to the Second World War portfolio investments accounted for approximately three quarters of all investments, although the growing involvement of the USA, which held more in the form of direct ownership, had begun to modify the picture.[13]

The dramatic surge in foreign investment activities in the post-war period was accompanied by a contemporaneous dual qualitative change in form and sectoral distribution. According to Hood and Young the strength of the recovery of private investment was indicated by the fact that most of it was direct rather than portfolio capital: 'between 1951 and 1964 ... around 90 per cent of the private total took the form of direct investment to establish overseas affiliates'.[14] A large part of this direct foreign investment was in the manufacturing sector.

For example, in 1974 45 per cent of British and US, 50 per cent of Canadian, and 70 per cent of West German (FRG) foreign investment was in manufacturing. The comparable figures for Japan and Italy were 35 per cent and 32 per cent respectively, but the trend was an upward one in both instances (see Tables 6.2 and 6.3). Thus

Table 6.2 Selected developed market economies: total stock of direct investment abroad in all industry and in manufactures, in 1971 and latest available year*

Country/total industry manufactures	Total stock					
	1971			1974		
	Dollars (million)		%	Dollars (million)		%
USA						
Total industry	101	313	100.0	137	244	100.0
manufactures	44	370	43.8	61	062	44.5
UK						
Total industry	23	717	100.0	32	277	100.0
manufactures	10	043	42.3	14	131	45.2
Canada**						
Total industry	6	524	100.0	9	390	100.0
manufactures	3	437	52.7	4	729	50.4
FRG						
Total industry	7	277	100.0	19	915	100.0
manufactures	5	796	79.6	14	032	70.5
Japan						
Total industry	3	962	100.0	10	620	100.0
manufactures	1	092	27.6	3	723	35.0
Italy						
Total industry	3	343	100.0	2	864	100.0
manufactures		881	26.4		907	31.7

* Years for USA are 1973 and 1976; for the FRG, 1971 and 1976; for Italy, 1972 and 1976.
** Mining and quarrying is included in Manufacturing.

Source: UN (1978) pp. 242-3; quoted in Table 6.1.

the importance of direct foreign investment in manufacturing in total foreign investment during the post-war period is indisputable. However, it should be noted that the relative predominance of manufacturing activities in foreign investment is unlikely to continue indefinitely, although growth in absolute terms with its attendant potential implications for similar structures of production will persist.

The high elasticity of demand for service-sector goods combined with the fact that the bulk of foreign investment is located in high-income economies (see 'Country shares: location, etc.', below) suggests a likely predominance of services in direct foreign investment in the medium term.

6.2.1 Country shares: ownership

The stock of direct foreign investment of developed market economies rose from $105.3 billion in 1967 to $287.2 billion in

Table 6.3 Selected developed market economies: stock of direct foreign investment in all industry and in manufactures in developing countries, 1971 and 1974.

| Country/total industry | Stock in LDCs | | | |
| | 1971 | | 1974 | |
manufactures	Dollars (million)	%	Dollars (million)	%
USA				
Total industry	22 904	100.0	29 050	100.0
manufactures	7 320	34.1	11 362	39.1
UK				
Total industry	4 511	100.0	5 059	100.0
manufactures	1 828	40.5	2 409	47.6
Canada				
Total industry	1 575	100.0	2 214	100.0
manufactures	. . .	. . .	. . .	. . .
FRG				
Total industry	2 044	100.0	6 015	100.0
manufactures	1 605	78.5	3 633	60.4
Japan*				
Total industry	. . .	. . .	5 678	100.0
manufactures	. . .	. . .	2 887	50.8
Italy				
Total industry	1 208	100.0	1 078	100.0
manufactures	292	24.2	345	32.0

*   Developing country totals are calculated by adding figures for Asia, Africa, Oceania (except Australia) and the Middle East.

Source: See Table 6.2.

1976. During this period the relative shares of the seven leading countries, accounting for the bulk of foreign investment, experienced noticeable changes (see Table 6.4). The Federal Republic of

Table 6.4 Shares of seven leading investor countries in direct foreign investment, 1967-76 (in billions of dollars and percentages)

	1967	%	1971	%	1973	%	1976	%
USA	56.6	53.8	82.8	52.3	101.3	51.0	137.2	47.6
UK	17.5	16.6	23.7	15.0	26.9	13.5	32.1	11.2
Switzerland	5.0	4.8	9.5	6.0	11.1	5.6	18.6	6.5
France	6.0	5.7	7.3	4.6	8.8	4.4	11.9	4.1
FRG	3.0	2.8	7.3	4.6	11.9	6.0	19.9	6.9
Canada	3.7	3.5	6.5	4.1	7.8	3.9	11.1	3.9
Japan	1.5	1.4	4.4	2.8	10.3	5.2	19.4	6.7

Source: UN (1978), p. 236; quoted in Table 6.1.

Germany and Japan, particularly the latter, made rapid advances. The share of the FRG more than doubled from 3 per cent in 1967 to 6.9 per cent at the end of the period. In the same span of time the Japanese share more than quadrupled, from 1.5 per cent in 1967 to 6.7 per cent in 1976. It is likely that their relative shares have continued to improve. The relative shares of the USA and UK declined from 56.6 per cent and 17.5 per cent to 47.6 per cent and 11.2 per cent, respectively. This change in relative shares was inevitable with the recovery of Germany and Japan, considering the dynamism of their economies and export performance, when they began to follow the pattern of foreign investment of developed market economies.

6.2.2 Country shares: location and composition

Most foreign investment is located in developed market economies, i.e. investors who are virtually all from developed market economies prefer to invest in similar economies (see Table 6.5). In 1975, 74 per cent of all foreign investment was located in developed market economies; of the remainder 6 per cent was located in OPEC countries, 3 per cent in tax havens, and only 17 per cent in non-oil developing market economies. This feature reaffirms the

Table 6.5 Stock of direct investment abroad of developed market economies by host country, 1967–1975

Host country and country group	1967	1971	1975
Total value of stock (billions of dollars)	105	158	259
Distribution of stock (percentage)			
Developed market economies of which:	69	72	74
Canada	18	17	15
United States	9	9	11
United Kingdom	8	9	9
Germany, Federal Republic of	3	5	6
Other	30	32	33
Developing countries of which:	31	28	26
OPEC countries*	9	7	6
Tax havens**	2	3	3
Other	20	17	17
Total	100	100	100

*   Algeria, Ecuador, Gabon, Indonesia, Iran, Iraq, Kuwait, Libyan Arab, Jamahiriya, Nigeria, Qatar, Saudi Arabia, United Arab Emirates and Venezuela.
** Bahamas, Barbados, Bermuda, Cayman Islands, Netherland Antilles and Panama.

Source: UN (1978) p. 237; quoted in Table 6.1.

observation made in the introduction that the operations of TNCs in developed market economies are quantitatively larger, and hence more significant than the apparent changes associated with the new international division of labour and developing market economies.

It may be surmised that, with the self-explanatory exception of investments in extractive industries, proximity to markets is an important determinant of location. The defining characteristics of such markets are the relatively high level of incomes and production skills, which only exist in developed market economies. The importance of proximity to markets is of particular relevance for the manufacturing sector since direct foreign investment is also prompted by the prospect of competition and/or tariff barriers in export markets.

The substantially greater importance of developed market economies for those TNC operations, which can modify similar structures of production, is underscored by the proportion of manufacturing investment, which is crucial for such modification, in total investment, located in these economies as compared with developing market economies. For a selected group of developed host countries 47.65 per cent of all direct foreign investment was in the manufacturing sector in 1974, a total of approximately $53.8 billion. By contrast, only 30.3 per cent of direct foreign investment in developing host economies was in the manufacturing sector in 1972, a total of $13.3 billion; of the remainder, investment in petroleum totalling $15.4 billion comprised 35 per cent, a virtually identical amount was in services.[15]

6.2.3 TNCs and the group of strategic industries

Although a larger amount of direct foreign investment is located in developed market economies, and a higher proportion of this investment is in the manufacturing sector, as compared to developing market economies, the participation of TNCs in the group of strategic industries is high in both sets of countries (see Table 6.6). Among the developed market economies Australia and Canada have the highest percentage of foreign ownership. For example, as measured by assets, 84 per cent of chemicals, 72 per cent of iron and steel, and 83 per cent of motor vehicles in Australia were owned by foreign investors in 1972-3. Similarly, in Canada 73 per cent of chemicals, 70 per cent of rubber (measured by output), 64 per cent of electrical machinery and 84 per cent of motor vehicles

Table 6.6 Indicators of foreign participation in selected industries in developed market economies and developing countries, selected years.

ISTC No.	(351-2)	(355)	Estimated percentage of foreign share of: (371)	(382)	(383)	(3843)	
Developed countries							
Australia	84(A)	...	72(A)	...	...	83(A)	1972/73
Austria	21(E)	56(E)	...	...	40(E)	...	1973
Belgium/Luxembourg	73(O)	70(O)	...	32(E)	...	...	1970
Canada	33(E)	25(E)	11(E)	...	64(A)	84(A)	1973
France	33(A)	48(A)	33(R)	37(A)	51(A)	21(A)	1973
Germany, Fed. Rep. of	...	...	...	...	...	...	1974
New Zealand	...	...	...	...	...	...	1969/70
Spain	...	...	...	...	50(O)	84(O)	1973
Sweden	...	...	...	...	...	...	1973
Turkey	54(A)	59(A)	14(O)	43(A)	...	38(A)	1974
Developing countries							
Argentina	37(O)	75(O)	61(O)b/	82(O)	33(O)	84(O)	1969
Brazil	51(O)	44(O)	41(O)	55(A)b/	33(A)b/	100(A)	1976
India	27(O)	52(O)	37(O)	52(O)	33(O)	10(O)	1973
Korea, Republic of	22(E)	...	37(O)	19(O)	...	...	1970
Mexico	67(O)	84(O)	...	31(O)	63(O)	...	1973
Peru	67(S)	88(S)	...	25(S)	62(S)	...	1969
Philippines	...	73(O)	...	...	...	43(A)	1973
Singapore	46(E)	76(E)	21(E)	...	...	...	1968

Code:
ISTC No.
(351-2) Chemicals
(355) Rubber
(371) Iron and Steel basic industry
(382) Non-electrical machinery
(3843) Motor Vehicles

Key: A = Assets
E = Employment
O = Output

Source: UN (1978) p. 273; quoted in Table 6.1.

(measured by assets) were owned by foreign investors in 1973. Indeed, in 1973 52 per cent of employment in manufacturing in Canada was provided by TNCs; in Australia TNCs provided 29 per cent of employment in manufacturing and owned 42 per cent of all assets.[16]

Substantial foreign participation is also evident in key sectors of the economy in the largest Latin American countries (e.g. Argentina and Brazil), and countries in southeast Asia like Singapore (see Table 6.6). In fact, with the exception of the USA and Japan, all developed and virtually all developing market economies, are significant hosts to foreign investments. In recent years, however, there has been an acceleration of direct foreign investment in the USA from other developed market economies.[17]

6.3 Actual impact of TNC operations on the economic autonomy of the State

The conspicuous presence of TNCs in the industrial sectors of developed market economies suggests that the spread of transnational corporations and national autonomy in production are not necessarily at odds. In fact, the impact of TNC operations on the similar structures of production has not been significant in totality, either through the re-organisation of the strategic industries on a global rather than national basis, or owing to 'sourcing' policy.

The history of industrial policies in the latecomer countries of the second round, discussed earlier in the book, demonstrated the determination of the State to acquire the kind of economic autonomy necessary for perceived political security; such industrial policies usually took the form of import-substitution to establish the basic industrial infrastructure.

The old industrial nations have also resisted the dismantling of strategic industries and their re-location to sites in other parts of the world which might enjoy a comparative advantage in that product; this resistance is particularly well illustrated by the implacable policies over the re-location of textile and clothing (especially the latter) to developing countries.[18] Thus the global spread of TNC operations may have led to foreign ownership of national industries but significant changes in national production structures have not occurred yet.

It may, however, be argued that although the array of physical productive facilities remain within the country, the control of production flows is vested in the hands of TNCs and this may substantially affect national economic autonomy. A look at the relationship between trade flows and home production will indicate the extent to which this may be true.

It has been found that in most countries, despite significant foreign presence (see Table 6.6) most of the output is sold on the local market rather than exported. According to an UNCTAD study US majority-owned foreign affiliates as a group exported 18.6 per cent of their total sales in 1961 and 23.3 per cent in 1974. For developing market countries alone, as a group, comparable figures during the same period were 8.4 per cent and 10.6 per cent respectively. However, for Asia and the Pacific region the over-all level was closer to the world average although the proportion of exports to total sales only increased from 23.3 per cent in 1966 to 24.9 per cent in 1974 (see Table 6.7).

From the perspective of imports, threats to national control of production come from heavy reliance of internal consumption on foreign produced goods, i.e. on globally rationalised production in the specific case of the TNCs. Since incoming trade generated by TNCs is a sub-set of national imports, the upper limit to such imported production by TNCs at any moment is represented by the value of total imports in relation to total apparent consumption.

According to the UNCTAD (see Table 6.8) total imports of manufactures as a percentage of apparent consumption in the EEC, the USA, and Japan as a whole rose from 5.7 per cent in 1959–60 to 9.6 per cent in 1975. The highest percentage of imports in apparent consumption in 1975 was in metals (17.7 per cent), and the lowest was in transport equipment (8.3 per cent). These aggregated data, of course, conceal significant geographical variations; for example, the EEC is a much bigger importer than either the USA or Japan.

In the case of the EEC countries the ratio of the volume of manufactured imports to GNP was 15.8 per cent in 1978 (see Table 5.8). However, the ratio of imports to gross output was significantly higher in a number of sectors for individual countries (see Table 6.9). This was the case for the UK, France, and to a lesser degree Germany, countries which, as substantial powers, might be expected to prevent excessive import penetration; in the case of the UK such import penetration was less unexpected since it was the declining country.

But the apparent significance of the degree of import penetration

Table 6.7 Exports of US majority-owned manufacturing affiliates in 1966 and 1974 (millions of dollars)

	Total exports		Exports to the USA		Exports to others		Exports as % of sales	
	1966	1974	1966	1974	1966	1974	1966	1974
World	8817	40998	2679	11228	6138	29770	18.6	23.3
LDCs	578	2792	219	1024	359	1768	8.4	10.6
Latin America	362	1421	129	509	233	912	6.2	6.8
Argentina	n.a.	295	n.a.	73	n.a.	222	n.a.	10.4
Brazil	n.a.	423	n.a.	175	n.a.	248	n.a.	5.5
Colombia	18	97	4	11	14	86	5.9	8.2
Mexico	49	233	23	152	26	81	3.2	4.7
Other Asia and Pacific	208	1184	88	480	120	704	23.2	24.9

Source: United States Department of Commerce, Bureau of Economic Analysis, (1976) *Survey of Current Business*, Washington D.C., **56**, No. 5, pp. 25–34.

Table 6.8 Developed market economies: major categories of imports as percentage of apparent consumption of manufactures in EEC,* the USA and Japan

	Total manufactures	Metals	Textiles	Clothing
Total imports				
1959–1960	5.7	10.9	6.3	3.7
1971–1972	8.1	14.3	11.1	10.3
1973–1974	10.1	16.6	13.4	13.2
1975	9.6	17.7	10.0	16.3
Imports from developing countries				
1959–1960	1.2	2.9	1.6	1.0
1971–1972	1.3	3.2	2.6	4.1
1973–1974	2.0	4.1	3.6	6.0
1975	2.0	3.5	3.3	8.6
Imports from centrally planned economies				
1959–1960	0.2	0.4	0.2	0.1
1971–1972	0.3	0.9	0.5	0.7
1973–1974	0.5	1.3	0.8	1.1
1975	0.5	1.1	0.8	1.3
Imports from developed market economies ‡				
1959–1960	4.3	7.6	4.5	2.6
1971–1972	6.5	10.1	8.0	5.6
1973–1974	7.6	11.3	9.1	6.1
1975	7.1	13.2	5.9	6.4

	Wood Products paper and printing	Chemicals	Transport and equipment	Machinery and other manfc †
Total imports				
1959–1960	8.8	6.9	3.2	4.4
1971–1972	9.0	9.4	6.6	9.0
1973–1974	10.5	12.2	8.3	10.8
1975	9.2	12.1	8.3	10.6
Imports from developing countries				
1959–1960	0.4	1.3	0.1	0.1
1971–1972	0.7	1.3	0.1	0.6
1973–1974	0.9	1.8	0.2	1.0
1975	0.8	1.7	0.2	1.2
Imports from centrally planned economies				
1959–1960	0.5	0.3	—	0.1
1971–1972	0.5	0.4	0.1	0.1
1973–1974	0.5	0.7	0.1	0.2
1975	0.5	0.6	0.1	0.2
Imports from developed market economies ‡				
1959–1960	8.0	5.3	3.1	4.2
1971–1972	7.9	7.7	6.4	8.3
1973–1974	9.0	9.8	8.0	9.6
1975	8.0	9.8	8.0	9.2

Sources: Office for Development Research and Policy Analysis of the United Nations Secretariat, based on United Nations, *Handbook of International Trade and Development Statistics*, 1976 (United Nations publication, Sales No. E/F.76.II.D.3) and Supplement, 1977 (United Nations publication, Sales No. E/F.78.II.D1).

* The six countries of the original EEC (Belgium, France, Germany, Federal Republic of, Italy, Luxembourg and the Netherlands) considered as one trading unit; i.e., excluding EEC intratrade.

† Excluding rubber, non-metallic mineral products and processed food products.

‡ Including imports from the original EEC, the United Kingdom, the United States and Japan, but excluding EEC intratrade.

Table 6.9 Ratio of imports, and exports to gross output in strategic manufacturing industries in Germany, France and the UK 1978

Sector	Germany		France		UK	
	imports	exports	imports	exports	imports	exports
Textiles	44.0	34.2	29.2	26.7	27.9	23.3
Clothing & footwear	37.3	12.3	15.3	17.4	24.6	15.2
Paper	25.6	15.7	25.6	13.9	32.0	8.8
Printing	8.4	10.3	4.2	7.4	3.9	7.4
Chemicals	14.0	25.6	28.3	34.0	18.4	25.6
Basic metals	15.3	23.0	25.8	27.2	21.4	19.2
Metal products	12.8	25.0	21.6	23.4	12.3	16.9
Non-electrical machinery	12.6	41.3	29.1	35.7	25.9	38.7
Elec. machinery	12.0	23.5	27.4	32.5	20.0	25.0
Trans. equipment	14.1	35.7	19.7	36.1	34.0	38.3

Source: UN (1981) *Economic Survey of Europe in 1980,* New York, pp. 234-5.

is qualified by a number of factors. Firstly, in the case of the EEC countries, including Britain, the ratio of the reverse flow of exports to gross output seems to outweigh the incoming flow of imports to gross output in each of the sectors (see Table 6.9).[19] Thus the impact of high levels of import on potential production capability is neutralised by exports from the same sectors.

The reason for imports and exports between countries in products from the same industry is product differentiation.[20] A country may specialise in the production of particular types of machinery or develop expertise in a specific range of vehicles (e.g. buses and saloon cars) in the transport equipment sector. But such production facilities could, if required, be converted to the production of the varieties imported (e.g. tractors and small cars) within the same sector; perhaps more pertinently, most vehicle factories can also be converted to produce armoured carriers and tanks. In the machinery sector components are interchangeable, and firms are able to adapt to the production of different types of machines.[21] Thus the basic fact remains that imports as a percentage of consumption in the particular industry may affect the degree of economic autonomy, but in so far as the industry exists in the country the structure of national production remains unaltered.

Secondly, a major proportion of the imports in these sectors are the outcome of intra-EEC trade. Since the EEC is one economic unit it is only surprising, on the face of it, that greater specialisation and therefore larger levels of imports did not occur in the normal course of events (see concluding section of previous chapter for detailed analysis of the process by which national governments ensured the survival of industries of the strategic group despite economic union). In effect, economic union among member countries of the EEC means that they expect to provide a unified political and military response to major international conflagaration which might involve them in total war. The institutional expression of this expectation is NATO.

Thirdly, intra-EEC economic interdependence owing to imports is not so high that it would prevent individual countries from pursuing other objectives requiring military action without co-operation from other member countries. But the fundamental point should be stressed that the EEC is what Karl Deutsch describes as a 'security community', i.e. there is no expectation of war among themselves in foreseeable circumstances.[22]

Developing market economies are also more dependent on imports for consumption of products of the group of strategic industries. Imports depend on the stage of industrial structure, conceptualised in terms of early, middle, and late industry, which in turn is determined by the level of per capita incomes, as it has been elaborated in Chapter 1. Thus a higher level of imports in a wider range of products is inevitable given the lower level of per capita incomes in developing market economies.

More important for the present argument is the fact that TNCs are responsible for only part of the import flows. For example, the share of TNCs in total US imports (including non-manufactures) in 1974 amounted to 32.1 per cent. For developed and developing market economies the respective levels of such TNC imports were 24.8 per cent and 37.4 per cent. In 1970 TNCs were also responsible for 50 per cent of US exports; comparable figures for the UK are 30 per cent (1975), and for Canada 59 per cent (1971).[23] Thus, even if 50 per cent of all trade in manufactures (i.e. as reflected in imports in relation to GNP) were the outcome of TNC global production it would still have been under 8 per cent of output in 1978 for EEC countries, which have a relatively high level of import penetration. The highest figure would be under 22 per cent for German textile and clothing imports and the lowest would be 6 per cent for German electrical machinery imports in 1978.

The loss of between 10 and 20 per cent of national consumption owing to the disruption of imports would not be significant because domestic consumption could easily be increased at the expense of exports. In any case, most of these prosperous economies could also reduce civilian consumption as well if necessary, and by a larger percentage during war without creating privation.

Finally, it should be observed that all trade generated by TNCs does not necessarily imply globally rationalised production. Exports by TNCs could be similar to exports by firms with an exclusively national base, although in reality TNCs rather than such firms dominate trade in manufactures. Only if production is primarily for export can a global-market industry/factory be considered to exist. This is true for raw materials production, in principle, because their location is dictated by geology, climate etc. But such production of manufactures primarily for the world market only occurs in, as yet, quantitatively limited free trade zones.

Reiterating the basic points, it is concluded by stressing that: (a) from the perspective of national economic autonomy the crucial point is that virtually all countries which have achieved a degree of industrialisation (e.g. up to the level of the NICs) have reproduced similar structures of production despite the operations of TNCs; (b) despite foreign ownership the control over the production flows will remain within the country to a significant extent.

6.4 Direct foreign investment and developing market economies

The conclusion reached in point b) of the preceding paragraph requires some qualification with respect to developing market economies. It cannot escape attention that a fundamental asymmetry exists in the flow of direct foreign investment. While developed market economies are both hosts to foreign investment and foreign investors themselves, developing market economies are only hosts. The latter are only modest foreign investors, a characteristic which sharply limits their relative decision-making authority regarding present and future access over the location and distribution of economic resources.[24]

According to the UN study quoted above, intra-regional investment in Latin America amounted to $192 million in 1974, or about 1 per cent of the total stock of direct foreign investment in the region.[25] This amount has certainly increased since, although precise figures are unavailable. A similar flow of intra-regional investment has occurred in Asia, and growth rates have been impressive: for instance, the share of Hong Kong in the stock of direct foreign investment in the Philippines increased from 1 per cent in 1973 to 3 per cent in 1976. However, both Hong Kong and Singapore have become conduits for capital originating from developed market economies, owing to tax considerations.[26] Thus developing market economies essentially remain hosts to foreign investments, and their role as investors is minimal.[27] In conclusion, it should be noted that developing market economies have virtually no direct foreign investments in developed market-economies, making the asymmetry stark.

6.5 Intra-firm trade and contemporary trade relations

Up to now the discussion has assessed the impact of direct foreign investment, particularly in manufacturing, on national production structures. In what follows the direction of the analysis will be inverted to examine the degree to which trans-national production (i.e. production related to TNCs) impinges on international trade in manufactures.

Three issues need to be discussed in order to assess the impact of TNCs on the evolution of contemporary trade relations. Firstly, the proportion of total international trade (particularly in manufactures) which now takes place within the firm, i.e. intra-firm trade. Secondly, the costs which would be incurred by TNCs if such trade were disrupted, and thirdly, the influence of TNCs on international trade policy. Owing to the strong differences in quality, quantity and nature of data available for various countries the discussion on the first issue will be organised separately for the USA, other developed countries and developing ones, respectively.

The empirical evidence concerning the relationship between TNC operations and international trade is not comprehensive, but preliminary figures (particularly for the USA, the major investor) indicate that intra-firm trade is a significant proportion of international trade, especially in manufactures. According to the UNCTAD study on which this part of the analysis draws extensively, intra-firm transactions constitute 'a substantial portion of international trade and are increasing in importance'.[28]

6.5.1 USA: quantitative dimensions of intra-firm trade

The most detailed evidence pertains to 298 US TNCs and their 5,237 majority-owned affiliates. Two other sources of evidence are imports into the US under headings 806.30 and 807.00 of the Tariff

Schedule, and imports from 'related-parties' abroad by firms operating in the US.

Evidence from the first source shows that in 1973 US TNCs accounted for about one-quarter of total world exports ($73 billion out of $309 billion), and for approximately one-fifth of world exports of manufactures; this includes exports of parent companies and majority-owned foreign affiliates abroad.

Between 1966 and 1970, total exports of US TNCs increased by 69 per cent, while world exports rose by 53%. The exports of manufactures by US TNCs grew by 73 per cent, compared to 65 per cent for world exports. An enlarged estimate using the same statistics but enlarging the coverage to include all US TNCs (3,400 in all) suggests that one-third of total US manufactured exports were on an intra-firm basis.

A further indication of the growing importance of intra-firm trade is provided by the imports into the US under headings 806.30 and 807.00 of the Tariff Schedule. Duties on imports under these provisions are only levied on the value of processing abroad, the original product having been exported from the US.

Between 1966, when the relevant tariff provisions were introduced, and 1979 such imports grew from $953 million to $11,937.7 million. Apart from the recession year of 1975 such imports have risen rapidly (26 per cent per annum) in the 1970s, registering rates considerably in excess of the rates of growth of total US manufactured imports.[29]

Imports were concentrated in the metal products' industries dominated by TNCs, notably motor vehicles, engines, office machines, electronic components and sewing machines. The bulk of LDC trade under these provisions is in electronic components and clothing.

One final source of evidence about intra-firm trade is the detailed information on 'related-party' imports now reported in the US by the Department of Commerce. A 'related-party' is defined, for the purposes of these estimates, as a firm in which at least 5 per cent of the voting stock is owned by the other party to the transaction. The parent firm may be either the buyer or the seller; and neither need have any US ownership. Thus the definition includes non-US firms and is broad enough to embrace transactions which do not constitute production within vertically integrated enterprise, but it is a more satisfactory basis for defining and measuring intra-firm trade than the 50 per cent ownership rule employed by the US Department of Commerce.[30] It is reasonable to assume that transactions between a parent and a minority-owned affiliate are of economic and political significance.

In 1977 US 'related-party' imports amounted to 48.4 per cent of total imports (excluding petroleum); 53.7 per cent of total imports from OECD countries and 43.4 per cent from developing countries were transactions between 'related-parties'.

In the same year 53.6 per cent of all manufactured imports were 'related-party' transactions; 61.1 per cent of manufactured imports from OECD countries and 37 per cent from developing countries were transactions between 'related-parties'. For semi-manufactures the corresponding figures were 37.6 per cent of all imports in this category, 43.4 per cent of such imports from OECD countries and 17 per cent from developing countries.[31]

However, it should be noted that a substantial part (36 per cent) of total 'related-party' trade consists of whole-sale (i.e. re-sale without further manufacture) imports by non-US firms. This phenomenon is not different from normal third party exports by the same firms to the US and therefore somewhat qualifies the magnitude of intra-firm trade suggested by 'related-party' trade data.

6.5.2 USA: composition and distribution of intra-firm trade

Several features of intra-firm trade are relevant to the present discussion. First, according to the UNCTAD study cited above (excluding paragraphs 3-6 immediately preceding), the share of parent company exports to their majority-owned foreign affiliates accounts for the major portion of all intra-firm trade. In 1970 US parent companies enjoyed a surplus of $2,379 million in trade with such affiliates, an amount equal to the US trade surplus.

Second, a survey of one hundred large US firms suggests that foreign affiliates also serve as important distribution outlets for finished goods. Such whole-sale transactions accounted for 59 per cent of all intra-firm exports from the US in 1975, rising from 53 per cent in 1970. During the same period finished goods accounted for a similar but declining share of intra-firm imports for the same sample of firms. The share of such intra-firm imports declined from 65 per cent to 59 per cent while raw material imports rose from 9 per cent to 15 per cent; intermediates accounted for 25 per cent in 1975.[32]

Although intra-firm trade in finished goods is akin to normal third party trade and thus does not constitute 'sourcing' policy, the use of foreign affiliates for distribution purposes is an integral part of corporate planning for TNCs. The end of this priviliged access would create difficulties for TNC exporters because exclusive marketing arrangements confer advantages.

Third, the major part of exports by US majority-owned foreign affiliates were also on an intra-firm basis: 61.5 per cent for all industries and 69.3 per cent for manufacturing. A significant proportion of all exports by affiliates were destined for other affiliates in third countries as opposed to the US parent; 70.3 per cent for all industries and 58.2 per cent in manufacturing.[33]

Fourth, in the manufacturing sector two of the group of strategic industries, and an important sub-sector in a third account for 70 per cent of all intra-firm trade of US TNCs; transport equipment accounted for 41 per cent, non-electrical machinery 18 per cent, and chemicals 11 per cent.

Finally, the case of the US for which the most detailed evidence is available, highlights the significance of intra-firm trade and its potential political impact on trade policies. The more limited evidence concerning other countries is surveyed briefly below and as Helleiner observes, '. . . the new political forces operative in the US are likely to be reproduced in other industrialised countries;[34]

6.5.3 The UK

According to an inquiry undertaken in the UK in 1966, of 1,466 manufacturing TNCs, both British and foreign, UK TNCs exported 27 per cent of their total exports to foreign affiliates. By contrast, TNCs of US origin and of other countries operating in the UK exported 56 per cent and 35 per cent, respectively, of total exports on an intra-firm basis.

Another survey of 30 leading UK TNCs operating 100 affiliates in 22 developing countries, although incomplete suggests that 25 per cent of all trade is intra-firm, the largest consisting of UK parent exports to affiliates. The proportion of imports by affiliates from the parent company in developing countries was highest in the metal and engineering industries, probably due to assembly operations, and lowest in the chemical sector.[35]

6.5.4 The Federal Republic of Germany

A survey of the foreign activities of the 27 most important TNCs of the Federal Republic of Germany (FRG) conducted in 1973 provides indications of the importance of intra-firm trade for TNCs owned in the FRG.

The 27 German-owned TNCs accounted for 35 per cent of all manufactured exports from the FRG, and approximately 60.2 per cent of direct foreign investment in manufacturing. Between 1966 and 1971 the percentage of their exports sold to foreign affiliates increased from 34 per cent to 43 per cent.

Firms in the electrical and automobile industries exported the largest percentage (59 per cent and 57 per cent respectively) of their total exports to foreign affiliates. In comparison the proportion for the chemical industry, the largest foreign investor, is relatively low (36 per cent). Some two-thirds of such intra-firm exports of parent companies to their foreign affiliates were for resale.

The operations of TNCs of FRG origin are centred primarily in developed market economies, and intra-firm trade with these countries is growing at a more rapid rate than that with developing market economies. The affiliates of FRG TNCs in such developing countries, in common with affiliates of US and UK parents, depend largely on imports from parent companies (15.2 per cent of sales) and export very little (1.9 per cent of total sales) to them.[36]

6.5.5 *Norway and Sweden*

A study of foreign subsidiaries of other countries operating in Norway, 421 of which had majority-ownership, showed a significant level of intra-firm trade; in 1972 8 per cent of the subsidiaries imported more than a third of their total raw materials and components from their parent company.[37]

Intra-firm trade data on Swedish-owned TNCs reveal that between 1965 and 1975 internal deliveries to foreign subsidiaries rose from 15 per cent of total exports to 29 per cent.[38]

Data on exports from Canada show that in 1971 59 per cent of total exports were on an intra-firm basis.[39]

6.5.6 *Developing market economies and intra-firm trade*

It has already been observed that direct foreign investment in manufacturing occurs primarily because proximity to markets enhances competitive ability, and pre-empts the threat of tariff barriers. A further reason which has assumed increased importance is differential wage costs, as between developed and developing market economies.[40]

During the past decade or so a growing number of firms from

developed market economies have located labour-intensive parts of the production process of certain manufacturing industries in developing market economies. Although low wages seem to be the main attraction, most of this type of investment has been located in the medium-income developing market economies; i.e. the NICs rather than countries with the lowest wages. Two reasons can be adduced for this preference: firstly, the market of the host country is an important consideration; secondly, a minimum level of development in terms of infrastructure, the availability of skills, and importantly, political stability are regarded as a prerequisite.

Thus in recent years countries like Brazil and Mexico in Latin America, and Hong Kong, South Korea, Taiwan, and Singapore in Asia have received most of the direct foreign investment in manufacturing among developing market economies.[41] However, the share of developing market economies as a group in total direct foreign investment in manufacturing has diminished from 31 per cent in 1967 to 26 per cent in 1976. The share of developing market economies, excluding OPEC countries and tax havens, has declined from 20 per cent to 17 per cent over the same period.[42]

In the context of this declining share, it is not surprising that developing market economies accounted for 62.3 per cent of total US intra-firm trade, and 91.1 per cent in manufacturing; the bulk of this trade was associated with operations in Canada and the EEC.[43]

In transactions with developing market economies petroleum products dominated intra-firm trade of US majority-owned foreign affiliates, confirming the earlier conclusion that the importance of these countries in international trade in manufactures has been exaggerated by the apparent successes of the NICs; rates of growth have been impressive but relative shares are still modest, except in a narrow range of products.

To express the same arguments in quantitative terms, 57 per cent of all exports of US majority-owned foreign affiliates in developing countries were on an intra-firm basis. Of these total intra-firm exports only 4.3 per cent were in manufactures.

In the manufacturing sector, which accounted for less than 5 per cent of all intra-firm trade of US majority-owned foreign affiliates in developing countries, 53 per cent of all exports were on an intra-firm basis. In certain Latin American countries the proportion reached 65 per cent. In other words, manufactures are a marginal item in the total intra-firm exports of US majority-owned foreign affiliates in developing countries but the majority of exports in manufactures are intra-firm. It should also be noted that the world-wide export activities of US majority-owned foreign affiliates in manufactures in developing market economies has been increasing rapidly, and quintupled between 1966 and 1974.

The importance of intra-firm trade for manufactured products in developing countries is underlined by data on US majority-owned affiliates in Brazil and Mexico. One analysis cited by the UNCTAD study shows that intra-firm trade represents a substantial part of manufactured exports by US majority-owned affiliates in Brazil and Mexico. In 1972 it accounted for 73 per cent and 82 per cent respectively, rising from 68 per cent and 54 per cent in 1960. It is noteworthy that intra-firm trade occurred in 10 out of 12 industrial sub-sectors in both countries.

In Mexico the bulk of intra-firm trade was accounted for by majority-owned affiliates of US TNCs. In 1972, 56 per cent of chemicals, 55 per cent of primary and fabricated metals, 70 per cent of non-electrical machinery, 89 per cent of electrical machinery, 100 per cent of transportation equipment, and 100 per cent of instruments exported by US majority-owned foreign affiliates in Mexico were on an intra-firm basis.

Although imports from parent companies by these affiliates have declined since 1966, such imports still accounted for 12 per cent and 18 per cent of total material production costs in Brazil and Mexico, respectively, in 1972; and 50 per cent and 58 per cent, respectively, of the affiliates' total import requirements. More recent evidence about Brazil shows that imports by 115 TNCs in 1974 were valued at $2.9 billion, or approximately one-third of total national imports.

A survey of Japanese and US TNCs in the Republic of Korea shows that over 50 per cent of their total imports of raw materials originated from parent companies or from the country in which the parent company was based. The proportion of imported intermediate inputs throughout most of manufacturing in Korea is high, particularly in firms with foreign participation. More than 60 per cent of intermediate inputs in the petroleum and electronic machinery industries, and between a quarter and a third in transportation equipment, machinery and metal industries were imported in 1975.

In conclusion it may be reiterated that the share of developing market economies in total intra-firm trade in manufactures is less than 9 per cent. In addition, although 57 per cent of all exports from developing countries were on an intra-firm basis, manufactures constituted only 4.3 per cent of such exports. Thus although intra-firm trade is important for developing country exports (53 per cent of manufactures) their relative importance for TNCs is not disproportionate. In this context it is interesting to note that developing countries probably encourage TNC participation in the export sector (e.g. Korea) as a guarantee of continuing access to markets in developed market economies, underlining the apparent importance of TNCs in the formulation of national trading policies — a feature to be discussed at greater length later in this chapter.[44]

Before assessing the importance of the phenomena discussed above for international trade policies it would be useful to summarise the main findings in point form:

(1)   Intra-firm trade constitutes a significant proportion of trade, particularly US trade; also over 61 per cent of imports from OECD countries.

(2)   Judging from the US experience, exports from parents to their majority-owned foreign affiliates tend to dominate this trade, particularly in the case of manufactures.

(3)   Finished products comprise an important part of intra-firm trade, somewhat qualifying the apparent significance of global production systems.

(4)   In the case of the US most exports by majority-owned foreign affiliates are also on an intra-firm basis; this is also the case for manufactures. A significant proportion of such exports is destined for plants in third countries.

(5)   Products of some of the strategic industries dominate intra-firm trade in manufactures.

(6)   The share of developing countries in total intra-firm trade is small but intra-firm trade does comprise a large part of their exports. Similarly, manufactures are a small percentage of total intra-firm trade of developing countries but the major part of trade in manufactures is intra-firm.

(7)   Finally, according to one estimate, 25 per cent of all international trade in manufactures is intra-firm.[45]

6.6 Economic importance of intra-firm trade to TNCs and the influence of TNCs on trade policy

The rapid growth of intra-firm trade and underlying changes in the international division of labour have important consequences for trade policy in the developed market economies. TNCs, particularly of US ownership, have been in the forefront of intra-firm transactions, and it is their impact on trade policy which needs to be understood. In this context, the impact of US TNCs on trade policy is of special interest since US policies towards the existing international economic order are likely to be decisive in determining the outcome of contemporary protectionist pressures because the US remains an indispensable market for other major economies.

Economic importance of intra-firm trade to TNCs: The purely quantitative importance of intra-firm trade is undeniable, as Helleiner has observed, 'a remarkably high proportion of international trade now takes place on an intra-firm basis in oligopolistically organised markets'.[46] This trade is also associated with transactions in intermediate products and technology gaps. Thus TNCs have a compelling incentive to internalise such transactions in order to minimise search and transaction costs and to capture their own share of available 'quasi-rents'.

As a result, national boundaries are a handicap for TNCs in their efforts to rationalise production globally, maximising global profitability. Such hindrances require adherence to an array of financial obligations and regulations like the payment of customs dues, fulfilment of administrative rules (e.g. relating to currency controls), and other prohibitions and regulatory devices, and complications due to differential (and often conflicting) national taxation and legal stipulations. These barriers are analogous to transport costs to the free flow of intra-firm resources. And TNCs find such barriers troublesome and costly like transport costs and prefer them to be as low as possible.

Thus TNCs are strong and powerful advocates of freedom in international exchange and payments. The free flow of financial and human capital, and technology trade is as important to them as free trade in goods and services; the shift to exporting services will make such freedom important for countries like the US. In addition, the link between factor and goods flows is extremely close in the context of the operations of particular TNCs.[47]

Firms are averse to the imposition of barriers by their own national government, which may not only impinge on their activities directly, but also, even when they do not, provoke retaliatory action abroad against their exporting or investing operations in sectors unrelated to those in which the original action was taken. The fear of a chain reaction precipitated by the actions of their own government is therefore a concern of TNCs even if it does not affect them directly in the first instance. The collapse of the liberal international economic order, which displays remarkable resilience despite considerable pressure, would greatly reduce the advantage of internationally rationalised production and leave 'the transnation corporations with many useless plants', a scenario they will resist.[48]

6.6.1 *The influence of TNCs on trade policy*

The ability of giant economic agents like TNCs in developed market economies to influence public policy, particularly economic policy, cannot be seriously doubted.[49] A study by Helleiner (which forms the basis of the discussion below), following the precedent set by Kindleberger's analysis of group behaviour, suggests that TNCs in the US have been able to exercise a dominant influence on US trade policy. It may be assumed that not very dissimilar patterns of political influence are exercised by TNCs located in other developed market economies.[50]

An examination of the structure of US trade barriers, as opposed to the over-all level of tariffs, shows a positive correlation between the height of US effective protection rates on the one hand and unskilled labour intensity on the other. Furthermore, most quantitative import restrictions and voluntary export restraints, e.g. on cotton (and eventually all other) textiles clearly protect unskilled labour-intensive products.

The analysis by Cheh also demonstrates that the (relative) size of US nominal tariff and non-tariff reductions in the Kennedy Round was negatively related to unskilled labour intensity as well as to the original level of protection, and positively to the industry's growth rate.[51] Preeg shows that the largest reductions were achieved in industries typified by advanced technology, product innovation, and large, often international firms.[52]

Cheh deduced from his evidence on the structure of US tariffs that trade policy was designed to minimise short-run labour adjustment costs. But as Helleiner points out, the limited effects of the US trade adjustment programme during the same period to ease adjustment costs do not make Cheh's explanation a plausible one.

Another analysis, in terms of bargaining theory, attributes the bias against labour-intensive products in the Kennedy Round to the weak negotiating position of developing countries who would have been the principal beneficiaries of lower barriers in such products. Since they were unable to offer significant reciprocal concessions, their interests received less than equal attention. However, a micro-level examination of recent shifts in attitudes toward trade policy suggests that the importance of TNCs has been underestimated.

It is argued that the recent shift in perceptions of organised US labour stems from changes in the economic environment brought about by the transformation of international exchange, i.e. the international mobility of capital. Organised US labour (represented by the AFL-CIO) has now shifted to a position of over-all protectionism. Labour and industry are now frequently at odds over trade policy within the same industry, whereas they previously typically concurred.

The explanation offered by Helleiner for the shift in attitudes of organised labour is the weakening of their bargaining position because of the international mobility of capital owing to the TNC. The imperfections in the international labour market which allowed US labour (as in other developed market economies) to be relatively highly rewarded has been progressively undermined by the possibility of locating production abroad — the 'run-away' plant as labour describes it. In particular, unskilled and semi-skilled labour, which enjoyed a privileged position (in international terms), finds itself seriously threatened.

In the past, organised US labour supported liberal trading arrangements because most AFL-CIO members were not in industries directly affected by international trade; indeed 56 per cent of the membership was not even in manufacturing. But the existence of non-competing groups differentiated by skills, industry and regions which protected wage and employment levels is threatened by enhanced international capital mobility. The position of the scarce factor labour has been significantly weakened in every US industry since the mobility of capital brought about by TNCs affects the labour market as a whole. This explanation acquires added cogency when one considers that although the attitude of the AFL-CIO has changed the composition of its membership has not.

In the contemporary period the particular combination of protectionism and liberalism which has emerged in the US can thus be explained in terms of two pressures: organised US labour and the TNCs, of which the latter is proving the more influential, judging by the continuing successes in reducing tariff barriers in manufacturing trade at the Tokyo Round of GATT.

The influence of TNCs on trade policy is further evidenced by the size of import duties upon primary and intermediate products, which are usually lower than average duties on finished goods. These are the products which dominate intra-firm trade (i.e. imports under provisions 806.30 and 807.00 for instance), and hence of special interest to TNCs. If such production is undertaken locally protection is afforded, but this would probably prompt market entry by TNCs who would prefer to manufacture locally themselves rather than buy at arm's length. And if this local production is taken over by internationally-orientated firms the pressure for protection is likely to subside.

The escalation of tariff levels with the stage of processing can be interpreted as the consequence of the absence of production in the US of certain raw materials. But even if this is true, as Helleiner points out, the continued escalation from semi-processed to processed is not fully explained since the raw material can be imported duty free and processed locally from the first stage of manufacture. However, this is not the case and can be imputed to the more effective pressure from the user than that from the particular producer.

In part, the explanation for this situation is that local producers are often vertically integrated with the final user, very likely a TNC, for which the duty has no significance. From a political perspective, the dispersal of users geographically, as compared to the particular producer, allows them to influence more Congress votes. Thus one may concur with Helleiner's conclusion that

> one can then explain this particular escalation in terms of the political power of transnational enterprises the bulk of whose intra-firm trade is in such intermediate products.[53]

Another indication of the impact of TNCs on trade policy (precisely, the structure of US trade barriers) is provided by the lower tariffs and larger reductions achieved in the Kennedy Round for products characterised by capital-intensity and research-intensity, products in which US firms trade internationally.

The introduction of value added tariffs under items 806.30 and 807.00 of the Tariff Schedule, discussed earlier in the chapter, also conferred benefits on TNCs (including trading firms), reflecting their influence over trade policy. Indeed the very rapid growth of imports under these provisions underlines the pre-eminence of TNCs, since the import of products exported for processing in the first instance is undoubtedly detrimental to the interests of labour.

Two final examples of the impact of TNCs on trading arrangements are the US–Canadian auto agreement which permitted a substantial rationalisation of the north American automobile industry; and the US government guarantees, insurance, and tax deferrals enjoyed by direct foreign investment, privileges unavailable to the importation by arm's length US investors of foreign bonds.

The institutional expression of the preferences of TNCs with respect to trade and investment policies took shape in the form of the Trilateral Commission. The Trilateral Commission, which includes among its members leading politicians like Carter and Kissinger and top industrialists from the western world and Japan, is also concerned with other issues, e.g. the governability of industrial democracies, but trade issues have figured prominently in its deliberations. It advocates freedom of exchange in international economic relations, both in trade and investment, representing the interests of the TNCs, which were instrumental in its creation.[54]

Notes

1. Of course, the spread of industrialisation itself introduces structural transformation by altering the international allocation of economic activity, e.g. by the creation of new locations of production.
2. The opportunities for investment in productive activities in the US were circumscribed to the degree that there was no shortage of local investment capital. The Japanese government discouraged foreign investment in Japan for nationalist reasons.
3. Adam in Radice (ed.) (1975) p. 90.
4. Woytinsky (1955) p. 205.
5. Ibid. p. 206-7.
6. Ibid. p. 221.
7. UN (1978) p. 236.
8. Streeton (1981) p. 314.
9. UN (op. cit.) p. 37 and pp. 213-19 for a detailed breakdown of firms by origin.

10.   Vaupel and Curhan (1969) p. 125.
11.   UN (Ibid.) p. 37.
12.   Hood and Young (1979) pp. 10-11; and Vernon (1973) p. 67.
13.   Hood and Young (Ibid.).
14.   Ibid. p. 12; also see OECD (1981), pp. 5-8, especially.
15.   UN (op. cit.) p. 244 and p. 260.
16.   Ibid. p. 263.
17.   The inflow of capital as a percentage of outflow (i.e. direct invest-
       ment) from the US rose steadily from 17.8 per cent in 1967-9 to 40.5
       per cent in 1976, at a time when direct investment outflow continued
       to rise; UN (ibid) pp. 238-9.
18.   See section 5.10 of previous chapter.
19.   Unlike the other countries however, Britain the declining country,
       was also losing shares in the world market.
20.   This is the thesis of Linder (1961).
21.   See Rosenberg (1976), pp. 141-72.
22.   See Deutsch (1968).
23.   UN (op. cit.) pp. 44 and 220.
24.   The situation of both developed and developing market economies
       as hosts to TNCs might seem implicitly to raise the question of TNC
       impact on the process of development. This is a large and important
       question and only a few cursory remarks can be made in the context
       of direct foreign investment in manufacturing. Firstly, the relative
       share of such investment in manufacturing in developing market
       economies is smaller than in developed market economies, as it has
       already been noted, and its absolute size is considerably smaller than
       the total invested in manufacturing in developed market economies
       by TNCs. Its impact on the development process is ambivalent, at the
       very least (see UN Transnational Corporations in Developing Coun-
       tries, The Case of Backward Linkages via Subcontracting (1981) pp.
       8-9; also Streeten, and Lal (1977). Most probably TNCs are unlikely
       to have initiated the process of industrialisation since they usually
       appear in a country in response to the availability of a market which
       has been created by local efforts.
25.   This excludes investment stock held by the major tax havens in the
       Caribbean region and by Panama amounting to several million
       dollars. See UN (1978) p. 51.
26.   Ibid. p. 52.
27.   Developing OPEC countries have usually invested in short-term
       securities, with some notable though quantitatively limited ventures
       like the Iranian Government purchase of stock in the giant Krupp
       enterprise in the Federal Republic of Germany.
28.   UNCTAD (1978) *Dominant Positions of Market Power of Transnational
       Corporations*, p. 13. Where otherwise not attributed all data in suc-
       ceeding pages are from this document — ch. 13, pp. 13-19.

29. Helleiner (1981) p. 36.
30. The difference between 'related-party' data and those pertaining to majority-owned foreign affiliates is important. The latter excludes non-US firms, and only includes firms with 50 per cent or more equity ownership. The 50 per cent ownership rule does not record transactions between US-based firms and minority-owned affiliates abroad; such transactions are likely to be a motivation for advocacy of an open international trading system as well. Furthermore, imports to the US from 'related-parties' abroad also encompass transactions which do not arise because of exports from US firms that are re-imported after processing abroad, i.e., those covered by items 806.30 and 807.00 of the Tariff Schedule; see Helleiner, (op. cit.) p. 37.
31. Ibid. p. 28.
32. UN (op. cit.) p. 44.
33. UNCTAD (1978) p. 13. Also see UN (ibid.) p. 221 for another estimate.
34. Helleiner (1977) p. 116.
35. Also see UN (op. cit.), which quotes a somewhat higher figure.
36. UNCTAD, (ibid.) pp. 18-19.
37. Ibid. p. 19.
38. Ibid. and UN ibid. p. 43.
39. UN ibid.
40. Actually it is more plausible that TNCs invested in these countries to cater for the local market and then began to export. The advantages which such firms would consequently enjoy compel other firms to follow suit. Only free trade zones cater primarily for the world market; also see Helleiner (1976).
41. These countries also have the more prosperous markets among developing countries, as measured by per capita income.
42. UN (1978) section III 33, p. 237.
43. However, this situation does not provide an accurate indication of the relative importance of developed and developing market economies for TNCs since the actual source of corporate profits is frequently unknown owing to the phenomenon of transfer pricing.
44. See Cohen (1975) p. 135.
45. Streeten (op. cit.) p. 314.
46. Helleiner (1977) p. 106.
47. Ibid.
48. UN (ibid.) p. 45. Also see Trilateral Commission Task Force Reports: 1-7. *The Triangle Papers*, (1977) pp. 75-98. And Freiden (1977) pp. 1-22; both these documents illustrate the political determination of TNCs to preserve an open international economic order.
49. E.g. Horowitz (ed.) (1969) and Mills (1956).
50. Kindleberger (1951).

51.   Cheh (1974).
52.   Helleiner (1977) p. 104.
53.   Ibid p. 111.
54.   Trilateral Commission, (op. cit.); Frieden (1977))op. cit.); Ullmann, *Foreign Affairs* (October 1976) pp. 1-19.

Conclusion

A distinctive hypothesis is put forward in this book to explain the fundamental roots of international trade disputes in manufactures, both in the contemporary period and since the industrial revolutions of the nineteenth century. Existing theories are unable to explain the systematic pattern and recurrent feature of such disputes, i.e. why such trade disputes between countries occur over the same markets or products and the reasons for their periodic recurrence during the past century or so.[1]

It is argued in the alternative hypothesis put forward that the real causes of international trade disputes in manufactures hinge on the division of the international political system into competitive nation-states. The insecurity of existence in an international political system, characterised by the competitive relations of nation-state actors, prompts latecomer countries to pursue the goal of industrial transformation once the distribution of power has been dramatically altered by the occurrence of industrialisation in firstcomer countries; military capability, on which the distribution of power and the status of countries is predicated, being heavily dependent on the level of industrialisation.

In this existential condition of international rivalry and concomitant insecurity the onset of industrialisation in Britain in the late eighteenth century set in motion a powerful new dynamic in the international political system. The State in the latecomer countries of Europe, Japan, the USA and eventually elsewhere, felt compelled to industrialise their own country in response to the threat posed by the presence of industrially, and therefore militarily, powerful nations elsewhere.

In this context, the military activities in Europe over two and a half centuries before the onset of British industrialisation, underline the impact of defence production on the basic contours of the manufacturing economy. This period of endemic wars and the evolution of the mass armies prepared the basis for the subsequent industrial transformation in Europe. The demand for mass-produced and standardised goods for the purpose of war stimulated innovation in the techniques of production and the adoption of new methods of organisation, lowering unit costs for the sizeable civilian demand which had previously only remained potential. The wars also accelerated the process of capital accumulation.

This particular path to industrial transformation of economies had a profound impact on the character of the civilian economy, which burgeoned with the progress of industrialisation. The timing of industrialisation itself was the result of the occurrence of the two and a half centuries of war and their mass character. The impact of such military activity and its needs have continued to mould the nature of industrial society since that distant period, although its contemporary influence is more readily observable.[2]

The State in the latecomer countries plays a decisive role in promoting industrialisation, which crucially involves the acquisition through imitation of a group of industries that can be considered 'strategic'. By directly establishing or assisting in their acquisition the State ensures a national defence capability and relative economic self-sufficiency.

A survey of countries in late-nineteenth century Europe, Japan and the USA bears this out in detail; a similar survey of two developing countries in the period following World War II offers even more convincing evidence. The latter two countries display extensive State involvement in the economy regardless of professed ideological preferences, highlighting the fundamentally nationalist impulses which motivate such intervention and the imperatives that derive from the extremely competitive market conditions faced by latecomers in the contemporary world. Finally, it is clear that the behaviour of the State in these two distinctive countries is indicative of the magnitude of State intervention in the economy, which is now recognised to have become commonplace in the so-called newly-industrialising countries.

The sponsorship of the group of strategic industries by the State may take the form of assistance to private entrepreneurs or their creation under public ownership. The particular method chosen is dictated by both the overall economic conditions encountered by latecomer countries and local class interests and pressures. The creation of publicly-owned production facilities occurs because private entrepreneurs may be unable to raise the necessary capital, since the competitor firstcomer countries are likely to have achieved a scale of operation that requires large investments, with correspondingly greater gestation periods and risks. In addition, the complex interdependence between the group of strategic industries makes it necessary to establish production in several industries rapidly, in order to reap the benefits of external economies of scale. On the other hand, the degree of involvement might be circumscribed if dominant groups within the country have access to capital. For example, in the case of the USA the inflow of European capital in the propitious circumstances of the late nineteenth and early twentieth centuries allowed private entrepreneurs to operate much of the industry which in Europe and Japan had been in public ownership. The State may also divest itself of public undertakings at some stage, as it did in nineteenth century Japan and the Republic of Korea in the 1960s.

A number of other instruments of State intervention affecting industry, both in the public and private sectors, include tariff barriers, public procurement, etc., all of which have been in evidence in latecomer countries.

Finally, it might be appropriate to note that given the decisive importance of the group of strategic industries for defence and relative economic self-sufficiency, the State will ensure their survival subsequent to the achievement of industrialisation. This potential necessity exists for all industrialised countries and the occasion when it is likeliest to arise is the context of competition over markets. The State then deploys its economic and political resources in the defence of its strategic industries and, historically this has recurred because of the competition offered by latecomers to the previously ascendant earlycomer, events to be recapitulated below.

Whatever its form, State intervention appears to have been instrumental in the establishment of similar production structures, through what can be viewed as a process of imitation. The evidence presented in the first chapter demonstrates that modern economic growth is characterised by patterns which are broadly similar for countries irrespective of the actual historical period in which they occur. The similarity is observable in terms of the growth patterns of different sectors and different manufacturing industries in relation to GNP per capita. It is also borne out by the comparison of a number of structural indicators, namely (a) a measure of the linkages both forward and backward which connect a single industry with every other industry, (b) the degree of triangularisation of the input-output tables and (c) the comparability of the input coefficients of the countries sampled.

On the basis of the evidence in the literature regarding the patterns of growth and the similarities of structure between countries it is possible to single out a group of industries that appears to have been strategic for the process of growth, in terms of their performance, as well as the role they have in the industrial structure; the strength of backward and forward linkages and the presence of economies of scale in particular. The industries are also the ones that appear to have been vital for defence production, and have historically attracted the keenest State intervention.

Thus it may be inferred that the process of imitation has not occured merely because of the absence of alternative paths to industrialisation. It has stemmed rather from the necessity of relying on the same key industries likely to be possessed by other industrialised adversaries. The compulsion towards imitation has been reinforced by the technical and economic interrelationships which exist among the strategic industries, making each necessary for the others, in order to achieve self-sustained growth.

The process of imitation institutes a crucial link between economic growth and international trade. Imports of strategic industry products are a critical factor in the process of imitation, since the first sustained spurt of industrialisation appears to be constituted by import-substitution in the latecomer countries. Obversely, these imports become a vital component of a flow of demand that guarantees growth and fosters dynamic economies of scale for the firstcomer exporting countries. As a result productive capacity in the latter inherently tends to exceed local consumption requirements. And the loss of export markets may precipitate a vicious cycle of stagnation and low productivity.

With the spread of industrialisation, the duplication of production structures implied by imitation unavoidably leads to the emergence of world-wide surplus capacity in the group of strategic industries. And since world industrialisation is an on-going process, latecomers also become firstcomers with respect to countries industrialising after them, and the inherent imbalance in international trade acquires endemic proportions, with trade disputes ensuing systematically with every new round of world-wide growth.

The presence of several major industrial powers in the international economy since the spread of industrialisation in the nineteenth century has led to conflicts over markets into the present period. The attempts to cartellise the world market and ensure stability, which began early in the twentieth century and became widespread during the 1930s failed to resolve the problem. It was only the intervention of the two great wars that temporarily resolved the problem of over-capacity by eliminating important economic actors.

During the post-war period, the decline of Britain's relative position in the world market for the strategic industries, which can be traced to the third quarter of the nineteenth century, resumed with the end of reconstruction in Germany. However, Britain was now joined by the USA with the emergence of Japan. The US, which had become the dominant exporting nation for the strategic industries in the aftermath of the Second World War, had begun to decline after the early 1960s. By contrast, Germany and Japan made significant inroads and set the stage for serious tensions over world market shares. To this can be added the incursion of the NICs in textiles and clothing although certain countries have emerged as competitors in other markets too, e.g. South Korea in shipping.

The strains in international economic relations and threats to liberal trading arrangements have become especially acute now. However, the international trading operations of transnational corporations in manufactured goods have introduced an influential new participant opposed to a collapse of the liberal international economic order.

Although TNCs have not altered the relatively self-sufficient economic systems evidenced by similar production structures across countries, their impact on international trade in manufactured products (including the strategic industries) has been significant. The intra-firm trade across national boundaries in which they engage explains their opposition to protectionism, which would disrupt it.

The future of the international economic order and, more importantly, the territorial-state system which defines its parameters, is uncertain. The international economy, as numerous scholars have noted, has outgrown the international political system. However, the durability of the territorial-state system is underlined by the continuing success of countries in maintaining national economic autonomy although the economically and politically powerful TNC system exercises pressures in a contrary direction. In addition, the hostility between socialist countries, who are economically self-sufficient and unaffected by the operations of TNCs tending to reduce economic autonomy, and capitalist

countries, makes the latter reluctant to allow economic transformations which affect their own economic autonomy. As one
scholar has argued, the dramatic social and political upheavals in
many latecomer countries which preceded industrialisation occurred because of competition between nation-states, and it should
therefore be reiterated that while such competition remains the
dominant reality of international relations, it would be premature to
speculate about the demise of the nation-state.[3] For the immediate
future, the presence of the TNC system is only likely to pre-empt
the sudden collapse of the liberal international economic order by
even greater internalisation of international trade within their intra-
firm operations.

Notes

1.   The shortcomings of existing approaches have already been discussed
     in the introduction to this book.
2.   According to one recent report it is anticipated that one important sub-
     sector of the transport industry will be shaped by a £500 billion
     investment in combat and trainer aircraft; 'Military needs will shape
     the airliners of 2000', *Financial Times* (21 August 1980) p. 6; also see
     Milward (1977) for a succinct summary.
3.   See Skocpol (1979).

Bibliography

Abegglen, J.C. and Hout, T.M. (1978) 'Facing up to the Trade Gap with Japan', *Foreign Affairs*, **57**, No. 1. pp. 146-68.

Adelman, I. (1979) (ed.) *Economic Growth and Resources*, (Proceedings of the Fifth World Congress of the International Economic Association Tokyo, Japan, 1977, Vol. 4), London.

Adreano, R. (ed.) (1966) *The Economic Impact of the Civil War*, Boston.

Allen, G.C. (1972) *A Short Economic History of Modern Japan*, London.

Allen, G.C. (1978) *How Japan Competes, A Verdict on 'Dumping'*, IEA, London.

Allen, G.C. (1967) *Japan as a Market and Source of Supply*, Oxford.

Allen, G.C. (1979) *British Industry and Economic Policy*, London.

Anderson, P. (1974) *Lineages of the Absolutist State*, London.

Andic, S. and Veverka, J. (1964) *The Growth of Government Expenditure in Germany since the Unification*, Finanzarchiv, Neue Folge, Band 23, Heft 3, Juli.

Apter, D. and Goodman, L.W. (eds.) (1976) *The Multinational Corporation and Social Change*, New York.

Aron, R. (1967) *Peace and War*, London.

Aronson, J.D. (1977) *Money and Power, Banks and The World Monetary System*, Beverley Hills, California.

Asakawa, K. (1929) 'Agriculture in Japanese History: A General Survey', *The Economic History Review*, Vol. II. No. 1.

Ashley, P. (1920) *Modern Tariff History: Germany, U.S. France*, London.

Ashton, T.S. (1955) *The Industrial Revolution, 1760–1830*, London

Ashworth, W. (1975) *A Short History of the International Economy Since 1850*, London.

Averitt, R.A. (1968) *The Dual Economy*, New York.

Bairoch, P. (1975) *The Economic Development of the Third World Since 1900*, London.

Balassa, B. (1969) *Trade Liberalization Among Industrialized Countries*, New York.

Balassa, B. (ed.) (1970) *Changing Patterns in Foreign Trade and Payments*, New York.

Baran, P.A. and Sweezy, P.M. (1966) *Monopoly Capital*, Middlesex, UK.

Barbera, H. (1973) *Rich Nations and Poor in Peace and War: (Continuity and Change in the Development Hierarchy of Seventy Nations from 1913–1952)*, Lexington, Mass.

Bardhan, P. (1978) 'External Economies, Economic Development and the Theory of Protection' in S.P. Singh (ed.) *Underdevelopment to Developing Economies*, Bombay.

Barker, E.J. (1912) *Modern Germany*, London.

Barkin, K.D. (1970) *The Controversy Over German Industrialization 1890–92*, London.

Batchelor, R.A. Major, R.L. Morgan, A.D. (1980) *Industrialization and the Basis of Trade*, Cambridge, UK.

Beard, C.A. and M.B. (1944) *A Basic History*, Garden City, New York.

Beard, C.A. (1956) *An Economic Interpretation of the Constitution of the United States*, New York.

Beasley, W.C. (1963) *The Modern History of Japan*, London.

Benoit, E. (1973) *Defence and Economic Growth in Developing Countries*, Lexington. Mass.

Bergsman, J. (1970) *Industrialization and Trade Policies*, Oxford.

Bergsten, C. and Krause, L.B. (1975) *World Politics and International Economics*, Washington, D.C.

Bergsten, C.F. (1976) *The Dilemmas of the Dollar: The Economics and Politics of U.S. International Monetary Policy*, New York.

Bergsten, F.C. (ed.) (1975) *Toward a New World Trade Policy: The Maidenhead Papers*, Lexington, Mass.

Bergsten, C.F. (1977) *Managing International Economic Relations: Selected Papers of C.F. Bergsten 1975–76*, Lexington, Mass.

Bergsten, F.C. and Tyler, W.G. (1973) *Leading Issues in International Economic Policy*, Lexington, Mass.

Berrier, R.J. (1980) 'Traditional Industrial Sectors Textiles and Steel', (Panel on the International Crisis — the French Response, International Studies Association), Los Angeles, California.

Bhagwati J.N. and Desai, P. (1979) *Planning for Industrialization and Trade Policies*, Delhi.

Black, C.E. et al. (1975) *The Modernization of Japan and Russia*, New York.

Blackaby, F.T. (ed.) (1978) *British Economic Policy 1960–74*, Cambridge, UK.

Blackaby, F.T. (ed.) (1978) *De-Industrialization*, London.

Blackhurst, R. et al. (1977) *Trade Liberalization, Protectionism and Interdependence*, Geneva.

Blackhurst, R. Tumlir, J. et al. (1978) *Adjustment, Trade and Growth in Developed and Developing Economics*, Geneva.

Bornstein, M. (1975) *Economic Planning, East and West*, Cambridge, Mass.

Braudel, F. (1972–73) *The Mediterranean and the Mediterranean World in the Age of Philip II*, Vol. 2. London.

Braudel, F. *On War and Its Consequences in the Age of Philip II*, London.

Brodie, B. (1965) *Strategy in the Missile Age*, Princeton.

Brooke, M.Z. and Remmers, H.L. (eds.) (1972) *The Multinational Company in Europe*, London.

Bryant, W.E. (1975) *Japanese Private Economic Diplomacy*, New York.

Bull, H. (1977) *The Anarchical Society*, London.

Buzzell, R.D. and Wierseman, F.D. (1981) 'Successful Share-Building Strategies', *Harvard Business Review*, pp. 135-44, January-February.

Cable, V. (1979) 'Britain, the New Protectionism and Trade with the Newly Industrializing Countries', *International Affairs*, **55**, No. 1, January.

Cafagna, L. (1973) 'The Industrial Revolution in Italy 1830–1914' Vol. IV ch. 6 in Cippola C.M. (ed.), *The Fontana Economic History of Europe*, London.

Cairncross, A.K. (1962) *Factors in Economic Development*, London.

Calder, K.E. (1982) Asia Pacific Community, Winter.

Calleo, D.P. and Rowland, B. (1973) *America and the World Political Economy*, Bloomington, Indiana.

Calleo, D.P. *et al.* (eds.) (1976) *Money and the Coming World Order*, New York.

Cambridge Economic Policy Review (1979) April 1979 No. 5. University of Cambridge, Department of Applied Economics.

Cameron, R.E, (1961) *France and the Economic Development of Europe 1800–1914*, Princeton.

Cameron, R.E. (1970) *Essays in French Economic History*, Homewood, Illinois.

Carr, E.H. and Davies, R.W. (1974) *Foundations of a Planned Economy 1926–1929*, Vol. 1, Middlesex, UK.

Casadio, G.P. (1973) *Transatlantic Trade USA–EEC Confrontation in the GATT Negotiations*, Hampshire, UK.

Caves, R.E. (1967) *Trade and Economic Structure Models and Methods*, Cambridge, Mass.

Chandler, L.P. (1970) *America's Greatest Depression 1929–1941*, New York.

Cheh, J.H. (1974) 'United States Concessions in the Kennedy Round and Short-run Labour Adjustment Costs', *Journal of International Economics*, **4**, No. 4.

Chenery, H.B. (1960) 'Patterns of Industrial Growth', *A.E.R.*, **50**, No. 4.

Chenery, H.B. and Hughes, H. (1972) 'Industrialisation and Trade Trends: Some Issues for the 1970's' in Hughes, H. (ed.) *Prospects for Partnership*, Baltimore.

Chenery, H.B. and Shishido, S. and Watanabe, T. (1962) 'The Pattern of Japanese Growth, 1914–1954', *Econometrica*, **30**, No. 1, January.

Chenery, H.B. and Syrquin, M. (1975) *Patterns of Development 1950–1970*, Oxford.

Chenery, H.B. and Taylor, L. (1968) 'Development Patterns: Among Countries and over Time', *The Review of Economics and Statistics*, **50**, No. 4, November.

Chenery, H.B. and Watanabe T,. (1958) 'International Comparisons of the Structure of Production', *Econometrica*, Vol. 26, No. 4, October.

Chenery, H.B. and Hughes, H. (1972) 'The International Division of Labour: The Case of Industry' in *Towards a New World Economy* (Papers of the Fifth European Conference of the Society for International Development), Rotterdam.

Cippola, C.M. (1976) *Before the Industrial Revolution— European Economy and Society 1000–1700*, London.

Clapham, J.H. (1955) *The Economic Development of France and Germany 1815–1914*, Cambridge, UK.

Claude Jr, Inis L. (1962) *Power and International Relations*, New York.

Clausewitz, C. von (1968) *On War*, Middlesex, UK.

Clough, S.B. (1939) *France, a History of National Economics*, New York.

Clough, S.B. (1964) *The Economic History of Modern Italy*, New York.

Clough, S.B. (1946) 'Retardative Factors in French Economic Development' *Journal of Economic History*, Supplement VI.

Clough, S.B. and Cole, C.W. (1946) *Economic History of Europe*, Boston.

Cohen, B.I. (1975) *Multinational Firms and Asian Exports*, New Haven.

Cohen, S.D. (1977) *The Making of U.S. International Economic Policy*, London.

Cole, G.D.H. (1952) *Introduction to Economic History 1750–1950*, London.

Colin, J. (1912) *The Transformations of War*, London.

Collier, B. (1980) *Arms and the Men*, London.

Condliffe, J.B. (1951) *The Commerce of Nations*, London.

Cooper, R.N. (1968) *The Economics of Interdependence: Economic Policy in the Atlantic Community*, New York.

Corden, W.M. and Fels, G. (1974) *Public Assistance to Industry*, London.

Corvisier, A. (1979) *Armies and Societies in Europe — 1494–1789*, Indiana.

Crawford, Sir J. and Okita, S. (eds.) (1978) *Raw Materials and Pacific Economic Integration*, London.

Crosser, P.K. (1960) *State Capitalism in the Economy of the United States*, New York.

Cukor, G. (1981) *Strategies of Industrialisation in Developing Countries*, London.

Curzon, V. (1978) *A Review of Some Major National and Sectoral Priorities*, (Institute Université d'Etudes Européennes; Centre d'Etude Industrielle), Geneva; unpublished paper.

Dale, R. (1980) *Anti-Dumping Law in a Liberal Trading Order*, London.

Davies, E. (1939) *National Capitalism*, London.

Davis, R. (1979) *The Industrial Revolution and British Overseas Trade*, Leicester.

Debray, R. (1977) 'Marxism and the Nation', *New Left Review*, Number 105, September–October.

De Cecco, M. (1971) 'Lo sviluppo dell'economia italiana a la sua collocazione internazionale' *Rivista Italiana di Scienze Economiche e Commerciali*, October.

Denton, G. *et al.* (1975) *Trade Effects of Public Subsidies to Private Enterprise*, London.

Desai, M. (1974) *Marxian Economic Theory*, Suffolk, UK.

Destanne de Bernis G. (1966) 'Industries industrialisantes et contenu d'une politique d'integration regionale', *Economie Appliquée*, no. 3–4.

Deutsch, K.W. (1968) *The Analysis of International Relations*, Englewood Cliffs.

De Vries, J. (1976) *The Economy of Europe 1660–1750*, Cambridge.

Diaz-Alejandro, C.F. (1971) 'The Argentine State and Economic Growth: a Historical Review', in Ranis, G. *Government and Economic Development*, New Haven.

Diebold Jr, W. (1952) *Trade and Payments in Western Europe*, New York.

Diebold Jr, W. (1980) *Industrial Policy as an International Issue*, New York.

Dobb, M. (1946) *Studies in the Development of Capitalism*, London.

Dobb, M. (1963) *Economic Growth and Underdeveloped Countries*, Surrey, UK.

Donges, J.B. (1980) 'Industrial Policies in West Germany's Not So Market-Oriented Economy', *The World Economy* Vol. 3. September 1980 No. 2, pp. 185-204.

Downes, A. (1957) *An Economic Theory of Democracy*, New York.

Duncan, W.C. (1973) *A Study in Economic Confrontation: US–Japanese Automobile Diplomacy*, Cambridge, Mass.

Dunham, A.C. (1955) *The Industrial Revolution in France, 1815–1848*, New York.

Dunkel, A. (1982) 'Development Forum', UN University Division of Economic and Social Information Vol. 10, No. 2.

Dunning, J.H. and Pearce, R. (1981) *The World's Largest Industrial Enterprises*, Aldershot.

Dutta-Chaudhuri, M. *Industrialization and Foreign Trade: an Analysis of the Development Experience in the Republic of South Korea and the Philippines*, ILO, ARTEP, Bangkok.

Economist (1982) 'Japan's Technology: Tomorrow's Leaders — a Survey', special article 19 June.

Elbaum, B. and Wilkinson, F. (1979) 'Industrial Relations and Uneven Development: a comparative study of the American and British Steel Industries', *Cambridge Journal of Economics*, No. 3.

Elvin, M. (1973) *The Pattern of the Chinese Past*, London.

Emmanuel, A. (1972) *Unequal Exchange: A Study of the Imperialism of Trade*, London.

Evans, D. (1974) *The Politics of Trade, the Evolution of the Superbloc*, London.

Fainsed, M. *et al.* (1941) *Government and the American Economy*, London.

Finer, S.G. (1975) 'State- and Nation-Building: the Role of the Military' in Tilly, C.H. (ed.) *The Formation of National States in Western Europe*, Princeton.

Fishlow, A. (1965) *American Railroads and the Transformation of the Ante-Bellum Economy*, Cambridge, Mass.

Fogel, R.W. (1964) *Railroads and American Economic Growth: Essays in Econometric History*, Baltimore.

Fogel, R.W. and Engerman (1971) *The Reinterpretation of American Economic History*, New York.

Fohlen, C. (1973) *The Industrial Revolution in France (700–1914)* Vol IV chapter 3, in Cippola, C.M. (ed.) *The Fontana Economic History of Europe*, London.

Foreign and Commonwealth Office (1979) *The Newly Industrializing Countries and the Adjustment Problem*, Government Economic Service Working Paper No. 18, January.

Frankel, F.R. (1979) *India's Political Economy, the Gradual Revolution, 1947–77*, Princeton.

Franko, L.G. (1976) *The European Multinationals*, London.

Franko, L.G. (1978) 'Multinationals: the end of U.S. Dominance', *Harvard Business Review*, November–December.

Franko, L.G. (1979) 'Industrial Policies in Western Europe: Solution of a Problem' *Journal of the World Economy*, January, Vol. 2, No. 1.

Fremdling, R. (1977) 'Railroads and German Economic Growth: A Leading Sector Analysis with a Comparison to the United States and Great Britain' *Journal of Economic History* Vol. XXXVII No. 3, September.

Frieden, J. (1977) 'The Trilateral Commission' *Monthly Review*, 29, No. 7, December.

Froebel, F., Heinrichs, J. and Kreye, O. (1980) *The New International Division of Labour*, Cambridge, UK.

Fuller, J.F.C. (1946) *Armament and History: A study of the Influence of Armament on History from the Dawn of Classical Warfare to the Second World War*, London.

Gallaher, J. and Robinson, R. (1972) 'The Myth of a "Twilight Era" in the History of Imperialism', in Wolfe, M. (ed.) *The Economic Causes of Imperialism*, New York.

Gerschenkron, A. (1966) *Economic Backwardness in Historical Perspective*, Cambridge, Mass.

Gerschenkron, A. (1968) *Continuity in History and Other Essays*, Harvard.

Gerstein, I. (1976) 'Production, Circulation and Value: the Significance of the "Transformation Problem" in Marx's Critique of Political Economy', *Economy and Society*, Vol. 5, No. 3.

Glamann, K. (1971) 'European Trade 1500–1750' Vol. 2. Chapter 6, in Cippola, C.M. (ed.) *The Fontana Economic History of Europe*, London.

Glyn, A. and Sutcliffe, B. (1972) *British Capitalism, Workers and the Profits Squeeze*, Middlesex, UK.

Golt, S. (1974) *The Gatt Negotiations 1973–75: A Guide to the Issues*, USA.

Golt, S. (1980) *The Gatt Negotiations 1973–79: the Closing Stage*, London.

Griffiths, R.T. (ed.) (1977) *Government, Business and Labour in European Capitalism*, London.

Grove, J.W. (1962) *Government and Industry in Britain*, London.

Guardian, (1980) Report on U.S. Economy, 31 May.

Gurley, J.G. (1976) *China's Economy and the Maoist Strategy*, New York.

Habakkuk, H.J. (1962) *American and British Technology in the 19th Century*, Cambridge.

Haber, G. and Stern, R.M. (ed.) (1961) *Equilibrium and Growth in the World Economy*, Economic Essays by Ragnar Nurkse, Cambridge, Mass.

Hacker, L.M. (1947) *The Triumph of American Capitalism*, New York.

Haldi, J. and Whitcomb, D. (1967) 'Economies of Scale in Industrial Plants', *Journal of Political Economy*, 75, No. 4, August.

Halliday, J. (1975) *A Political History of Japanese Capitalism*, New York.

Hanabusa, M. (1979) *Trade Problems Between Japan and W. Europe*, (Royal Institute of International Affairs), Saxonhouse.

Hawtrey, R.G. (1930) *Economic Aspects of Sovereignty*, London.

Hayward, J. and Narkiewicz, O.A. (eds,) (1978) *Planning in Europe*, London.

Heckscher, E.F. (1934) *Mercantilism*, London.

Hedberg, H. (1972) *Japan's Revenge*, Bata, UK.

Helleiner, G (1973) 'Manufactured Exports from less Developed Countries and Multinational Firms', *Economic Journal*, 83, March.

Helleiner, G.K. (1977) 'Transnational Enterprises and the Political Economy of U.S. Trade Policy', *Oxford Economic Papers*, 29, No. 1. March.

Helleiner, G.K. (1980) *International Economic Disorder: Essays in North-South Relations*, London.

Helleiner, G.K. (1981) *Intra-firm Trade and the Developing Countries*, London.

Henderson, W.O. (1975) *The Rise of German Industrial Power 1834–1914*, London.

Henderson, W.O. (1958) *The State and the Industrial Revolution in Prussia*, Liverpool.

Henderson, W.O. (1961) *The Industrial Revolution on the Continent 1800–1914*, London.

Herbert, N.E. (1940) *Japan's Emergence as a Modern State*, New York.

Hexner, E. (1946) *International Cartels*, Durham, North Carolina.

Hieronymi, O. (1980) *The New Economic Nationalism*, London.

Hilferding, R. (1981) *Finance Capital*, London.

Hilgerdt, F. (1945) *Industrialization and Foreign Trade*, League of Nations, Geneva and (1942) *The Network of World Trade*, League of Nations.

Hilton, R. (ed.) (1976) *The Transition from Feudalism to Capitalism*, London.

Hirschman, A. (1969) 'The Political Economy of Import-Substituting Industrialization in Latin America' in Nisbet, C.E. (ed.) *Latin America, Problems of Development*, New York.

Hirschman, A. (1958) *The Strategy of Economic Development*, New Haven.

Hobsbawm, E.J. (1969) *Industry and Empire*, Middlesex, UK.

Hobsbawm, E.J. (1979) 'The Development of the World Economy', *Cambridge Journal of Economics*, 3, No. 3.

Hobsbawm, E.J. (1977) *The Age of Capital*, London.

Holloway, J. and Picciotto, S. (1978) *State and Capital, a Marxist Debate*, London.

Hood, N. and Young, S. (1979) *The Economics of Multinational Enterprise*, London.

Hopkins, R.F. and Mansbach, R.W. (1975) *Structure and Process in International Politics*, New York.

Horowitz, D. (ed.) (1969) *Corporations and the Cold War*, New York.

Howard, E.D. (1907) *The Cause and Extent of the Recent Industrial Progress of Germany*, London.

Howard, M. (1976) *War in European History*, Oxford.

Hudson, M. (1977) *Global Fracture*, New York.

Hughes, A. and Singh, A. (1979) *Mergers, Concentration and Competition in Advanced Capitalist Economies: an International Perspective*, Department of Applied Economics, Cambridge, UK.

Hughes, H. (ed.) (1973) *Prospects for Partnership, Industrialization and Trade Policies in the 1970's*, Baltimore.

Hymer, S. (1979) *The Multinational Corporation: A Radical Approach*, Cambridge, UK.

Ike, M. (1947) 'Taxation and Landownership in the Westernization of Japan', *Journal of Economic History* Vol II, No. 2. November 1947.

Imlah, A.H. (1958) *Economic Elements in the Pax Britannica, Studies in British Foreign Trade in the Nineteenth Century*, Cambridge, Mass.

ILO (1982) *Women Workers in Asian Industry*, ARTEP, Project Idea, Bangkok.

Jacoby, N.H. (1975) *The Business–Government Relationship: A Reassessment*, California.

Jessop, B. (1977) 'Recent Theories of the Capitalist State', *Cambridge Journal of Economics*, Vol. 1 No. 4, December.

Jessop, B. (1982) *The Capitalist State*, Oxford.

Johannsen, Dr. G.K. and Kraft, H.H. (1937) *Germany's Colonial Problem*, London.

Johnson, P.S. (1980) *The Structure of British Industry*, London.

Jones, L.P. (1975) *Public Enterprise and Economic Development: the Korean Case*, Seoul.

Kahn, H. (1961) *On Thermonuclear War*, Princeton.

Kaldor, M. (1978) *The Military in Third World Development in Disarmament and World Development*, Jolly, R. (ed.), Oxford.

Kaldor, M. (1979) *The Disintegrating West*, London.

Kaldor, M. (1980) *The Third World Military Order*, London.

Kaldor, N. (1957) *A New Model of Economic Growth*, London.

Kaldor, N. (1967) *Strategic Factors in Economic Development*, New York.

Kaldor, N. (1976) 'Inflation and Recession in the World Economy', *Economic Journal*, December.

Kalecki, M. (1972) *The Last Phase in the Transformation of Capitalism*, New York.

Kapoor, A. (1972) *Foreign Investments in Asia: A survey of problems and prospects in the 1970s*, Princeton.

Kecskemeti, P. (1958) *Strategic Surrender: the Politics of Victory and Defeat*, Stanford.

Keesing, D.B. and Wolf, M. (1980) *Textile quotas against Developing Countries*, London, Trade Policy Research Centre, London.

Kemp, T. (1969) *Industrialization in Nineteenth Century Europe*, London.

Kemp, T. (1978) *Historical Patterns of Industrialization*, London.

Kemp, T. *Economic Forces in French History*, London.

Kennedy, G. (1974) *The Military in the Third World*, London.

Kennedy, G. (1975) *The Economics of Defence*, New Jersey.

Kennedy, G. (1983) *Defence Economics*, London.

Kenwood, A.G. and Lougheed, A.L. (1971) *The Growth of the International Economy 1820–1960*, London.

Kidron, M. (1968) *Western Capitalism since the War*, London.

Kindleberger, C.P. (1951) 'Group Behaviour and International Trade', *Journal of Political Economy*, No. 59, pp. 30-47.

Kindleberger, C.P. (1961) 'Obsolescence and Technical Change', *Oxford University Institute of Statistics Bulletin*, August.

Kindleberger, C.P. (1973) *The World in Depression 1929–1939*, London.

Kindleberger, C.P. *et al.* (1977) *Multinationals from Small Countries*, Cambridge, Mass.

Knorr, K. (1956) *The War Potential of Nations: The Struggle for Power and Peace*, New York.

Knowles, L.L.A. (1932) *Economic Development in the 19th Century: France, Germany, Russia and the United States*, London.

Kobayashi, U. (1922) *Military Industries of Japan*, London.

Kojima, K. (1971) *Japan and a Pacific Free Trade Area*, London.

Kolko, J. (1974) *America and the Crisis of World Capitalism*, Boston.

Krasner, S. (1976) 'Statepower and the structure of International Trade', *World Politics*, **28** No. 3. April.

Krauss, M.B. (1979) *The New Protectionism, the Welfare State and International Trade*, Oxford.

Kravis, I.B. and Lipsey, R.E. (1971) *Price Competitiveness in World Trade*, New York.

Krueger, A.O. (1980) 'The Impact of Foreign Trade on Employment in the U.S.', in Black, J. and Hindley, B. (eds.) *Current Issues in Commercial Policy and Diplomacy*, London.

Krueger, A.O. *et al.* (eds) (1981) *Trade and Employment in Developing Countries*, Chicago.

Kuznets, S. (1957) 'Quantitative Aspects of Economic Growth of Nations II, Industrial Distribution of National Product and Labor Force', *Econ. Develop. and Cul. Change*, No. 5, July.

Kuznets, S. (1966) *Modern Economic Growth*, New Haven.

Lal, D. (1979) *Market Access for Semi-manufactures from Developing Countries*, Geneva.

Lal, S. (1981) *Developing Countries in the International Economy*, London.

Lal, S. and Streeten, P. (1977) *Foreign Investment, Transnationals and Developing Countries*, London.

Lal, S. (1979) 'The Indirect Employment Effects of Multinational Enterprises in Developing Countries', ILO Working Paper, Geneva.

Lal, S. (1980) *The Multinational Corporation: Nine Essays*, London.

Lal, S. (1980) 'Exports of Manufactures by Newly-Industrializing Countries: Survey of Recent Trends', *Economic and Political Weekly*, **XV** No. 49, 6 December 2051-62, **XV** No. 50, 13 December 1980.

Landes, D.S. (1969) *The Unbound Prometheus: the Technological Change and Industrial Development in Western Europe from 1750 to the Present*, Cambridge.

Laumas, P.S. (1976) 'An International Comparison of the Structure of Production', *Review of Economics and Statistics*, May.

Lazonick, W. (1979) 'Industrial Relations and Technical Change: the Case of the Self-acting Mule', *Cambridge Journal of Economics*, Vol. 3.

League of Nations (1920) International Financial Conference 1920, *Relief Credits and the Promotion of Exports: A Summary of Government Measures*, London.

League of Nations (1929) *Economic and Financial Section Memorandum on Production and Trade, 1913, and 1923-27*, Geneva.

League of Nations (1932) *Review of World Production 1925-31*, Geneva and (1939) *World Production and Prices 1938-39*, Geneva.

League of Nations (1939) International Instutute of Intellectual Co-operation; International Studies Conference. Tasca, H.J. *World Trading Systems: Study of American and British Commercial Policies*, Paris.

League of Nations International Institute of Intellectual Co-operation; International Studies Conference. (1938) Condliffe, J.B. *Markets and the Problem of Peaceful Change*, Paris.

Lee, S.P. and Passell (1979) *A New View of American History*, New York.

Lenin, V.I. (1973) *Imperialism, the Highest Stage of Capitalism*, Peking.

Leveson, I. and Wheeler, J.W. (1980) *Western Economies in Transition: Structural Change and Adjustment Policies in Industrial Countries*, Colorado.

Levine, A.L. (1967) *Industrial Retardation in Britain, 1800-1914*, London.

Lewis, W.A. (1978) *The Evolution of the International Economic Order*, New Jersey.

Linder, S.B. (1961) *An Essay on Trade and Transformation*, New York.

Lipsit, V.D. (1978) 'Economic Development in Meiji Japan and Contemporary China: a Comparative Study', *Cambridge Journal of Economics*, Vol. 2. No. 2.

Lockwood, W.W. (1954) *The Economic Development of Japan*, Princeton.

Lockwood, W.W. (1968) *The State and Economic Enterprise in Japan*, Princeton.

Lowinger, T.C. (1976) 'Discrimination in the Government Procurement of Foreign Goods in the U.S. and Western Europe', *Southern Economic Journal*, **42**, January.

Lutz, V. (1962) *Italy, a Study in Economic Development*, London.

Macbean, A. (1978) *A Positive Approach to the International Economic Order, Part I, Trade and Structural Adjustment*, London.

MacKinnon, R. (1979) 'Foreign Trade Regimes and Economic Development: a Review', *Journal of International Economics*, **9**. No. 3. August.

Maddison, A. (1967) *Economic Growth in the West, Comparative Experiences in Europe and North America*, New York.

Maddison, A. (1919) *Economic Growth in Japan and the U.S.S.R.*, London.

Magdoff, H. (1969) *The Age of Imperialism, the Economics of U.S. Foreign Policy*, New York.

Maizels, A. (1970) *Growth and Trade*, Cambridge, UK.

Maizels, A. (1963) *Industrial Growth and World Trade*, Cambridge, UK.

Maizels, A. (1968) *Exports and Economic Growth of Developing Countries*, N.I.E.S.R., Cambridge.

Malmgren, H. (1971) *Coming Trade Wars* Foreign Policy, Winter.

Malmgren, H.B. (1972) *International Economic Peacekeeping in Phase II*, New York.

Mandel, E. (1975) *Late Capitalism*, London.

Mandel, E. (1978) *The Second Slump*, London.

Mandel, E. (1972) *Decline of the Dollar: A Marxist View of the Crisis*, New York.

Manglapus, R.S. (1976) *Japan in Asia: Collision Course*, New York.

Marfels, C. (1978) 'The Structure of the Military Industry Complex in the U.S. and its Impact on Industrial Concentration', *Kyklos*, **31**, Fasc. 3.

Marx, K. (1954) *Capital*, Vol. I, Lawrence and Wishart, London.

Mason, E.S. (1960) 'The Role of Government in Economic Development', *AER* Vol 1. No. 3.

Mathias, P. (1969) *The First Industrial Nation: An Economic History of Britain*, London.

Mathias, P. (1979) *The Transformation of England*, London.

Maunder, P. (ed.) (1979) *Government Intervention in the Developed Economy*, London.

McClelland, C.A. (1966) *Theory and the International System*, London.

Meier, G.D. (1970) *Leading Issues in Economic Development*, Oxford.

Miles, C. (1976) 'Adjustment Assistance Policies: a Survey' in Whiting, A. (ed.) *The Economics of Industrial Subsidies*, HMSO, London.

Mills, C.W. (1967) *The Power Elite*, Oxford.

Milward, A.S. (1977) *The Economic Effects of the Two World Wars on Britain*, London.

Mitchell, B.R. and Deane, P. (1962) *Abstract of British Historical Statistics*, Cambridge, UK.

Mitchell, J.D.B. (1976) *Labour Issues of American International Trade and Investment*, Baltimore.

Miyohei, S. (1977) *The Japanese Economy and Southeast Asia in the New International Context*, Tokyo.

Mokyr, J. (1977) 'Demand *vs* Supply in the Industrial Revolution', *Journal of Economic History*, Vol. 37, No. 4, December.

Monroe, W.F. (1975) *International Trade Policy in Transition*, Lexington, Mass.

Moore, R. and Upham, M. (1979) 'British Steel's "Dreadful" Programme', *New Statesman*, **98**, No. 2543, 14 December, pp. 937–8.

Morgenthau, H.J. (1960) *Politics Among Nations: the Struggle for Power and Peace*, New York.

Morrison, T.K. (1976) *Manufactured Exports from Developing Countries*, New York.

Mosley, H. 'Monopoly, Capital and the State: Some Critical Reflections on O'Connor's Fiscal Crisis of the State', *The Review of Radical Political Economics*, Vol. II. No. 1. Spring 1979.

Mottershead, P. 'Industrial Policy' in Blackaby, F.T. (ed.) (1978) *British Economic Policy 1960–1974*, Cambridge, UK.

Moulder, F.V. (1977) *Japan, China and the Modern World Economy*, Cambridge, UK.

Mulhall, G. (1899) *The Dictionary of Statistics*, Fourth Edition, London.

Mumford, L. (1934) *Tecnics and Civilization*, London.

Nash, G.D. (ed.) (1964) *Issues in American History*, Boston.

National Consumer Council (1978) September.

Nef, J.U. (1944) 'War and Industrial Civilization 1640–1740' *Review of Politics*, Vol. VI.

Nef, J.U. (1944) 'Wars and the Rise of Industrial Civilization 1640–1740' *Canadian Journal of Economics and Politics*, Vol. X.

Nef, J.U. (1950) *War and Human Progress*, London.

Negandhi, A.R. (1979) *Quest for Survival and Growth*, Athenaum Verlag, Germany.

Nettels, C. (1952) 'British Mercantilism and the Economic Development of the 13 Colonies', *Journal of Economic History*, No. 2.

Norman, E.H. (1975) *Origins of the Modern Japanese State: Selected Writings of E.H. Norman*, New York.

Nove, A. (1972) *An Economic History of the U.S.S.R.*, Middlesex, UK.

Nurkse, R. (1961) *Equilibrium and Growth in the World Economy. Economic Essays by Ragnar Nurkse*, Harberier, G. and Stern, R.M., Cambridge, Mass.

Ohlin, B. *et al.* (eds.) (1977) *International Allocation of Economic Activity*, London.

Ono, G. (1922) *War and Armament Expenditures of Japan*, Oxford.

Okita, S. (1975) *Japan in the World Economy*, Tokyo.

Owen, R. and Sutcliffe, B. (eds.) (1972) *Studies in the Theory of Imperialism*, London.

Ozawa, T. (1974) *Japan's Technological Challenge to the West 1950–1974*, Cambridge, Mass.

OECD (1978) *The Impact of Newly-Industrializing Countries on the Pattern of*

World Trade and Production in Manufactures, Department of Economics and Statistics, Mimeo, Paris.

OECD (1979) *Adjustment for Trade, Studies on Industrial Adjustment Problems and Policies,* Development Centre, Paris.

OECD (1981) *International Investment and Multinational Enterprises: Recent International Direct Investment Trends,* Paris.

Paretti, V. and Block, G. (1956) *Industrial Production in Western Europe and the United States, 1901 to 1955, Banca Nazione del Lavoro Quarterly Review,* No. 39. December (Industrial statistics, 1900–1959, OEEC, Paris, 1960).

Patterson, G. (1966) *Discrimination in International Trade: The Policy Issues (1945–65),* New Jersey.

Pavitt, K. and Warboys, M. (1977) *Science, Technology and the Modern Industrial State,* London.

Peacock, A.T. and Wiseman, J. (1967) *The Growth of Public Expenditure in the United Kingdom,* London.

Perroux, F. (1965) *Les Techniques quantitatives de la planification,* Paris.

Pettman, R. (1975) *Human Behaviour and World Politics,* London.

Pollard, S. (1981) *Peaceful Conquest, the Industrialization of Europe 1760–1970,* Oxford.

Polyani, K. (1957) *The Great Transformation: the Political and Economic Origins of our Time,* Boston.

Post, C. (1982) 'Origins of U.S. Capitalism' *New Left Review,* No. 133 pp. 30-51, May–June.

Prest, R. (1976) 'The Economic Rationale for Subsidies to Industry', in Whiting, A. (ed.) *The Economics of Industrial Subsidies,* HMSO, London.

Pratt, E.A. (1921) *British Railways and the Great War,* London.

Pratt, E.A. (1970) *A History of Inland Transport and Communication,* Trowbridge, Wilts.

Pratt, E.A. (1915) *The Rise of Rail-Power in War and Conquest: 1833–1914,* London.

Pryor, F.L. (1972) 'The Size of Production Establishments in Manufacturing', *The Economic Journal,* Vol. 82, June.

Radice, H. (ed.) (1975) *International Firms and Modern Imperialism,* Middlesex, UK.

Rangarajan, L.N. (1978) *Commodity Conflict: The Political Economy of International Commodity Negotiations,* London.

Ranis, G. (ed.) (1971) *Government and Economic Development,* New Haven.

Reich, R.B. (1982) Review Article, *New York Review of Books,* Vol. XXIX, No. II. January, 24, pp. 37-41.

Reich, R.B. (1982) 'Why the U.S. Needs an Industrial Policy', *Harvard Business Review,* January–February.

Reid, G.L. and Allen, K. (1970) *Nationalized Industries,* Middlesex, UK.

Renshaw, G. (ed.) (1981) *Employment, Trade and North–South Co-operation,* ILO, Geneva.

Reynolds, C.W. (1970) *The Mexican Economy*, New Haven and London.

Riddell, A.R. (1980) *Adjustment or Protectionism, the Challenge for Britain of Third World Industrialization*, London.

Robertson, R.M. (1964) *History of the American Economy*, New York.

Rosenstein-Rodan, P.N. (1943) 'Problems of Industrialisation of Eastern and South-Eastern Europe', *Economic Journal*, June–September.

Roemer, J.E. (1976) *U.S.–Japanese Competition in International Markets*, Berkeley, California.

Rosecrance, R. (1973) *International Relations: Peace or War?*, New York.

Rosenberg, N. (1972) *Technology and American Economic Growth*, New York.

Rosenberg, N. (1976) *Perspectives on Technology*, Cambridge, UK.

Rosenberg, N. and Ames, E. (1971) *Changing Technological Leadership and Industrial Growth* in N. Rosenberg (ed.) *The Economics of Technological Change*, Middlesex, England.

Rostow, W.W. (ed.) (1965) *The Economics of Take-Off into Sustained Growth*, New York.

Rostow, W.W. (1960) *The Stages of Economic Growth*, New York.

Rostow, W.W. (1962) *The Process of Economic Growth*, New York.

Rostow, W.W. (1971) *Politics and the Stages of Growth*, Cambridge, Mass.

Rothschild, E. (1982) 'Reagan's Case Against the Economy', *New York Review of Books*, **XXIX**, No. 6. 15 April.

Rowthorn, B. and Hymer, S. (1970) 'Multinational Corporations and International Oligopoly: the non-American Challenge', in Kindleberger, C.P. (ed.) *The International Corporation*, Cambridge, Mass.

Sampson, A. (1977) *The Arms Bazaar*, New York.

Santhanam, K.V. and Patil, R.H. (1972) 'A Study of the Production Structure of the Indian Economy: an International Comparison', *Econometrica*, **40**, No. 1.

Sau, R. (1977) 'Towards a Marxian Theory of International Trade and Capital Flows' *Economic and Political Weekly of India*, Special Number, **XII**, Nos. 33 and 34.

Saul, S.B. (1960) *Studies in British Overseas Trade 1870–1914*, Liverpool.

Saunders, C. (1981) *The Political Economy of New and Old Industrial Countries*, London.

Sayers, R.S. (1965) *The Vicissitudes of an export economy: Britain since 1880*, Sydney.

Sayle, M. (1978) 'Will Japan lead us to World War III?' *New Statesman*, **96**, No. 2477, September.

Schacht, H. (1937) 'Germany's Colonial Problems', *Foreign Affairs*, January.

Schiller, H.I. and Phillips, J.D. (eds.) (1970) *Super State Readings in the Military–Industrial Complex*, Illinois.

Schlote, W. (1952) *British Overseas Trade from 1700–1930's*, Oxford.

Schmitt, H.O. (1979) 'Mercantilism: A Modern Argument', *The Manchester School*, No. 2, June.

Schneider, W. (1976) *Food, F.P. Raw Materials and Cartels*, New York.

Schwartz, G.G. and Choate, P. (1980) *Being Number One: Rebuilding the U.S. Economy*, Lexington, Mass.

Scitowski, T. (1969) 'Growth — Balanced or Unbalanced' in Abramovitz, L. *et al. The Allocation of Economic Resources*, Stanford.

Semmel, B. (1970) *The Rose of Free Trade Imperialism: Classical Political Economy, the Empire of Free Trade Imperialism 1750–1850)*, Cambridge, UK.

Shirokov, G.K. (1973) *Industrialization of India*, Moscow.

Shuntaro, S. (1968) 'The Role of Government in the Postwar Economic Development of Japan', in Klein, L. and Ohkawa, K. *Economic Growth*, New York.

Simpson, D. and Tsukui, J. (1965) 'The Fundamental Structure of I–0 Tables: An International Comparison', *Review of Economics and Statistics*, No. 4.

Singh, A. (1977) 'U.K. Industry and the World Economy: a case of Deindustrialization', *Cambridge Journal of Economics*, Vol. 1. No. 2, June.

SIPRI (1971, 1975a) *The Arms Trade with The Third World*, Stockholm.

Sklar, H. (ed.) (1981) *Trilateralism: the Trilateral Commission and Elite Planning for World Management*, Boston, Mass.

Skocpol, T. (1979) *States and Social Revolutions*, Cambridge, UK.

Smead, E.S. (1969) *Governmental Promotion and Regulation of Business*, New York.

Sprout, H. and M. (1962) *Foundations of International Politics*, Princeton.

Stearns, P.N. (1975) *The Lives of Labour*, London.

Steindl, J. (1952) *Maturity and Stagnation in American Capitalism*, Oxford.

Stewart, F. (1977) *Technology and Underdevelopment*, London.

Strange, S. and Tooze, R. (1981) *The International Politics of Surplus Capacity*, London.

Streeten, P. (1981) *Development Perspectives*, London.

Sugihara, K. (1980) 'Patterns of Intra-Asian Trade, 1899–1913', *Economic Review*, Osaka City University, No. 16.

Supple, B. (1976) *The State and the Industrial Revolution 1700–1914*, in *The Industrial Revolution*, General Editor Carlo M. Cippola, England.

Sutcliffe, R.B. (197) *Industry and Underdevelopment*, Philippines.

Sweezy, P.M. (1970) *The Theory of Capitalist Development*, New York.

Taylor, A. (ed.) (1973) *Perspectives on U.S.–Japan Economic Relations*, US–Japan Trade Council, Cambridge, Mass.

Tharakan, P.K.M. (1979) *The International Division of Labour and Multinational Companies*, Saxonhouse, England.

Toder, E.J. *et al.* (1978) *Trade Policy and the U.S. Automobile Industry*, New York.

Trezise, P.H. *et al.* (1980) *The Impact of Japan's Economic Growth on the World's Economy in 1980*, Washington.

Trilateral Commission (1977) *Task Force Reports 1–7, the Triangle Papers,* New York.

Tsurumi, Y. (1976) *The Japanese are Coming (A Multination Interaction of Firms and Politics),* Cambridge, Mass.

Tumlir, J. (1977) 'Can the International Economic Order be Saved?', *The World Economy,* Vol. 1, No. 1.

Tumlir, J. (1978) 'The New Protectionism, Cartels and the International Order' in Ryan Amacher (ed.) *Challenges to Liberal Economic Order,* Washington.

Turner, L. (1979) *Europe and the Newly-Industrializing Countries, (RIIA),* London.

Tyler, W.G. (1976) *Manufactured Export Expansion and Industrialisation in Brazil,* in J.C.B. Mohr, Tubingen.

Ullman, R.A. (1976) 'Trilateralism: "Partnership" for What?', *Foreign Affairs,* October.

UN (1962) *The Economic and Social Consequences of Disarmament,* New York.

UN (1981) *Transnational Corporation Linkages in Developing Countries, the Case of Backward Linkages via Subcontracting,* New York.

UN Economic and Social Council (1974) *The Impact of Multinational Corporations on Development and on International Relations,* New York.

UN Economic and Social Council (1978) *Transnational Corporations in World Development,* Commission on Transnational Corporations, New York.

UNCTAD (1978) *Dominant Positions of Market Power of Transnational Corporations,* Geneva.

UNCTAD (1978) *Intra-firm Transactions and Their Impact on Trade and Development,* Seminar Programme, Report Series, No. 2, May, Geneva.

UNCTAD (1977) *Handbook of International Trade and Development Statistics,* Geneva.

UNIDO (1979) *Industrial Priorities in Developing Countries, The Selection Process in Brazil, India, Mexico, Republic of Korea and Turkey,* New York.

UNIDO (1979) *World Industry Since 1960: Progress and Prospects,* New York.

UNIDO (1981) *Development of World Industry,* New York.

US Department of Commerce (1980) Bureau of the Census, *Statistical Abstract of the U.S.,* 101st edition, Washington.

Vatter, H.G. (1975) *The Drive to Industrial Maturity, The U.S. Economy 1860–1914,* USA.

Vernon, R. (1966) 'International Investment and International Trade in the Product Cycle', *Quarterly Journal of Economics* 80, May.

Vernon, R. (1973) *Sovereignty at Bay, the Multinational Spread of U.S. Enterprises,* Middlesex, UK.

Vernon, R. (1970) *The Technology Factor in International Trade,* New York.

Vernon, R. (1981) *International Trade Policy in the 1980's: Prospects and Problems,* Cambridge, Mass.

Vernon, R. (ed.) (1974) *Big Business and the State, Changing Relations in Western Europe*, London.

Vernon, R. and Aharoni, Y. (1981) *State-Owned Enterprises in the Western Economies*, London.

Wade, B.S. and Kim, L.L. (1978) *Economic Development of South Korea, the Political Economy of Success*, New York.

Wadhva, C.D. (ed.) (1977) *Some Problems of India's Economic Policy*, second edition, New Delhi.

Wallerstein, M.B. (1980) *Food for War — Food for Peace, United States Food Aid in a Global Context*, Cambridge, Mass.

Warnecke, S.J. (ed.) (1978) *International Trade and Industrial Subsidy Policies*, London.

Weber, M. (1980) 'National State and Economic Policy' in *Economy and Society*, **9**, No. 4.

Webster, R.A. (1975) *Industrial Imperialism in Italy 1908–1915*, Berkeley, California.

Weeks, J. (1977) *The Sphere of Production and the Analysis of the Crisis of Capitalism, Science and Society*, **XLI**, No. 3, Fall.

Wells Jr, L.T. (ed.) (1972) *The Product Life Cycle and International Trade*, Boston.

Werner, B. (1965) *Industrialization and Economic Development in Brazil*, Homewood, Illinois.

Whynes, D.K. (1979) *The Economics of Third World Military Expenditure*, London.

Wilcox, C. et al. (1962) *Economies of the World Today*, New York.

Williams, J.R. (1972) *British Commercial Policy and Trade Expansion 1750–1850*, Oxford.

Williams, T.I. (ed.) (1978) *A History of Technology 1900–1950*, Oxford.

Williams, B. (1962) *The Whig Supremacy, 1714–1760*, Oxford.

Williamson, J.A. (1922) *A Short History of English Expansion*, London.

Williamson, J.A. (1968) *A Short History of British Expansion*, New York, and (1944) *Great Britain and the Empire, a Discursive History*, London.

Winter, J.M. (ed.) (1975) *War and Economic Development*, Cambridge, UK.

Wolf, J.B. (1951) *The Emergence of The Great Powers 1685–1715*, New York.

World Bank Development Report (1980), Washington.

Woytinsky, W.S. and Woytinsky, E.S. (1955) *World Commerce and Governments, Trends and Outlook*, New York.

Wright, O. (1942) *A Study of War*, Chicago.

Yamamura, K. (1977) 'The Role of Meiji Militarism in Japan's Technical Progress', *Journal of Economic History*, **XXXVII**, No. 1, March.

Yoshino, M.Y. (1976) *Japan's Multinational Enterprises*, Cambridge, Mass.

Yoshitake, K. (1973) *An Introduction to Public Enterprise in Japan*, Tokyo.

Youngson, A.J. (1967) *A Study in Development Economics*, Edinburgh.

Zeitlin, J. (1979) 'Craft Control and the Division of Labour: Engineers and Compositors in Britain' *Cambridge Journal of Economics*, No. 3.

Index